BACKROADS & BYWAYS OF

UTAH

BACKROADS & BYWAYS OF
UTAH

*Drives, Day Trips, &
Weekend Excursions*

CHRISTINE SJÖQUIST

THE COUNTRYMAN PRESS

A division of W. W. Norton & Company

Independent Publishers Since 1923

Copyright © 2017, 2011 by W. W. Norton & Company

For information about permission to reproduce selections from this book, write to Permissions, The Countryman Press, 500 Fifth Avenue, New York, NY 10110

For information about special discounts for bulk purchases, please contact W. W. Norton Special Sales at specialsales@wwnorton.com or 800-233-4830

Library of Congress Cataloging-in-Publication Data
Names: Sjöquist, Christine, author.
Title: Backroads & byways of Utah / Christine Sjöquist.
Other titles: Backroads and byways of Utah
Description: 2nd edition. | New York, NY : Countryman Press, a division of W.W. Norton & Company, 2017. | Includes index.
Identifiers: LCCN 2017020358 | ISBN 9781682680827 (pbk.)
Subjects: LCSH: Utah—Guidebooks. | Scenic byways—Utah—Guidebooks. | Automobile travel—Utah—Guidebooks.
Classification: LCC F824.3 .S56 2017 | DDC 917.9204—dc23 LC record available at https://lccn.loc.gov/2017020358

The Countryman Press
www.countrymanpress.com

A division of W. W. Norton & Company, Inc.
500 Fifth Avenue, New York, NY 10110
www.wwnorton.com

978-1-68268-082-7 (pbk.)

10 9 8 7 6 5 4 3 2 1

To David: Thanks for all the journeys we've
had, and for all those yet to come.

Contents

Introduction

U tah boasts vast amounts of open land and extremely varied terrain. It has mountain peaks that stand more than 13,700 feet above sea level, broad valleys, high planes, and many varieties of desert: red rocks, vermillion cliffs, buffed sandstone canyons, rounded arches, lunar landscapes, dramatic gorges, and expansive salt flats. Within a few hours of each other are high fortified alpine highways and wild dirt roads stretching across broad, low-lying desert basins. To drive for an afternoon in this state is to visit more landscapes than you might see driving for days in other parts of the country. To experience all of them is to travel to nearly every continent in the world—except, on most days, Antarctica—flora-, fauna-, and geology-wise. And Utah has six national parks and numerous national monuments and state parks to celebrate and preserve these vistas.

Because roughly 75 percent of Utah's population lives along the **Wasatch Range**, the remainder of the state's lands are quite open and untainted by the trappings of civilization. More than three-quarters of Utah's land is publicly owned, making the state third in the country for publicly owned land as a proportion of total area—ranking behind only Alaska and Nevada. The general openness of the landscape and straightness of the roads enable relatively speedy long-distance travel. Thus, many of the drives in this book will be in excess of 100 miles. The list of suggested routes will begin with a tour of the Wasatch Canyons near Salt Lake City. The rest are then listed in clockwise order, beginning in the northeastern corner of the state and working around to many remote and gorgeous sections of road. Each route has been chosen to represent the most interesting, beautiful, visually diverse, and historically and culturally relevant sections of road and surrounding points of interest.

Each drive listed in this book has been embellished with interesting historical, geological, scenic, and factual information. Keep your eyes open for

ASPENS HIGH ON MT. TIMPANOGOS' SHOULDER

advisories that warn about climate-related hazards such as the potential for snow closures or excess heat, as well as other possible dangers such as long stretches of road without services.

Utah is a large state—the thirteenth-largest in the Union—with only one major urban population, which runs the western Wasatch Front. Nearly everyone traveling to Utah by plane will almost assuredly fly into **Salt Lake City** via the **Salt Lake City International Airport**, a major hub just 5 minutes west of downtown. Be prepared: In the western United States, people are accustomed to driving long distances. And since Utah is crisscrossed by several major interstates, and speed limits are relatively high, most people consider a 200- or 300-mile drive totally reasonable for a weekend trip. But do not worry; the overwhelming majority of Utah's freeways now boast a speed limit of 80 miles per hour, making this one of just six states in the country with such a high limit.

Though Salt Lake City is certainly worth visiting, it will not be included in this book. (If you are interested in reading more about this city—or other cities in Utah—on your journey, you may want to check out Countryman's *Great*

Destinations: Salt Lake City, Park City, Provo & Utah's High Country Resorts or *Utah: An Explorer's Guide.*) With regard to rural exploration across the state, read the tips and alerts below.

NATIONAL PARKS PASS

Utah has a bounty of national parks and monuments. In fact, it has thirteen in all—or seventeen, if you count the four national trails—with yet more abutting its borders. For those planning to spend any serious amount of time in the state, it is almost assuredly worth the money to purchase an annual pass. Formerly known as the Golden Eagle Pass—now the **America the Beautiful–The National Parks and Federal Recreational Lands Pass**—it grants unlimited access to all national parks and monuments (as well as some other government-run parks) for a year from the date of purchase for $80. Compared with the cost of one-week passes to individual parks (usually around $20 apiece), this could very well be worth the money—especially

MOUTH OF KOLOB CANYON

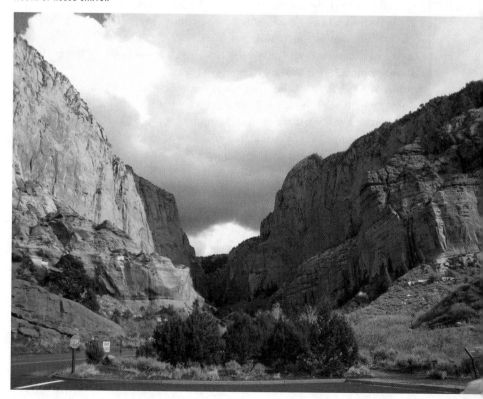

Utah History

The last major ice age, the Wisconsin glaciation, lasted from about 70,000 BC to 10,000 BC. During that time, the world was a much cooler, wetter place. The Great Basin, a massive bowl centered on but bigger than Nevada, had no outlet to the ocean; during this wet time, it became a huge holding area for water. Several times, a massive lake in northern Utah (more than a quarter the size of the state) filled, drained, and refilled. Its last major stint ended about 12,000 years ago, when a weakness along its shores gave way, releasing **Lake Bonneville** in a catastrophic flood across southern Idaho. Prior to the natural dam breaking, the lake's waters would have been up to 800 feet over present-day Salt Lake City.

It wasn't until after the ice started to recede that Utah became inhabited by humans. In fact, right around 11,000 years ago, the first groups of people started leaving evidence of their existence. This evidence has been found across the state, with the oldest being in **Danger Cave** (see chapter 15), in the **Bonneville** desert. Utah's most ancient residents lived a transient lifestyle, apparently spending all waking hours just trying to stay alive. The first permanent peoples in Utah to live in larger groups and leave major traces were the Anasazi and Fremont. Partially nomadic, these people also planted basic crops and even raised animals for consumption. This relatively stationary lifestyle allowed for the manifestation of more advanced culture, such as tool- and basketmaking. These were the ancestors of the **Ute**, **Paiute**, **Shoshone**, **Bannock**, and **Gosiute** tribes.

Far from any coasts, Utah wasn't inhabited by Europeans until quite recently. Some of the first Euros to see the region were the Spanish explorer-priests **Dominguez** and **Escalante** (after whom many features of Utah's southern region are named). These two, stationed in Santa Fe, came into the area on an exploratory mission to open a direct passageway from south to north in 1776. These men made it well into northern Utah—near **Dinosaur National Monument** and the **Uinta Basin**—before a particularly cruel early winter swept in and ushered the party hastily back south. After this expedition came the eighteenth-century Spanish miners, whose presence in the **Uinta Mountains** is evidenced by remaining infrastructure, tools, and the altered earth they left behind.

The next known Europeans to enter the area were all itinerant in nature: trappers, traders, and other passers through. Among the roster were **Kit Carson** and **Antoine Robidoux**, who established self-named trading posts in the 1830s and '40s; **William Henry Ashley**, namesake of the Ashley National Forest; and **Étienne Provost**, whose name appears in numerous places across the state. Settlement beyond these trading posts was nonexistent.

One of the earliest and most influential explorers of the Intermountain West, **John Wesley Powell**, ventured into the region via the **Green** and **Colorado Rivers** on two separate occasions. At the time of his voyages (1869 and 1871), white-water boating wasn't even a concept—and these rivers served up some very serious rapids. On his trips, Powell scrupulously observed and recorded the west's enormous and otherwise uncharted landscape. In addition to noting the geology and ecology of the area, Powell actually detailed this new white-water phenomenon in his immaculate journals.

Finally, in 1848, Utah saw its first large, permanent settlements—facilitated by the arrival of Latter-day Saints in Salt Lake Valley in July of that year. Contrary to demeaning rumors accusing the Mormons of mistaking the Great Salt Lake for the Pacific Ocean, they actually had specifically planned and prepared to settle in the Great Basin. Suffering persecution wherever they lived, the Mormons desired a home completely isolated from society. So with this specific wish, they set about establishing an empire in Utah, hoping to even create a sovereign nation of their own. Though they did a remarkable job of embedding a network into the state and beyond, they were never able to create their own country.

for those planning to visit other under-the-radar types of federally operated destinations such as **American Fork Canyon** near Lehi (chapter 3 in this book) or the **Mirror Lake Highway** in the **Uinta Mountains** (chapter 5).

(LACK OF) CELLULAR PHONE SERVICE

Be aware that in Utah, cellular phones are often completely without service. Long distances between townships and mountainous topography, combined with sparse rural population (and therefore low demand for cellular technology) renders predictably bad-to-nonexistent backroads cell service. If you're heading well off the beaten path, it doesn't hurt to occasionally check your phone for service, making a mental note of the last point on the approach where the phone picked up solid reception. Distance from an urban center is not the only predictor of cell service; it is possible to lose service rapidly when driving or hiking into Utah's steep-walled, winding canyons. For people accustomed to readily available phone use, Utah's lack of cell service can be a real shock. Keep in mind that it can potentially amplify the isolation should something go wrong in rugged and remote situations.

NATURAL HAZARDS

Where there's natural beauty, there's potential for danger. Utah's grandeur is typified by trademark ruggedness, barrenness, isolation, and other flavors of inhospitableness. While these create beautiful vistas, these features and landscapes are not the type to foster life—particularly untrained human life perhaps out of touch with man's vulnerability in nature. All of these potential hazards, of course, are amplified exponentially by frequent lack of human company, cell phone service, and rescue resources.

WATER: TOO LITTLE

Ranking high in Utah's biggest threats is its polarized and fickle climate: extreme temperatures and the lack (or sudden surplus) of water. Lack of water is, by far, the region's most common threat to the unprepared—particularly in southern Utah. To prevent dehydration, always pack extra water in the car (or in the backpack, if hiking). Depending on the season and strain of the activity, it is not excessive to bring *at least* a gallon of water per person, per day.

WATER: TOO MUCH

Considering the above advisory, it's strange to find that *too much* water can be a threat in Utah as well—yet every year people fall victim to flash flooding in this state. These floods generally occur in narrow canyons (slot canyons and other narrow river canyons) and are especially hazardous, as they often take their victims by complete surprise. Most accidents occur when people are recreating off the grid. Though it may be sunny and cloudless in their immediate vicinity, floods can form as a result of distant storms. These can easily inundate a drainage system and send a wall of rushing water downstream with no warning, packed with debris that will kill. Your best precaution is to meticulously check the weather before spending any time in a canyon system and to stay well clear of any slot canyons if there is rain forecasted anywhere in the region.

The other surplus-water-related threat, though much less violent, is mud. Some of Utah's soil, when mixed with rain, can create roads so slick or sticky that they become impassible for days at a time, stranding those on the "other" side from civilization. Especially if you are exploring Utah's old lake beds and salt flats, be sure to monitor the weather. Though a road may appear dry, more than a foot of car-sticking mud could be lurking just beneath the surface, ready to eat a passing car. Extraction from such a mess requires the payment of a hefty fee to a fancy, military-grade tow truck operator, as most typical wreckers cannot do this type of job!

SUN

Sunblock. Sunscreen. Hat. Protective clothing. All the things Mother suggested will be of indescribable use here! Utah, regardless of season, can burn the skin senseless. Summer heat means bodies are scantily clothed and exposed. Winter snow forms a blanket of white on the ground that acts as a mirror and absolutely blasts skin with ultraviolet rays. Add to that the state's relatively high elevation, roughly 300 days of sun a year, and you've got premature aging. Be prepared!

MOUNTAINOUS TERRAIN

Dramatic topography can be in and of itself a threat to the unwise. The fact is that gravity exists 24 hours a day, 7 days a week—and not all ground is stable. Be cautious near long drop-offs, even when walking on a trail. And be mindful when walking off-trail. Much of Utah's wilderness consists of fragile desert or high-alpine terrain easily damaged by foot traffic. Additionally, complicated mountain topography can easily render even experienced hikers lost. Be careful to keep your bearings and be diligent about returning exactly along the approach path you came up.

LIONS AND TIGERS AND BEARS: UH-OH

Animals, too, can present a lethal danger. It's obvious that mountain lions and bears are a threat. (But don't worry—tigers only exist in zoos in Utah.) However, don't forget the smaller (snakes and spiders) and the less obvious threats (moose and mice). Some people underestimate the potential danger of black bears, assuming they're less threatening than grizzly bears, but American Fork Canyon had its first modern lethal encounter in 2006. In that particular case, food was left very near the sleeping victim and not properly tied off far from the campsite.

Moose, too, are highly dangerous, testy, and unpredictable. They appear dumb, lanky, and homely—but they have a mean temper, particularly around their offspring, and can easily trample a person. Snakes exist in plentiful numbers in Utah; it's got the perfect climate. Be particularly on the lookout for rattlesnakes—they are the most lethal of the state's serpents. But fortunately, the rattle affixed to this snake usually (though not always!) serves as fair and generally sufficient warning to back away. Upon hearing this noise, simply pause, locate the sounding snake, and calmly (or with as much calm as can be mustered) leave its vicinity. It is important not to kill an appropriately rattling snake; research is beginning to show that these rattlesnakes are gradually being selected out of the population, rendering quiet (and much more dangerous) snakes more prevalent.

Finally, mice carry hantavirus. It is excreted in their waste and saliva, and it can easily become airborne if the dust containing their droppings is disturbed. If particles of infected waste are inhaled, the disease can be caught by unlucky humans.

Animal danger should not keep people out of the wilderness, but wildlife should be treated with respect (whether or not they pose a human threat). Give them space to operate without harassment, and don't tempt them into destructive habits.

VEHICLE AWARENESS

As almost all of these drives leave cell service at some point (and some for the majority of the route), drivers are responsible for making sure their vehicles will last the drive. Depleting the gas tank, flatting a tire, and running too low on oil are easy problems to prevent, but difficult to fix when in the backcountry. In the event something does go awry, it's best to have extra water, clothing, and food in the car. And don't forget to double-check the spare tire for proper air pressure before departing.

All of that said, Utah is one of the nation's most beautiful and rewarding states to visit. Don't shy away from its adventures. Simply come prepared to be responsible for your own well-being.

BACKCOUNTRY SKIER IN LITTLE COTTONWOOD CANYON'S WHITE PINE BASIN

1
SALT LAKE CITY INTO LITTLE COTTONWOOD CANYON

ESTIMATED LENGTH: About 25 miles one-way from downtown Salt Lake City to the top of Little Cottonwood Canyon

ESTIMATED TIME: A bit more than 30 minutes pure driving to Alta; a short half day for a round-trip journey with a few stops

HIGHLIGHTS: This trip is a short and sweet jaunt up Little Cottonwood Canyon. Being so near to Salt Lake City, quite beautiful, and endowed with a bit of interesting history—as well as phenomenal modern recreation and dining—it's worth the excursion. Along the way are the mysterious-seeming subterranean **Mormon vault**, **Snowbird Resort**, the **"Hellgate,"** and **Alta Ski Area**. Spring through fall, this canyon opens itself up to rock climbers and boulderers, road bikers, and hikers. In winter, this canyon fills with skiers and snowboarders (skiers only at Alta!). The resorts, also open in summer, offer hiking trails, summer lift and tram rides, and restaurants and pubs. Occasional live music and other festivals take place during the peak of summer.

Done in conjunction with the **Big Cottonwood Canyon** route (chapter 2 of this book), this route will amaze the viewer with geological contrast. Pristinely U-shaped, and very smooth, the white granitelike rock of Little Cottonwood was polished out by glaciers; it seems like the angular and blocky, burnt-orange quartzite of Big Cottonwood belongs in another mountain range entirely.

GETTING THERE: Thanks to the I-215 beltway encircling Salt Lake City, the Cottonwood Canyons couldn't be easier or quicker to reach. From the southeastern corner of this square-shaped interstate loop, take Exit 6, and head east on UT-190. This highway climbs eastward and uphill, turning naturally into South Wasatch Boulevard as it dips to the south. Stay on this road as it heads south along the base of the Wasatch for just over 2 miles. Turn left, following signs, to head uphill on UT-210 and into the very obvious ascending canyon. (Starting near the appropriate I-215 exit, the route to the canyons is signed the entire way. Big Cottonwood is the home of Brighton and Solitude Resorts; to get to Little Cottonwood, follow signs to Alta and Snowbird Resorts.) As of the writing of this book's second edition, there was no fee to enter the canyon; however, visitors soon may be required to purchase a day pass.

Before even entering Little Cottonwood Canyon, the driver must first ascend to its base. The **Salt Lake Valley,** at around 4,300 feet in elevation, sits the better part of a vertical mile beneath the *base area* of Alta (8,950 feet) at the end of the canyon road. Not to mention that the tip-top of Snowbird, **Hidden Peak**, has an elevation of 11,000 feet. Clearly glacially sculpted, the white walls of this canyon are actually not granite. They are composed of quartz monzonite, commonly mistaken for granite—also an igneous, intrusive rock, its quartz composition is roughly 5 to less than 20 percent by mass (whereas granite contains 20 percent quartz). Remember that, and you'll know more than most people in Salt Lake City about the canyon's geology.

In winter, be sure to check the road report (Utah Police Department of Greater Salt Lake via Facebook or Twitter; to receive critical updates only, text

"CanyonAlerts" to 53535), especially after a big snowstorm, to make sure the highway up-canyon is in fact open; with such steep sides, and such a narrow bottom, the canyon must be closed often for preventative blasting and clearing.

This rock was quarried by the Latter-day Saints (LDS) Church for use in the **Salt Lake Temple**, **Utah capitol building**, and **LDS Church Office Building**. Not actually mining from within the ground, they simply blasted and (cleanly) broke up already-fallen boulders. This caused great dismay among rock climbers, as it destroyed a lot of the classic boulder problems in the canyon. This LDS quarrying largely took place near the mouth of the canyon, but it also reached farther up as well. Parking at any of the numerous shoulder pullouts (or stopping at the park-and-ride at the mouth of the canyon, used heavily in winter by **Utah Transit Authority** ski shuttle buses) and walking even just slightly into the scrub oak forests will reveal many boulders with obvious blasting marks.

Even the Mormons have mistakenly labeled Little's rock type in the name of their **Granite Mountain Records Vault**. This obvious large hole in the rock about a mile into the canyon on its northern side is a deep, underground storage facility owned by the LDS Church and is heavily guarded. Created for the safekeeping of church documents in case of an apocalyptic event, the vault also contains more than 35 billion genealogical files, mostly on microfiche—a collection that was started back in the 1930s.

Needing a secure place to store these temperature-sensitive records, the church discussed many possible locations, including downtown buildings and other canyons. But the solid quartz monzonite walls of Little seemed a perfect and safe place. After initial testing, excavation began in 1960 using diesel fuel and ammonium sulfate. Ten-foot sections were blasted at a time, with alternate days being used to remove the fallen stone. The tunnels were complete enough by 1963 to begin storing items. The structure consists of

No Dogs Allowed!

Little Cottonwood Canyon and Big Cottonwood Canyon are both part of Salt Lake City's municipal watersheds. Because of this, and the already-high use of these canyons, the Salt Lake City government strictly forbids the presence of dogs in these canyons, regardless of whether they are on a leash. There are very few exceptions to the rule, and the penalty for disobeying can be a fine of several hundred dollars and, in extreme cases, can include jail time. Those with pets should leave them at home; even dogs left in parked cars are considered illegal. Alternative dog-friendly canyons are **Mill Creek Canyon**, east of Salt Lake City, at the end of 3800 South Street; and **City Creek Canyon**, north of the city's **Capitol Hill**. (In City Creek, dogs are only permitted downstream of the obvious water treatment center a few miles up the canyon.)

three nearly 700-foot-long tunnels with a few cross tunnels. The doors to the vaults are allegedly capable of sustaining a nuclear blast. Not too unlike something from *The Twilight Zone*! Today, private persons can pay a pretty penny to have their own goods stored in the vault as well.

On the way up the canyon, several hiking trails depart from obvious pull-outs on either side of the road. Most of these head up the southern side of the canyon, starting several miles up in the canyon where walls become less steep and rocky; if they started closer to the mouth of the canyon, the hikes would dead-end in cliffs and steep talus piles. A trail departing to **Red Pine Lake** and **White Pine Lake** begins at a rather large parking area (on the south side of the road) 5.5 miles up canyon. The hike to Red Pine Lake from here is about 3 steep miles, gaining almost 2,000 feet of elevation in that short distance. The White Pine Trail is just an extended version of this, lasting 4.5 miles each way, and gaining 2,540 feet in elevation. At the parking lot, all of this information

RIDGELINE BETWEEN RED PINE AND WHITE PINE LAKES IN LITTLE COTTONWOOD is clearly spelled out on a kiosk map. Hiking into either lake makes it obvious that the Wasatch Range is a huge area of wildlands. These trails are used by rock climbers in summer to approach yet higher alpine climbs; in winter, skiers and snowboarders ride down them, particularly White Pine, which can be accessed from Snowbird with just a bit of hiking.

Snowbird is about 8 miles up Little Cottonwood Canyon and is the first resort encountered on the drive up. Most famous as a ski and snowboard resort, Snowbird reports more than 500 inches of snow each winter—sometimes in excess of 800 inches. One of Utah's biggest, and certainly one of its most "hardcore" areas, it has 2,500 acres, 3,240 feet of vertical drop, and a base-to-summit tram that completes the trip in just 10 quick-seeming minutes via a 1.6-mile cable. This tram, a Snowbird institution since 1971, also operates during the summer, and for a few dollars brings those unable (or unwilling) to hike up to an incredible view. Those who do hike to the top can ride the tram down for free, saving their knees for another hike! During the winter, the resort is absolutely hopping, but in summer its restaurants remain open—from fine New American and Continental dining at the **Aerie** (in the **Cliff Lodge**) to basement and patio bars serving beers and burgers. Many, many restaurants and hotels operate at Snowbird; those curious should investigate further by calling the resort or checking online.

The **Cliff Lodge** is Snowbird's most obvious and largest hotel, with eleven stories (and a glass wall entirely exposed in its floor-to-ceiling atrium), three restaurants, multiple pools, and the world's largest privately held Oriental rug collection. Evidence of the 1989 World Cup rock climbing competition is visible on its external walls, in the form of still-attached holds. On its tenth floor is the **Aerie**, Snowbird's finest dining spot. With an incredible wine list (more than 1,100 selections, earning the restaurant a 2015 Best of Award of Excellence from *Wine Spectator* magazine), almost floor-to-ceiling windows, incredible down-canyon and mountainside views, and a high-caliber American and Continental menu, this is among the finer restaurants in the Salt Lake City area (and for those who don't know, this town is actually rich in culinary arts from around the globe). A sushi menu is available at Aerie as well. Those without reservations or who are looking for a quicker meal can sit at the sushi bar, just outside of the main restaurant.

Just slightly uphill is **Alta Ski Area**. Deliberately avoiding the "resort" moniker, Alta prefers to reserve itself for those who appreciate the less fast-paced aspects of skiing. Today (and likely forever), snowboarders are not allowed at Alta—unless they are skiing. Though not as big or as flashy as its neighbor, Snowbird, Alta is more beloved by many. It is a mountain characterized by semi-secret stashes that must be hiked to, chutes and bowls, and tree runs that are divided up from one another.

In the summer, this slope-and-bowl mountain terrain holds a collection of small alpine lakes. Intermixed forest and fields sit in Albion Basin beneath

Utah's Own Alpe d'Huez

Anyone who's watched the **Tour de France** knows about the famous mountain stage called **l'Alpe d'Huez**. Perhaps the most legendary and classic mountain stage on the world's most prominent bike race, the mountain has a nearly identical profile (in terms of distance and grade) to that of Utah's own Little Cottonwood Canyon. Both are just about 8.5 miles in length, climbing about 3,500 feet, with an average pitch of around 9.2 percent. The only difference is that the French version has switchbacks, and the Little Cottonwood version is more or less a straight shot, with meandering curves being the only thing that hides the ride and keeps the rider from giving up. And such similar mountains are an ocean apart.

A tip for road bikers: This canyon is one of the Wasatch's more beautiful, challenging canyon rides. Yet, with a fair amount of traffic on a pretty narrow roadway, this can be quite unpleasant during the day. Also, such a steep descent causes many drivers to burn their brakes. Not so terrible for other drivers, the pungent smell of burning brakes is sometimes present on this hike and can make sucking wind on a hill climb quite undesirable. The perfect solution to this problem is to wake up extra early and start riding by 5 AM. Riding at this time in the middle of summer means avoiding almost all of the vehicular traffic. It also provides ideal temperatures. Midday summer riding in this canyon can be pretty sadistic; the canyon's bowl-shaped bottom bakes in the sun and can be a cooker.

Devil's Castle, a massive limestone cliff that actually has multiple rock climbs reaching all the way to its peak (as well as a nontechnical hiking trail that ascends to the summit via the shoulder). Several trails crisscross the area, making almost all of it easily accessible on foot and by mountain bike during the post-snowmelt summer months (July and August in most seasons).

Wildflowers bloom intensely here in the summer, giving cause for the Alta installment of the Wasatch **Wildflower Festival** (Cottonwood Canyons Foundation: www.cottonwoodcanyons.org). This 3-day weekend affair brings many people to walk these slopes when they are absolutely painted with vibrant flowers of all colors. (Just one of the days takes place at Alta; the others occur at Snowbird Resort and in Big Cottonwood Canyon, at Brighton and Solitude.) Albion Basin has more than 300 species of wildflowers, and because of its high altitude, they don't come into full bloom until right in the middle of summer. The festival features guided walks, food, and live music. Hikes of varying difficulties are offered, so not everyone must be at a high fitness level.

Alta, as with many, many ski resorts across the western United States, was originally a mining town. In its heyday during the 1860s and '70s, it had flourishing mining operations, supported by a community with twenty-six bars, six breweries, and uncounted other nonpious goings on. Notice the name

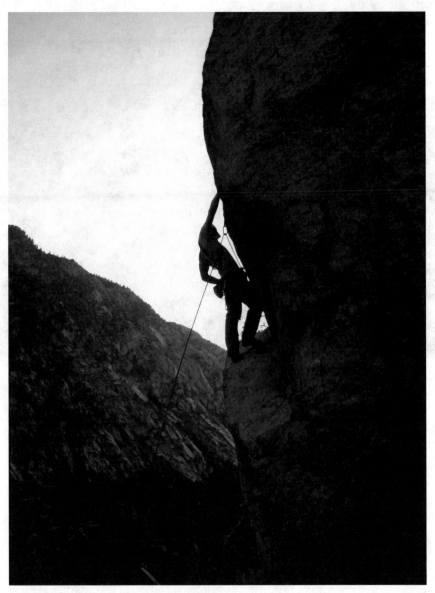

ROCK CLIMBER ON THE NORTHERN SIDE OF LITTLE COTTONWOOD

"Hellgate" around Alta: On the way up the canyon, immediately before Alta, two giant limestone fins come down and almost meet, nearly pinching off the canyon at that point. The Mormons named this section of Little Cottonwood Hellgate, as if the rock formation were literally the gate to Alta's "satanic," beer-drinking mining lifestyle. Like most mining towns, Alta died quickly when its limited resources ran out and left its residents stranded high above Salt Lake City with no viable economy. Also, as with many such ghost towns,

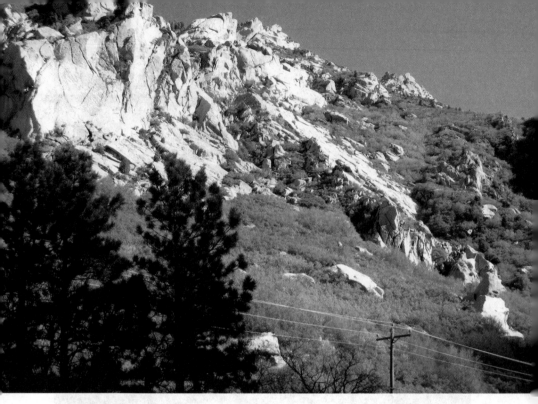

Alta saw a revival as a ski resort. Alta actually became one of Utah's first ski areas when it opened in 1938 (just behind Brighton, which opened in 1936). Since then, the facility has obviously grown, but it has remained a stiff arm's length from typical large-scale resort business practices.

Those interested in the mining history of the canyon can check out **Grizzly Gulch** via a hike. Along the way, this crosses many tailings piles and random mining equipment. A 2.2-mile walk with 1,240 feet of elevation gain reaches the **Prince of Wales Mine**. In operation from 1872 through the Great Depression, this mine shaft was roughly 900 feet deep, leading down to a maze of tunnels. Today a metal grate has been placed over the shaft, lest unsuspecting backcountry skiers plunge into it. The original hoisting machine still sits there today. To get there, park 8.25 miles up the canyon, at the old **Forest Service Garage**. A road leading up behind the Alta municipal offices turns into a jeep road and eventually a trail that steadily climbs into the gulch.

Alta Ski Area marks the end of this driving route. To return, simply turn back to the west, downshift (to save the brakes), and head back toward Salt Lake City. Again—a road more than 8 miles long with an average grade of 9.2 percent should be taken slowly. Remember the burnt-brake smell on the way up?

It is very possible to link this drive with **Big Cottonwood Canyon** (chapter 2 of this book), which runs parallel to, and just north of, Little Cottonwood on

UT-190. Right next to Little, but a much different canyon geologically, Big is home to **Brighton** and **Solitude** ski resorts.

IN THE AREA

Accommodations

CLIFF LODGE, Snowbird. Moderately priced. Snowbird's largest hotel, with guest rooms, a spa, pools, and three restaurants. Call 1-800-232-9542. Website: www.snowbird.com.

Attractions and Recreation

ALTA SKI AREA, UT-210, Little Cottonwoods Canyon, Alta. Ski area with summer activities and hiking. Call 801-359-1078. Website: www.alta.com.

SNOWBIRD, UT-210, Little Cottonwood Canyon, Snowbird. Ski and snowboard resort in winter, summer resort in summer (with tram rides to resort top). Many restaurants and pubs. Call 801-933-2222. Website: www.snowbird.com.

Dining

AERIE RESTAURANT, Cliff Lodge, Snowbird. Expensive. Open Tuesday through Saturday for dinner only; reservations strongly recommended. American and Continental cuisine, with a sushi bar. Call 801-933-2181. Website: www.snowbird.com.

Other Contacts

UTAH TRANSIT AUTHORITY. Operating winter ski shuttle buses running from the parking lot at the mouth of Little Cottonwood Canyon (in addition to standard metro bus lines). Call 1-888-743-3882 or 801-743-3882. Website: www.rideuta.com.

WASATCH WILDFLOWER FESTIVAL. Taking place for 3 days (only one of which is held at Alta; the others feature the flowers at Snowbird, as well as Brighton and Solitude Resorts in Big Cottonwood Canyon) in the middle of July. Call Alta Visitors Bureau at 1-888-258-2840. Websites: www.discoveralta .com and www.cottonwoodcanyons.org/events/wasatch-wildflower-festival/.

2

SALT LAKE CITY INTO BIG COTTONWOOD CANYON

ESTIMATED LENGTH: About 30 miles one-way from downtown Salt Lake City; add about 11 miles to descend into Park City over Guardsman Pass (open in summer only)

ESTIMATED TIME: Just over half an hour as a straight shot to the top of Big Cottonwood Canyon (or an hour to reach Park City); about a half-day with a few stops and a quick hike

HIGHLIGHTS: Much like its sister, Little Cottonwood Canyon, Big is the home of two ski areas, a lot of hiking, and a very steep road perfect for biking. Also like Little, Big Cottonwood is part of the city's watershed and is a no-pets-allowed area. However, the road to the top of Big is quite a lot longer than that in Little; it stretches for almost 15 miles (instead of Little's 8.3). Furthermore, at the top of Big, the road does not end (unlike in Little); it actually continues up and over the ridgeline at **Guardsman Pass**, descending into **Park City**, arriving in **Deer Valley**—but don't expect to take this road in winter. Turning into a dirt road east of its crest, it is closed during the long snowy season. Along the way, the route is flanked with the **Mount Olympus** and **Twin Peaks Wilderness** and the numerous foot trails that access them. By definition, these are not reachable by vehicle, but they provide pristine environments in which to ski tour and hike.

GETTING THERE: The I-215 beltway that encircles the expansive Salt Lake metropolitan area makes it possible for almost every place in Salt Lake City to be within 20 minutes of the mouth of Big Cottonwood Canyon, barring major traffic. To access Big Cottonwood, depart from the far southeastern corner of this beltway, taking Exit 6, and heading east and uphill on Fort Union Boulevard/UT-190. This climbs eastward and uphill, turning naturally into Wasatch Boulevard as it heads south. At a very obvious junction, signs will point eastward into Big Cottonwood Canyon (UT-190) and toward Brighton and Solitude Resorts, prompting a left-hand turn.

LEFT: SKI TOURING ATOP REYNOLD'S PASS, BIG COTTONWOOD CANYON

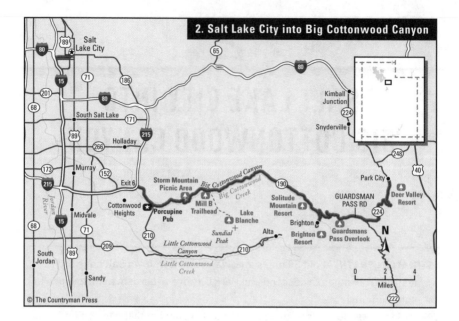

© The Countryman Press

(Do not stay straight here or follow signs to Alta and Snowbird; those are in Little Cottonwood Canyon, which runs parallel to Big, a few miles farther south.) In winter, be sure to check ahead of time for a road report (text "CanyonAlerts" to 53535 for critical updates). Especially after big snowstorms, this highway is frequently closed for up to several hours; given its steep sides and such a narrow bottom, the authorities must perform preventative blasting and clearing.

In summer, **Big Cottonwood Canyon** is one of the most popular hiking destinations for Salt Lake City-ites. In winter, its two ski resorts, **Brighton** and **Solitude**, its massive backcountry, and the annual 500-plus inches of snowfall make it a world-class ski playground. Though it seems many miles away, Park City and its ski hills are actually just over the ridge from Big Cottonwood as the crow flies. Many backcountry skiers take advantage of this fact, often riding the Canyons Village at Park City's lifts and then embarking on a major ski tour into and through Big Cottonwood Canyon.

The history of Big Cottonwood dates back roughly 900 million years—to the time when its quartzite and slate rock structures formed. Both metamorphic rock types, the mountain's rust-colored quartzite originated as sandstone, while the black slate came from shale. Compressed under high pressure, both turned (or "metamorphosed") into these more compact, but visually similar, versions of their originals. Especially low in the canyon, this orangish-red and very blocky, striated quartzite is the obvious and dominant rock type.

Just as in Park City and Little Cottonwood Canyon—and as all across Idaho, Wyoming, and Colorado—Big Cottonwood's ski resorts are a successor industry to earlier mining towns. In 1863, the first mine in the canyon, Evening Star, was opened. In the 1870s and '80s, more than 2,400 miners would come to live up near Brighton and Solitude, working at literally hundreds of assorted mines, living geographically and culturally segregated from the young, very Mormon Salt Lake City below. These towns flourished for just a few decades, then died out as quickly as they appeared. As in other mining towns, the resources here were finite, and this isolated settlement had no recourse once the mines became obsolete. Massive timber harvesting took place during the intervening years, but the canyon's local economy would not properly rekindle until Brighton opened in 1936, followed by Solitude in 1957.

Since the beginning of human settlement in Salt Lake Valley, Big Cottonwood has provided a beautiful retreat from city life—with picnic grounds and long, mountainous hikes, these canyons' resources are spread out, yet quite near the city. Today, this is the most popular sport climbing area immediately near Salt Lake City, and it is one of its best backcountry skiing zones.

When getting in the car, remember to leave the dog at home. Even if a dog remains in the vehicle the entire time, its presence is still highly illegal in Big Cottonwood. Law enforcement is serious about the preservation of the city's watersheds and will happily award a several-hundred-dollar fine (and

SPRING SNOW HIGH IN BIG COTTONWOOD

possibly even a jail stint) to anyone disobey-ing this simple law.

Porcupine Pub is conveniently located for people traveling to Little or Big Cottonwood Canyons. A large, nice but casual restaurant and pub, this popular joint serves draft beer, massive (and delicious, heaping) nachos, and a full menu that is perfectly befitted to skiing, hiking, and mountain biking appetites. Burg-ers, steaks, salads, and other entrees top the menu, with great daily specials offered. Located right at the southwestern corner of Fort Union Boulevard and Big Cottonwood Canyon Road junction, this is one of the last stops to be had before entering the canyon. Those who miss it on the way up should hit it on the way down.

Storm Mountain Picnic Area is the first major recreation area, located just 2.75 miles up-canyon. R. D. Maxfield Jr. decided to make his home here in the early twentieth century—and this has been a leisure site for many decades since, with a stage built by the Civilian Conservation Corps in the 1930s. Today, this popular day-use spot has plenty of open streamside space, a small outdoor stage, and a good bit of rock climbing, too. To enter, a day fee must be paid. (Note: No drinking water is available here; a $2 fee applies for vehicles with more than five persons.)

Four and a half miles into the canyon is the extremely obvious **"S-Curve"** of the road. Tucked in the folds of this curve (as well as lying to the outside of the curve) are a few dozen parking spots. This is a heavy-recreation-use spot, again with a generous amount of climbing (located above the upper fold of the curve) and a few hiking trailheads. On the lower bend of the S-Curve is one of Big Cottonwood Canyon's most well-known hiking trailheads, called **Mill B**.

A 3-mile trail to **Lake Blanche** departs from here. This striking alpine lake is encircled by rock spires skirted by talus and smattered thinly with evergreen trees. **Sundial Peak**, elevation 10,320 feet, sits immediately near the lake, with other summits surrounding it in the distance—**Dromedary Peak** (11,107 feet), **Sunrise Peak** (11,275 feet), and **Monte Cristo** (11,132 feet). Very dissimilar in appearance from the canyon bottom, the gray stone of this basin has been polished smooth by ancient glaciers in many places. To get there, head east (up-canyon) out of the lower parking lot in the S-Curve (Mill B). Go about 0.25 mile on the asphalt trail to a bridge that crosses a creek. The trail to Lake Blanche (now no longer paved) is signed, forks up from here, and is very easy to follow. The remainder of the hike is just under 3 miles. Before you reach Lake

Blanche (located at the terminus of the trail), other side trails will take quick jaunts to Lake Lillian and Lake Florence—both fine-looking lakes themselves.

For an almost zero-walking-time alternative, leave the Mill B parking lot and carefully cross the S-folds of the road to the north, toward a small alcove and stream. Hardly uphill from the road at all, the obvious stream forms a waterfall. Hiking along the trail (that heads uphill and to the right) leads to a few tiers of cliffs; these are some of the most popular rock climbing walls in the canyon. Beware, though—the approach to these is on steep, loose talus, and it can be dangerous to walk for those not accustomed to such scrambling.

Continue uphill, undistracted by infrastructure of any kind, and simply enjoy the scenery. Consider taking a hike along the way, as nearly every bend in the road reveals another pullout with another trailhead. Given enough time, these can be explored either with or without a map. During the winter, many of these serve as excellent backcountry skiing access points.

Nearly at the top of the canyon are Brighton and Solitude Resorts, Solitude being the lower of the two and having an apt name. Though "just" 1,200 acres in size, it has an almost 2,050-foot vertical drop, and hardly any crowding whatsoever. Perhaps because of its "old-fashioned" lifts, or the fact that the surrounding resorts are more expansive and famous, it enjoys seemingly less congestion than its competitors. In winter, too, it is one of the Wasatch's most popular Nordic skiing spots, with 20 kilometers worth of groomed trails at this facility. In the summer, hiking, biking, disc golf, scenic lift rides, and dining are all options. But of course, summer arrives a bit tardy in the high Wasatch, so

Ride Big Cottonwood

Big Cottonwood Canyon is just another of the Salt Lake area's great canyon road rides for mountain bikes. This is its most serious single-hill climb, too, with an in-canyon distance of 14.7 miles to Solitude and an elevation gain of 4,584 feet. And that's not counting the initial climb from the valley to the canyon's mouth, which adds another 600 or 700 vertical feet, depending on the point of origin.

Those wanting to take it even further can top out at **Guardsman Pass** (the turnoff to which is just slightly before Solitude Resort) by continuing on the switchbacks to an elevation of 9,700 feet (and a total distance of 16.9 miles), with final grades as steep as 15 percent. The reason for this not typically being part of the ride profile is that this topmost section of road eventually turns to dirt, and many people don't want to ride their multi-thousand-dollar bikes on dirt. For more information on this canyon, or other rides in the area, check out www.saltlakecycling.com. This awesome website gives ride profiles, lengths, elevation, descriptions, tips, and reports.

HIGH BIG COTTONWOOD BACKCOUNTRY

don't expect to be mountain biking up here in May; with the mountain's base elevation of 7,988 feet, it takes a little while before the slopes are clear of snow.

Brighton, founded in 1936, is the uppermost resort in the canyon and is favored among snowboarders and skiers who like to jib in its four terrain parks. Outside of these jumps, rails, and pipes, Brighton has 1,745 vertical feet spread across 1,050 acres and the usual eastern Wasatch 500 inches of annual snow—that's almost 42 feet of snowfall in an average year. Open from 9 AM to 9 PM in the height of ski season, night skiing is another of its special assets. In the summer, Brighton welcomes the public to visit for low-key dining, hiking, and fishing. Silver Lake, just a 1-mile walk from the base area, is stocked with trout and may be fished by anyone with a proper Utah conservation license.

To extend this drive all the way east and into **Park City**, backtrack just a few hundred yards from Brighton, and make a right turn to follow Big Cottonwood Canyon Road/UT-190 as it makes switchbacks farther up the sides of the canyon and toward **Guardsman Pass** (closed in winter), the top of which is 16.9 miles from the mouth of the canyon. In the short distance from the turnoff (just over 3 miles), the road climbs nearly another 1,000 feet to an elevation of 9,700 feet, changing from pavement to dirt as it zigzags with grades as steep as 15 percent.

To return to Salt Lake City, either do an about-face at the top of Guardsman, or extend the trip by heading down and east into Park City. From the top of the pass, the road (now UT-152) winds down through forests, fields, and the chairlifts of **Deer Valley Resort**, T-ing into UT-224. Take a left on this, turning north, and end up in **Park City** (and if you drive even farther north, I-80). Alternatively, head south on UT-224 into **Midway** (the home of **Soldier Hollow**

Resort, location of the 2002 Winter Olympics Nordic skiing events) and then, optionally, east into **Heber City**. These small rural communities sit in scenic valleys reminiscent of western Montana. South of Heber and Midway, US-189 takes a southwesterly direction into **Provo Canyon**. Taking this toward Provo will land you right in the center of the **Provo Canyon Scenic Drive** (part of chapter 3 in this book). Following this road to the west leads through Provo Canyon and into Provo-Orem; turning north on the Alpine Highway/UT-92 toward **Mount Timpanogos** finishes chapter 3's drive by winding along high, European Alps-esque mountainside and down into **American Fork Canyon**.

IN THE AREA

Attractions and Recreation

BRIGHTON RESORT, 12601 Big Cottonwood Canyon Road/UT-190, Brighton. Call 801-532-4731 or 1-800-873-5512; text "CanyonAlerts" to 53535 for critical road updates in winter. Website: www.brightonresort.com.

SOLITUDE RESORT, 12000 Big Cottonwood Canyon Road/UT-190, Solitude. Winter and summer resort with hiking, mountain biking, disc golf, dining, and lodging available in summer. Call 801-534-1400; text "CanyonAlerts" to 53535 for critical road updates in winter. Website: www.skisolitude.com.

Dining

PORCUPINE PUB, 3698 East Fort Union Boulevard/7200 South/UT-190, Salt Lake City. A moderately priced American restaurant and beer pub. Great "appy hour" 2:30–5:00 PM. Monday through Friday and other specials. Family friendly. Call 801-942-5555. Website: www.porcupinepub.com.

Other Contacts

SALTLAKECYCLING.COM. A highly informative, Salt Lake City–specific website with road cycling route descriptions and elevation profiles.

WASATCH WILDFLOWER FESTIVAL. Taking place for 3 days, and held at Brighton, Solitude, and Alta (in Little Cottonwood Canyon) in the middle weekend of July. Call the Alta Visitors Bureau at 1-888-258-2840. Websites: www.discoveralta.com and www.cottonwoodcanyons.org/events/wasatch-wildflower-festival/.

3

ALPINE LOOP TO AMERICAN FORK CANYON

ESTIMATED LENGTH: 26 miles

ESTIMATED TIME: 2 hours with some sightseeing

HIGHLIGHTS: Popular for both motorists and fit cyclists alike, this mountain route climbs steeply out of the expansive Wasatch Front metropolis and high into the mountain range itself. Beginning at about 4,830 feet elevation, it climbs roughly 3,200 feet to reach an altitude of 8,060 feet. The actual "scenic" business lasts just over 30 miles, with each end of the scenic drive within about 10 minutes of I-15. This road offers a virtual trip abroad: tight, Tour-de-France-style switchbacks; narrow, looping roads; craggy peaks; and canyon-bottom riverside driving.

GETTING THERE: This route travels south to north, from the Provo area up to the lesser-known Lehi and Highland area by way of Provo Canyon and American Fork Canyon. The starting point for this trip sits in the northeastern corner of the Provo-Orem continuum, at the intersection of Orem's 800 North Street (UT-52) and University Avenue (US-189). From here, follow US-189 north out of town. Alternatively, to drive the route from north to south, depart from I-15 at Exit 284 for Highland/Alpine, and head east on UT-92. This busts directly through sprawling farmland-turned-new-build territory, making a beeline dead east for American Fork Canyon. As of 2017, the cost to enter American Fork Canyon was $6, payable to the Uinta-Wasatch-Cache National Forest; annual America the Beautiful passes are accepted.

Before departing from town, take a look around and check out what Provo and Orem have to offer. Around the world, Salt Lake City holds the reputation for being the Mormon capital of the world. Though in many ways

LEFT: SUMMIT OF ALPINE LOOP

3. Alpine Loop to American Fork Canyon

(especially in the historical sense) it deserves this title, Provo also serves many important roles in modern Latter-day Saints Church functioning—particularly in education. Here, Brigham Young University and the Missionary Training Center (as well as other institutions) attract a surprisingly diverse collection of Mormons who come from around the world to study and settle here. Though most of the dining options around the city are understated and appear somewhat drab, don't underestimate the tastiness of the many ethnic cuisines prepared by Mormon immigrants.

Utah Lake, the largest freshwater lake in the state, has about 150 square miles of surface area. Just south of the famous Great Salt Lake, and hardly any higher, this is the last pooling place for Great Basin runoff before the **Jordan River** flows terminally into the Great Salt Lake. There, water's only escape is evaporation, leaving behind its saline content and making the Great Salt Lake roughly ten times as salty as the ocean.

To the east of Utah Lake and **Utah Valley** looms the southern portion of the **Wasatch Mountains**—more than 7,000 vertical feet higher. **Mount Timpanogos**, the most famous and visually impressive peak in the range, peaks at 11,750 feet above sea level; Utah Lake's surface touches just around 4,500 feet. **Mount Nebo,** the southernmost mountain in the Wasatch Range, stands taller than any of its sister peaks, at 11,928 feet. Though tall, Nebo is also rather hard to spot; not a distinct, pointy peak, this mountain is recognizable as double peaks on the southern end of a long, clean ridgeline.

Beneath the distinctly angular peaks of the Southern Wasatch, narrow canyons drain the massive snowfields that accumulate in winter—as the western side of the Wasatch receives an average of more than 500 inches of snow annually. Many mountain streams collect beneath the mountainside, eventually flowing into the valley and adding to the abundant freshwater of Utah Lake.

As Utah Lake contains a vast supply of fresh mountain water and the climate of Utah Valley behaves rather hospitably, this area has long been inhabited by humans—first by the Timpanogotzis ("Fish Eaters"). Unlike many tribes in North America's interior, who were forever chasing good climes, these fish eaters lived a stable life in one location. The weather neither froze nor baked them; the lake fed and watered them.

Their first encounter with Europeans was likely with the famed Franciscan explorer-priests Escalante and Dominguez in September 1776. However, approaching winter chased the explorers out of Utah and back toward Mexico—they stayed here but briefly. Aside from trappers, traders, outlaws, and other transient Europeans, this valley would remain left alone and undeveloped for several decades.

July 24, 1848, would become one of the most significant days in history for Utah and the Intermountain West. After several months of rugged

MT. TIMPANOGOS FROM ALPINE LOOP BYWAY

Winter Road Closure Extended!

Before embarking on this route anytime from October through May, be sure to check with the **Utah Department of Transportation** (801-965-4000) to be sure the road is in fact open. The lofty elevation of this mountain pass and its more than 500 inches of annual snowfall close the road each winter—sometimes as early as October, and usually lasting into May or June. Naturally, the time frame is different every year, so be sure to check online for up-to-date information.

cross-country travel, Brigham Young and his Latter-day Saints followers arrived in the Salt Lake Valley. Being of peculiar beliefs and practices, the Mormons had endured persecution and societal rejection since their church's founding—especially in the church's pre-1890 days when polygamy was an acknowledged practice. Banished from city after city and state after state in just a matter of decades, the LDS deliberately sought a deserted and utterly isolated place to establish their own society away from other religions and politics. As Utah was utterly isolated—far from any coasts, and also quite far from the Oregon Trail or any major throughway—it would be the perfect location.

Other would-be European residents of the Salt Lake Valley had little interest in it for the exact same reasons that made it perfect for the Mormons—much too isolated and arid, and a challenging environment to coax into sustaining a large population. However, the industrious values and pious nature of these Latter-day Saints gave them the perfect credentials for the job. Organized and hungry for a home, they set about voraciously laying down roots. Salt Lake City was pre-planned and under construction by the fall of 1848—just a few months after the Mormons' historical arrival.

Fields were planted and plans set in motion. Encouraged by news of success, more LDS pioneers began to arrive by great handcart parades, and church leaders ordered more satellite communities to be founded. Colonizing efforts began and pilot groups went out, establishing other towns across Utah in the name of building a Mormon empire.

Provo was established in March 1849. Though at first a small village, it quickly grew in size and importance. The completion of the first transcontinental railroad at Promontory Point, just north of Salt Lake City, would leave many retired rail workers in the Salt Lake Valley, and allowed for much easier arrival of non-Mormons to this open, promising landscape. Never being ones for "heathens," many Mormons slipped south out of Salt Lake and focused more on the settlement of nearby Provo. While Salt Lake City will always remain the historical capital of Mormonism, today Provo seems in many ways to be a more spiritually pure cultural center for the Saints.

In modern times, Provo is the training ground for blossoming Mormons. On its soils sit two of the church's most important educational centers: **Brigham Young University** and the **Missionary Training Center** (actually part of BYU). BYU and the MTC remain especially connected to the church, as both are funded by it and were established expressly for church members. Though Orem's **Utah Valley University** is technically not a Mormon institution, many thousands of the area's youth receive a degree from it every year. Together these institutions comprise roughly 70,000 students and faculty.

Though technically two separate townships, Orem and Provo operate nearly as one, and flow into each other seamlessly, sharing many of the same streets and community facilities. Anyone requiring food will notice that the area is teeming with national midlevel chain restaurants. For a locally flavored bite, head to the intersection of **University Avenue** and **Center Street**; park your car and walk in any direction to find dozens of small eateries featuring almost as many cuisines. Given the general monocultural ambience of Utah Valley, it may come as a surprise that this small intersection features restaurants representing the cuisine of countries from Korea to India, most of which are run by first-generation immigrants. Why are they here? As the Mormon Church spreads around the world, international members have been inspired to live in Utah, quite often specifically for an education at BYU or to be trained at the MTC.

Lodging in Utah Valley is almost exclusively of the budget-to-average national-brand variety—dependable yet unadorned. The one major exception to this rule exists outside of Provo at the **Sundance Resort** (described later in this chapter). Sleepy visitors in the valley can choose between any imaginable chain, from a Hampton Inn to a Best Western to a Marriott. As with most of the valley's restaurants, these hotels are clustered around University Avenue, downtown, and near I-15.

Head toward Provo Canyon and out of the city from Orem's 800 North Street (UT-52) and University Avenue (US-189). Those wanting to check out the canyon as pedestrians, Rollerbladers, or cyclists can pick up the Provo River Parkway here or at any of the numerous access points between Utah Lake and its terminus at Nunn's Park. (For more information, visit www.utahmountainbiking.com and navigate to this ride from the Utah Valley region trails page.) This paved 14-mile trail heads up and into Provo Canyon, providing a peaceful way to get some exercise and enjoy nature away from US-189. Tracing along the Provo River, this pathway climbs into the canyon, but it has a very tame grade and is extremely popular among casual cyclists, joggers, families, and stroller pushers. Be aware that in town the path often plunges underneath streets via narrow tunnels, and careless riders with too much speed can cause a serious collision with others.

Drivers: Point the wheels north-northeast and head out from Orem on US-189. This range is overseen by the Uinta-Wasatch-Cache National Forest. Leaving Utah Valley, this pavement ribbon begins to ascend into **Provo Can-**

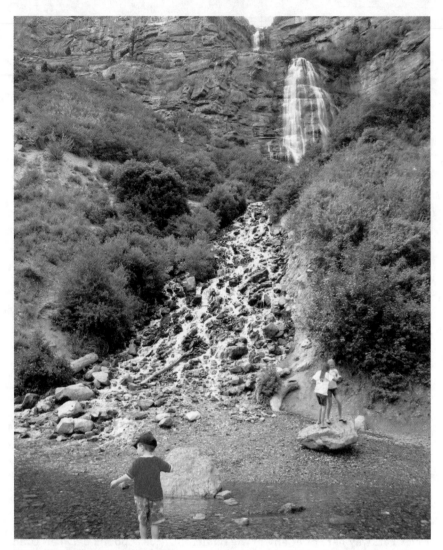

KIDS PLAYING BENEATH BRIDAL VEIL FALLS

yon, which is drained by the **Provo River**. Though the Wasatch Range isn't necessarily famous for fly fishing, Provo River offers some of the best trout fishing in the area. Its entire course consists of roughly 70 miles, from the Uinta Mountains' **Washington Lake** at 10,450 feet elevation down to Utah Lake. In the lower and middle sections of this river swim brown, cutthroat, and rainbow trout—roughly five thousand fish per river mile. For a guided trip, equipment retail or rental, or just online fishing forecasts, check out **Fish Heads Fly Shop**, located in Heber City, or call the **Park City Anglers** in Park City.

As US-189 climbs into the canyon, the first stop along the way is **Canyon Glen Park**—just one in a series of many city-park-type alcoves with tables and green space in this canyon. This particular locale's bonus for picnickers is its distinctly smaller crowds than those in the Bridal Veil Falls vicinity. From this park you can also access the **Great Western Trail**. This enormous, often very rugged path leads all the way from Mexico to Canada through the western United States, crossing five states: Arizona, Utah, Wyoming, Idaho, and Montana. It adds up to 4,455 miles, yet it is still wild, rough, and sometimes crudely patchworked—much less developed than its more famous cousin to the east, the Appalachian Trail. Sixteen hundred miles of the GWT pass through Utah, incorporating many of the state's most popular and scenic trails near Bear Lake, Brighton Ski Resort, Mount Timpanogos, Fish Lake, Bryce Canyon National Park, and Grand Staircase-Escalante National Monument. The trail is still under development, so hiking the entirety of it takes great navigational skills and self-sufficiency in the wilderness.

Three miles into the canyon is the location of one of its most famous attractions: **Bridal Veil Falls**. Off this two-tiered cataract falls, a ribbon of water cascades steeply down vertical limestone cliff bands for a total of 607 vertical feet. Clearly visible off to the south side of the road, these can also be seen by taking the short, paved hiking trail that ventures yet closer from the signed pull-off for Nunn's Park/Bridal Veil Falls. To hike the trail, turn right (and away from Nunn's Park) from this exit; hike up canyon on the most obvious broad paved path. The falls are about half a mile away.

Cyclists' Dream

For hardcore road cyclists, the Alpine Loop is one of Utah's finest mountain rides. Cyclists can follow more or less the exact same path as this chapter's driving route, looping easily back south through town at the "end" of this scenic drive.

To begin the ride, cyclists can pick up the Provo River Parkway, a paved pedestrian and bike path, at an access point right at the mouth of Provo Canyon on 800 North. Head east into the canyon, and rejoin the main road and scenic route in the **Bridal Veil Falls** area.

As the Alpine Loop climbs high onto the shoulders of Mount Timpanogos, the way becomes quite narrow and must be shared with vehicles. Because of the steep and winding nature of the road, most drivers should be maneuvering attentively—but that should never be taken for granted, and bikers should be extremely cautious.

During spring, a magic window of good weather sometimes avails in May. This is a time when the road is still closed to vehicular through traffic but is sometimes clear of snow. During this period, and before the true heat of Utah summer kicks in, this can be one of the most enjoyable paved bike rides in the state, utterly scenic and free of traffic.

During winter, keep an eye out for ice climbers on this flow. Though there are numerous ice-climbing areas in the canyon, this is one of the most popular. This famous ice-climbing route, called Stairway to Heaven, is so named because of its terraced nature; it is one of the taller water ice climbs in the United States. Many climbers stick to the first pitch of the route, called the Apron, but climbers wishing to continue can go on for multiple pitches above that. For more information, check out the guidebook *Beehive Ice*, published in 2016 by Nathan Smith and Andrew Burr.

Nunn's Park, just across the highway and under the bridge from Bridal Veil Falls, makes a good base camp for those checking out the falls. Like a typical city park, this has shade trees and green grass. Here there are more than twelve campsites (for $15 per night), pit toilets, and different pavilions for hire during the summer months. All camping is handed out first come, first served; pavilions must be reserved and paid for ahead of time. The park's namesake, L. L. Nunn, was an early hydroelectric-power thinker, who operated the first 44,000-volt water-powered plant in America here, back in 1897. Converting the potential and kinetic energy of the Provo River into electricity, he provided power for mines in the Mercur, Utah,

Bridal Veil Falls Tram

From 1967 through 1996, a six-passenger aerial tram shuttled guests from the Bridal Veil Falls parking area to the Eagle's Nest Lodge atop the falls. The lodge wore many hats throughout its lifetime, and the tram was the only reasonable means to reach it. But both the tram and the lodge were set up in a difficult area with fickle weather and inconsistent business. The tram was claimed by locals to have been the world's steepest, but hard evidence is lacking on this point.

The lodge itself changed ownership many times, and during its tenure from roughly 1961 to 1996, it functioned sometimes as a restaurant, sometimes as a special-events venue. The nature of its location—precipitously perched on a mountainside—left it and the tram quite exposed to the elements, particularly avalanches. When one such slide finally destroyed the tram in early 2006, the restaurant, whose only access had been via the tram, closed "temporarily." Unable to raise funds to restore and reopen, the owners finally gave up trying in 2007 when the Forest Service required a mandatory $100,000 environmental study to be conducted before it would consider allowing the restaurant to begin operating again.

The final blow came in July of that year, when a wildfire burned 240 acres in the vicinity, including the restaurant itself, as well as four of the five tram cables; the other was later snipped and removed. Today the site remains vacant, with few good solutions proposed for future use of the land.

Sundance Film Festival

Though you won't find the festival here at the Sundance Resort, the fact that the two share the same name is not a coincidence. Like the resort, the now-world-famous independent film festival was also the brainchild of actor Robert Redford—a man who has led a life using his stardom to promote the arts and practice philanthropy. Established in 1981, Sundance is the most influential independent film festival in the world to date, taking place primarily in Park City, but also flowing over into Salt Lake City and beyond. Sundance fills the local theaters in January, and its busyness gridlocks the small mountain town. Tickets are nearly impossible to get last-minute, but with advance planning or a steel will, they can be acquired. Good luck parking, though!

area. There are still traces left over from the hydropower plant days—as well as a plaque to commemorate its existence.

Next up is **Vivian Park**, just under 6 miles into the canyon (and about 2.5 miles up from Bridal Veil Falls). Historically, this area has been an attraction for travelers and recreationalists of various wants and needs since 1888. Originally, Billy's Place was a stop for Provo Canyon travelers to dine and recover. Around 1900, its role switched to that of a canyon retreat, complete with restaurants, guest cabins, and live music (See "Bridal Veil Falls Tram," below). When the world started getting smaller, people could travel farther away to bigger resorts, such as Sundance Resort (later in this chapter), and this retreat became defunct. Today, a tiny village of miniature-looking homes is tucked into the forest here. Nearest US-189 is the public recreation area with picnic tables, pit toilets, and greenery. There is also a fishing area (for children twelve and under only). From the west end of the park (departing from its central parking lot) is the **Provo River Parkway** (as described earlier in this chapter). This 14-mile paved pathway leads back down the canyon, through town, and to Utah Lake.

About 7 miles into the canyon, and still barely above 5,200 feet of elevation, the route departs from Provo Canyon, turning left (northwest) onto the Alpine Loop (UT-92) and begins to seriously climb. Just 2 miles after this turnoff comes the **Sundance Resort**, nearly 2,000 feet higher than the Alpine Loop–US-189 junction just a few miles back. For most, the name Sundance signifies more than just a ski resort. Sharing the same name and founder with the Sundance Film Festival, this Robert Redford–owned ski area is one of the smallest and most beautiful in Utah. Much more of a retreat than a tram-driving, crowd-pushing resort, the restaurants and the arts culture are the only features that compete with its natural beauty.

Robert Redford, who famously played the Sundance Kid in *Butch Cassidy and the Sundance Kid*, became enamored of Utah during his many shoots in the area. He purchased a fledgling ski area on this site in 1969 and transformed it into the modern-day resort. Today, it's a peaceful stop in any season for lunch or even a multiday stay. Everything at Sundance—from the cuisine to the architecture—draws from and highlights the natural environment.

The dining at Sundance is some of the best in the area, and people regularly drive from Provo and beyond just to enjoy dinner here. Those needing sustenance may choose from many options. Two restaurants, the Tree Room and the Foundry Grill, both present options to sit down and enjoy local game and vegetables, as well as seafood, fresh fish, and more. Hearty, seasonal cuisine is cooked up with fine skill at both places, with the **Tree Room** being the much more formal of the two. This AAA four-diamond, *Wine Spectator* Award–winning affair serves modern American and Continental cuisine with a western flair and heavy use of local, organic, and generally top-notch ingredients.

The **Foundry Grill** provides a meal to those wearing jeans, towing children, or simply desiring a less formal or less pricey experience. Also serving regional American cuisine, this menu is nothing to pooh-pooh. The offerings span the range from salad, pizza, and pasta to halibut and filet mignon. But this is no iceberg lettuce salad bar or greasy pizza; the salads are lush, green, and creative; and the pizza is wood-fired.

For those in a rush or wanting to move on, **The Deli** is a Sundance-flavored general-store-type affair, offering everything from gift baskets and wine to specialty sauces and dressings to preserves, fresh baked goods, snacks, and chilled soda. Those not wishing to drive any farther for the day should consider unwinding with a beverage. In the resort center, the **Owl Bar** serves libations nightly across a historic Victorian rosewood bar that was actually used back in the 1890s in Thermopolis, Wyoming, at a watering hole that Butch Cassidy and the Wild Bunch often visited.

While at the resort, there are numerous activities to check out any time of the year. In the summer the resort offers fly fishing, mountain biking, hiking, cross-country horseback riding, and moonlit lift rides. In winter, snowboarding, Nordic skiing, and downhill skiing obviously draw most of the visitors. But year-round, the resort sports a spa and hosts various nature programs like night owling and nighttime snowshoeing, as well as children's programs. The Spa at Sundance has gained national notoriety and has been featured in a number of magazines such as *New York*, *Travel + Leisure*, and *Spa*.

The **Sundance Art Studio** is another year-round affair completely atypical of a ski resort. Here artists-in-residence work; their art can be seen in exhibits around Sundance. These artists also oversee and instruct daily 2-hour workshops designed for guests. Check out the glassblower studio and take a class there if time allows. The gallery and glassblower studio are both located right in the Art Studio, and clinics are offered multiple times daily.

After leaving Sundance, prepare for ever-steepening and narrowing roadways as the pavement now begins to ascend into the high shoulders and cirques of the tall Wasatch Range and Mount Timpanogos. The steepness of

American Fork Rock Climbing

Look around on this leg of the trip and notice the many dozen limestone cliffs rising at all heights throughout the canyon. Though many of these cliffs appear rotten and crumbly, a few dozen of them actually consist of relatively compact, sturdy rock. The faces and caves of these "better" cliffs have been a destination for technical rock climbing for decades.

Technical rock climbing began in a much different style than that done today on these gray rocks. It developed out of mountaineering; as rock climbing moved away from high summits, a new sport arose on sheer rock faces, pushing physical and technical difficulty. First following cracks, these routes stuck to the natural "lines" in rock, and climbers' falls could be protected with ropes and removable gear. Yosemite is one of the famous birthplaces of rock climbing in North America, during the 1960s and 1970s.

ROCK CLIMBER AT THE DIVISION WALL IN AMERICAN FORK CANYON

However, during the 1990s, a new type of technical climbing became popular that didn't require a crack for placing protection. Sport climbing, as it's called, implemented the use of bolts drilled into rock. Climbers, now able to clip their ropes into these bolts with carabiners, could climb faces of rock—totally independent of removable gear. Sport climbing, by nature, was much faster and more accessible than traditional climbing. It required much less gear and emphasized placement of protection much less. Rather than spending time finding the right cam for a crack, a climber could simply clip a pre-placed bolt and move on.

With the new ease and speed of protection, climbers could now focus on harder moves and routes. "Whippers," where a climber falls off a route, became the norm, as climbers could now "work" routes and moves until they gained the fitness, skill, and memory necessary to "send" them, or complete them in one push from the ground.

Since sport climbing's inception in the '90s, it has revolutionized climbing, pushing climbers beyond what they could do with traditional gear. Though many extremely difficult routes have gone up on traditional gear, it is thanks to sport climbing that these ascensionists had the strength and skill to apply to traditional climbing.

(continued on next page)

Though today many sport climbing areas have been developed around the country, this canyon is special. American Fork Canyon was once one of the sport's pioneering epicenters in the United States and is therefore considered a historically significant location for climbers around the world. So even though the routes are polished, climbing snobs should appreciate it for what it's worth and imagine bolting some of these lines back in the 1990s!

Popular walls today include the Hell Cave, home of some of the canyon's most difficult routes; the Division Wall, with many 5.10s–5.12s; and the Escape Buttress, a south-facing 5.10 haven. For a vastly more thorough guide, check out *Climber's Guide to American Fork/Rock Canyon*, by Stuart and Bret Ruckman.

the terrain forces the road to narrow severely and fold into switchbacks; at points, the vistas look more like Europe's Alps than like central Utah.

From here, it's hard to believe that only 60 miles west, as the crow flies, lie the salt flats of the Great Salt Lake Desert and the Dugway Proving Ground (see chapter 16). Just 6 miles beyond the Sundance Resort, the Alpine Loop Road tops out. At an elevation of 8,030 feet, the Alpine Loop is draped over the high shoulders of Mount Timpanogos, a broad fortress of a peak. Take a deep breath (of thin air!) and begin to descend. Keep speed in check and watch for oncoming traffic and bikers—this is one of the more popular bike rides in Utah.

Six miles of truly stunning descent brings the road through Pyrenees-style switchbacks and down almost 2,000 vertical feet (to an elevation of 6,070 feet)—a drop symmetrical to the climb on the southern side of the pass. At the bottom of this steep decline, this road meets up with **American Fork Canyon**. To enter the canyon, a day fee of $6 per vehicle (as of 2017) must be paid at the **Uinta-Wasatch-Cache National Forest** tollbooth; America the Beautiful passes are accepted.

American Fork Canyon, like all the major Wasatch drainages, runs east-west and cuts deeply into the tall range, carving severely steep, narrow slots into the already-impressive, craggy Wasatch Range. Though not many people find themselves readily occupied in the canyon—no overlooks, no restaurants, no gift shops—it nevertheless is a beautiful canyon in and of itself, offering multiple Forest Service picnic grounds and campgrounds. Beware here—though this area is not overtly dangerous, trail accidents, animal attacks, and weather incidents cause injury and death every year. Education on basic wildlife behavior and taking precautions can help avoid these situations.

Heading down American Fork Canyon and toward Lehi (the nearest township in the Utah Valley), visitors pass by **Timpanogos Cave** very near the western end of the canyon, near its mouth.

Timpanogos Cave National Monument represents one of the largest, most publicly accessible caves in the region. Though the approach to the actual cave does require physical effort, the hike can be called reasonable by most standards. To reach the cave, all visitors must follow a 1.5-mile paved path that gains almost 1,200 feet of elevation from the parking lot to the cave's mouth. Though the path becomes quite steep in some places, it remains broad and smooth. Climbing out of the canyon floor and onto its southern slopes gives perspective and showcases the steepness of the V-shaped mountainsides.

The cave typically opens May through October. During this time, the park operates tours through three major chambers: Timpanogos Cave, Middle Cave, and Hansen Cave. To enter, all visitors must be part of a guided trip. These cost $8 per adult ($6 for juniors up to 15; $4 for children under 5; free for infants 2 and under) and can be reserved by calling the park. During the summer, booking ahead is highly recommended.

The first of the caves to be discovered was Hansen Cave, found by cougar-tracking Martin Hansen, all the way back in 1887. In the intervening time, before coming under government protection, much of Hansen Cave was vandalized and its features destroyed. Timpanogos and Middle Caves remained just a rumor until 35 years later, when they were each discovered by separate parties. Because of their delayed discoveries, these two caves' interiors were better protected and remain well-preserved today. The interior of the limestone complex is densely featured with speleothems, including stalactites and stalagmites, cave bacon, popcorn, flowstone, and rock straws called helictites.

Leaving the Timpanogos Cave and heading west, the ride is all but done. Soon enough the canyon opens up, quite abruptly, dumping traffic into Utah

Bear Attack: A Word of Caution

Though American Fork Canyon is generally safe and popular among visitors, it doesn't hurt to remember that it is also home to wild animals. In the early summer of 2007, a family camped at the Timpooneke Campground to celebrate Father's Day and christen the new tent that Dad had received as a gift. That night a black bear made its way into the campground, likely lured by the scent of food in the campsite. The animal mauled a sleeping eleven-year-old boy, dragging him from the tent and killing him.

At the time of the incident, this attack stood as the first lethal bear mauling in the state's written history. This type of attack can largely be avoided by keeping your campsite clear of enticing scents—by tying food high up in a distant tree or keeping it locked in the car, well away from the campsite—and carrying bear spray at all times. Regardless of precautions and existing warnings, wildlife is always a concern and should never be fed—for the sake of the animals and of the people.

Valley and the suburbs of Highland. To return to the interstate, stay on US-92, which travels due west, intersecting with I-15 in about 8 miles—no turning necessary. If biking, head south-southeast on any number of roads to return to the car. The main roads heading back toward Provo Canyon are UT-146 (Canyon Road), later 100 East Street, US-89 (State Street), and finally UT-52 (800 North Street, heading east). The total road bike loop is almost exactly 70 miles.

IN THE AREA

Accommodations

SUNDANCE RESORT (See "Attractions and Recreation" below)

Attractions and Recreation

FISH HEADS FLY SHOP, 32 South Main Street, Heber City. Retail and rental shop, guide services. Call 435-657-2010. Website: www.fishheadsflyshop.com.

NUNN'S PARK, Utah Country Park Department. For pavilion reservations or general questions, call 801-851-8640. Website: www.utahcountyonline.org.

PARK CITY ANGLERS, Park City. Gear rental, guide services. Call 435-658-3474. Website: www.parkcityanglers.com.

SUNDANCE ART STUDIO, Sundance Resort Center (see Sundance Resort). Gallery open Saturday and Sunday only; Art Studio open daily, check website for workshop schedule and to make reservations. Call 801-223-4535. Website: www.sundanceresort.com.

SUNDANCE RESORT, 8841 North Alpine Loop Road, Sundance. Call 1-866-259-7468 (or **Tree Room Restaurant**, 801-223-4200, and **Foundry Grill**, 801-223-4220). Website: www.sundanceresort.com.

TIMPANOGOS CAVE NATIONAL MONUMENT, 2038 Alpine Loop Road, American Fork. Call 801-756-5239 (headquarters) or 801-756-5661 (summer only). For tour reservations (recommended), call 801-756-5238. Website: www.nps.gov/tica.

VIVIAN PARK, 5828 North South Fork Road (US-189), Provo Canyon. For pavilion reservations or general questions, call 801-851-8640. Website: www .utahcountyonline.org.

Dining

THE DELI, Sundance Resort Center (see Sundance Resort). Open daily, morning through evening. Call 801-223-4211. Website: www.sundanceresort .com.

FOUNDRY GRILL, Sundance Resort Center (see Sundance Resort). Open for breakfast, lunch, and dinner Monday through Saturday, and brunch on Sunday only; closed between meals. Call 801-223-4220. Website: www .sundanceresort.com.

OWL BAR, Sundance Resort Center (see Sundance Resort). Open evenings Monday through Friday, and earlier on weekends. Call 801-223-4222. Website: www.sundanceresort.com.

TREE ROOM, Sundance Resort Center (see Sundance Resort). Fine, formal dining; American and Continental cuisine. Open for dinner only Tuesday through Saturday, closed Sunday. Reservations encouraged. Call 801-223-4200. Website: www.sundanceresort.com.

Other Contacts

BRIGHAM YOUNG UNIVERSITY, 150 East Bulldog Boulevard, Provo. Call 801-422-4636. Website: www.byu.edu.

GREAT WESTERN TRAIL. Trail system spanning the western United States from Mexico to Canada, passing Arizona, Utah, Wyoming, Idaho, and Montana on the way.

MISSIONARY TRAINING CENTER, 2005 North 900 East, Provo. Call 801-422-2602. Website: www.mtc.byu.edu.

SUNDANCE FILM FESTIVAL, Sundance Institute, 1825 Three Kings Drive, Park City. Call 435-658-3456. Website: www.sundance.org.

UTAH DEPARTMENT OF TRANSPORTATION. Responsible for road maintenance, issuance of reports. Call 801-965-4000. Website: www.udot.utah .gov.

UTAH VALLEY UNIVERSITY, 800 West University Parkway, Orem. Call 801-863-7149. Website: www.uvu.edu.

NEARING LOGAN FROM THE SOUTH ON US 89/91

4

LOGAN CANYON TO BEAR LAKE

ESTIMATED LENGTH: 39 miles from Logan to Bear Lake

ESTIMATED TIME: Half a day (with return trip)

HIGHLIGHTS: Along the way, the road climbs up and out of **Logan**, through **Logan Canyon** and along the **Logan River**. Ascending more than 3,000 vertical feet to a crest of 7,799 feet, it then descends into the **Bear Lake Valley** toward **Bear Lake**, which spans the Utah-Idaho border and is the second-largest freshwater lake in Utah (behind Utah Lake). The more the road climbs, the fewer and farther between the city-park-like picnic grounds, and the more the landscape transforms from typical Utah mountain lands to Montana- or Wyoming-like hills. Narrow twists and cliffs at the bottom of the canyon give way to a broader landscape at the top with rolling, grassy slopes.

GETTING THERE: Logan is one of just a handful of medium-sized towns in Utah not attached to an interstate or an urban conglomerate and yet not deriving its main industry from tourism. As it is separated from I-15 by a mountain ridge and about 20 miles (as the crow flies), there is no single way to get there. If coming from the south, the fastest way is via US-89/US-91, departing from I-15 in Brigham City. This major, oft-divided highway heads northeast, climbing up high through mountain passes before dipping back down again into the Cache Valley. If you are coming from the north, access can either be had by taking US-91 south from Idaho and directly into Logan or by taking UT-30 east from I-15 at Exit 385.

Logan is one of Utah's neatest, most genuine midsize towns. Not a mere dot on a map, a tourist town, or a sprawling suburb, this university town has roughly 49,000 residents and a beautiful post in the **Cache Valley** next to **Logan Canyon**, which cuts deeply into the **Bear River Range**. At the colder

4. Logan Canyon to Bear Lake

Idaho

Swan Flat · Bridger Peak · 89

Beaver Mountain Ski Area · 243 · SWAN FLAT RD

White Pine Lake · Steam Mill Hollow Trailhead · Beaver Creek Lodge

Naomi + Peak · Peter Sinks · 89

Bear Lake State Park · Garden City · Bear Lake

Mount Naomi Wilderness · Tony Grove Lake · FR-003 · Tony Grove Memorial Ranger Station Historic District

Bear River · Smithfield · 218

Bear River Range

Rendezvous Beach · Laketown · 30

Cache Valley · 91

Logan Canyon · Logan River · 89

Uinta-Wasatch-Cache National Forest

Utah State University · Second Dam · Wind Caves

Logan · 30 · Cache Valley Visitors Bureau · Main Street · First Dam Park · Stokes Nature Center · Crimson Trail · Spring Hollow Campground · Bridger Campground

Saddle Creek

89 · 165

101 · Hyrum · Blacksmith Fork Canyon · 101

N

Blacksmith Fork · Hardware Ranch

0 · 3 · 6 Miles

© The Countryman Press

---

end of Utah's diverse climate spectrum, Logan has seasons more closely resembling those in Wyoming than those in other towns in Utah.

Hungry people in Logan need look no further than **Main Street**. This strip of pavement running north–south is littered with restaurants of every genre and price range, from counter-style sub shops to Mexican cantinas and contemporary American dining. For a statewide favorite, visit Logan's **Indian Oven**. Opened by a native of India—also a restaurateur since 1989—this casual restaurant offers an extensive menu of authentic Indian cuisine with ample vegetarian offerings. Open for lunch and dinner only, the restaurant unfortunately closes its doors on Sundays, like many Utah establishments.

Le Nonne is Logan's favorite dispensary of Italian cuisine, serving traditional, high-end fare in an upscale, remodeled historic home. This place is yet another favorite in the area—and actually in the state—and is always one of the top-ranked restaurants in northern Utah. Again, this restaurant closes on Sundays, so plan ahead if you wish to dine here. It is primarily a dinner establishment, though lunch is served on Thursday and Friday. Make a reservation!

If you need a place to crash, Main Street is again the place to go. Many national hotel and motel chains have assembled along this street. **University**

DOWNTOWN LOGAN

Inn represents Logan's locally run hotel-style quarters. Owned by **Utah State University**, this stately hotel offers a range of options, from classic rooms to deluxe suites. Right on campus, this can be a relatively serene location in town, except perhaps on the weekends. The **Beaver Creek Lodge** is one of the more special deluxe hotels in the area, but it is in Logan Canyon (27 miles east of town; described later in this chapter).

While you're sleeping or dining on Main Street, it doesn't hurt to stop in at the **Cache Valley Visitors Bureau**. This group distributes a wealth of information (some free, some visitors must pay for) pertaining to Logan, Logan Canyon, Cache Valley, Bear Lake, and Utah in general. Even if you are just driving through and never exit the car outside of town, illustrated maps can shed some light on the significance of the views.

US-89 enters **Logan Canyon** by heading east from the city center as 400 North Street. This canyon, carved by the **Logan River** (ah *ha!*), is also cooled subtly by the river during summer, bringing temperatures here to a more humane level than in the sun-baked valleys. About 39 miles long from Logan to **Garden City**, US-89 parallels the river, climbing high through different landscapes and ending in the Bear Lake Valley, near the shores of the strikingly blue-green Bear Lake.

Before plunging into the Bear River Range Canyon, take a glance back across the Cache Valley and notice the very obvious horizontal terraces ringing the valley. During the last ice ages, which ended as recently as 12,000 years ago, this valley was submerged under hundreds of feet of Lake Bonneville's waters, just as the Salt Lake Valley was. The cool and moist climate of that time caused the **Great Basin** to fill with a lake that spanned from **Cedar City** to **Red Rock Pass** (near the Utah-Idaho border and I-15)—350 miles in length, and almost half as wide. What is today Logan sat under more than 600

26.2 Miles of Fall Foliage

The **Top of Utah Marathon**, one of the area's most famous events, is a 26.2-mile suffer-fest (with shorter versions) that begins in **Blacksmith Fork Canyon** at 6:55 AM on the third Saturday in September each year. Starting at **Hardware Ranch**, a refuge for moose, elk, and deer during the Bear River Mountains' harsh winter months, it runs down this canyon along UT-102, and finally into town. The race has become quite popular among runners for its supreme beauty and, possibly, because it's a gradual downhill course.

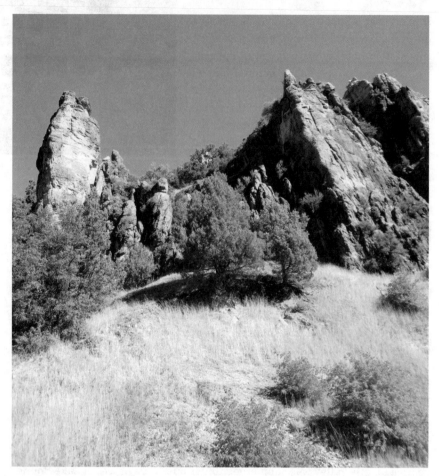

LIMESTONE SPIRES IN LOWER LOGAN CANYON

feet of water. During these times, the fauna was vastly different than today, with musk oxen, wooly mammoths, bison, and camels cruising the shoreline.

Those with any questions about the vast expanses of the **Uinta-Wasatch-Cache National Forest** (which is where the route is about to enter) should stop by the **Logan Ranger District Visitor Center** on the way. Situated cleverly at the mouth of the canyon, right on the roadside and well signed, it is open in all seasons (but closed on weekends!). Here visitors can pick up maps, ask about camping, get advice on recreation, or purchase keepsakes and postcards.

The first several potential stops happen in quick succession right after you enter the canyon. The first is one of a series of three low-head dams (cleverly named **First Dam**) pooling the Logan River's waters. Around this mini-reservoir sits a city park with picnickers, casual fishermen, and the like. Built up with bathrooms and fishing docks, the park is well manicured and user-friendly.

Those wanting to get stoked about the flora and fauna in Logan Canyon should move right along to the **Stokes Nature Center**, just 0.6 mile upriver of the canyon's mouth. This organization educates any curious person on Logan Canyon's environment, from fish to birds—and it can enrich an otherwise uninformed drive. A largely program-based operation, this center offers many educational events to the general community in addition to schools and groups. Check online for the current schedule. Park on the south side of the road and walk another tenth of a mile up canyon to pick up a short trail across US-89. This trail leads to the center after just another few hundred yards of walking. From here, too, the **River Trail** can be picked up. Perfect in length and pitch for a jog or casual walk, this 3.7-mile trail runs parallel to the Logan River and is sheltered from the highway by trees and bushes. Use your newly gained knowledge from the nature center to observe the canyon bottom.

Moving up canyon, the trail, road, and river all pass the **Second Dam** and the **Logan City Power Plant**, in operation since the early 1900s—during a time when power bills were assessed based on the number of light bulbs operating in a household. Today, this turbine provides the valley with roughly a sixth of its power. This pullout also offers another chance to picnic and use the restroom, but it won't be the last opportunity.

Three miles into the canyon is the first car camping site, **Bridger Campground**. Located in the Rocky Mountains at 5,400 feet, this sucker is closed down by snow every year, typically between October and May. If arriving during a questionable season, call the Logan Ranger District Visitor Center to double-check.

The **Third** (and final) **Dam** is the next stop, where from another campground, **Spring Hollow**, the hiking options start to branch out a bit. On the eastern edge of the campground, the **Riverside Nature Trail** follows the Logan River. Along it, small placards interpret the environs, identifying and naming different plant and animal species. Wetlands near the campground render the area abundant with waterfowl and other critters not extraordinarily common in dry Utah.

The other path leading away from this area is the 3-mile **Crimson Trail** that heads to **Guinavah Campground**. This trail was named after ye olde Brigham Young College. Formerly based in Logan (now Brigham Young University in Provo), its graduating students held ceremonious walks along this trail, wearing the school's then-red and gold colors. Along the way, this steep trail passes by a striking band of limestone called the **China Wall**. Because limestone is fossilized seabed, it often contains preserved sea creatures. This section of rock happens to contain a lot; take the time to look for and find them. Connecting to the Riverside Nature Trail, this route loops right back to the Spring Hollow Campground, after a total of 4 trail miles.

As you climb higher into the canyon, more campsites and picnic areas continue to litter the roadside. A little over 4.5 miles after US-89 enters the canyon, it passes by **Wind Caves** and **Cave of the Winds Trail**. (These caves are also visible from the DeWitt Picnic Area, back down the road about a quarter of a mile.) It may surprise Utahans that sandstone is not the only type of rock that forms arches; here, wind and water have carved a triple arch into limestone. This cave-like formation seems like a gazebo with skylights. The trail to reach the caves stretches about 2 miles each way and provides a more panoramic, zoomed-out view of the canyon below. In the autumn, this trail provides stunning views of the colorful deciduous foliage.

Just about 19 miles into the canyon, its narrow floor broadens in the **Tony Grove** area. Not named for a gentleman called Tony, this portion of the canyon actually got its name from a group of late nineteenth-century elite (or "high-toned") who regularly vacationed here during the summer. Taking the Tony Grove Canyon Road to the left (northwest), park after just 0.25 mile. Here stands a 1907 log structure that served as the home of the area's first ranger. Now part of the **Tony Grove Memorial Ranger Station Historic District**, this cabin stands in the company of a cluster of somewhat newer buildings. Erected in the 1930s for all kinds of forestry use, these have served as training and guard stations as well as nurseries. Still in operation today, the structures have been maintained throughout their lives.

Those who wish can continue along US-89 toward Garden City; others can embark on a deeper-yet detour up and to **Tony Lake**, which sits near the perimeter of the **Mount Naomi Wilderness**. This 45,000-acre protected area was set aside as such in 1984 by the United States Congress. A total of 7.5 miles of pavement climb from US-89 to this glacial lake, which sits at an elevation of 8,043 feet. A natural lake by origin, Tony Lake has also been enlarged by the construction of a dam in 1939—though it's still quite small, at just over 25 acres. The lake is supplemented with pit toilets, picnic tables, and a few dozen campsites. Fishing is possible here, but the high elevation of the lake serves to kill many fish during the cold winter months.

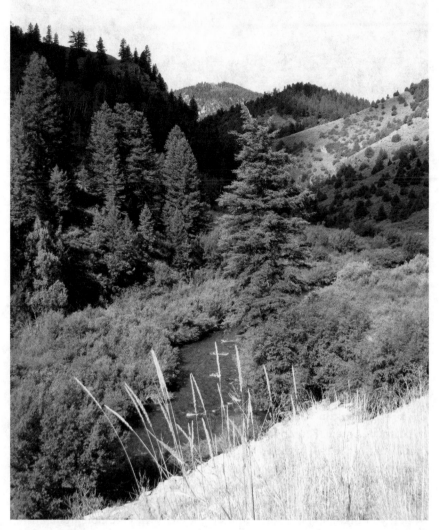

MIDDLE LOGAN CANYON

At the lake, a signed nature trail traipses along the shores, depicting a bit of the area's wildlife and geology. A "backcountry" trailhead here serves as the gateway to a number of different hiker- and horse-friendly trails. Heading to the northeast, a trail leads to **Naomi Peak**, elevation 9,979 feet (gaining roughly 1,900 vertical feet over 4 miles); to the south a trail leads to **White Pine Lake**, passing various high-elevation springs and ponds. Because of the general moistness of this area, moose are a common sight every year; beware—though these animals appear goofy and docile, they can in fact be quite fierce. Though they won't bite or eat a person, they will charge, ram, and trample anyone—particularly a person too near, or interfering in any way

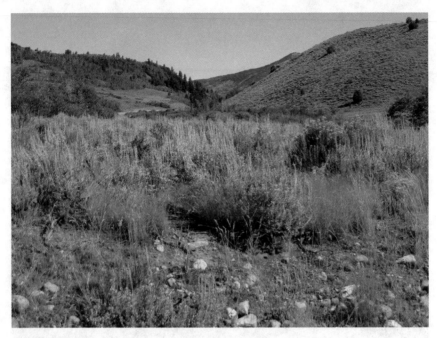

BROAD TOP OF LOGAN CANYON

with, a baby moose (called a calf). To park here, all vehicles must pay $6 for a day-use fee, which helps to maintain the trailhead restrooms.

About 3 miles and a few more campground and picnic areas farther along US-89 are **Franklin Basin** and the **Steam Mill Hollow Trail**. Heavy beaver trapping between 1820 and 1840 nearly wiped out the species in this area (not unlike in the rest of the country), but intervening decades have allowed them to repopulate. Therefore, curious visitors should keep an eye out for their dams. Made of sticks, these hollow, dome-shaped mounds block water flow and, like small huts, actually provide a home to the beavers. Along this trail, if you hike long enough you may get lucky and stumble upon buried stolen gold. Apparently, during the late 1800s, two robbers evading a posse fled into these hills and buried a serious quantity of gold here.

The turnoff to Beaver Mountain is 25 miles from the mouth of the canyon on the main road. The northernmost ski area in Utah, **Beaver Mountain** gets about 20 percent less snowfall than the famous Wasatch resorts such as Snowbird and Alta (though still more than 400 inches annually), and has 1,600 vertical feet of drop and almost 700 skiable acres. But with an insulating drive from Salt Lake City and Park City, it also has vastly less crowding. The resort was first opened by the Seeholzer family in 1932 and is still run by the same family today. In its early decades, the resort experienced growing pains and changed locations a few times, but it seems to have permanently settled where it is—its home since 1949.

During winter, snowmobilers (in addition to snowboarders and skiers) come to Beaver Mountain. In summer, it is possible to hike and mountain bike there, as well as to stay in guest accommodations (yurts or heavy-duty permanent tents) or in the full-service RV park. Check online or call for an event schedule; sometimes the resort even hosts summer concerts.

For more lodging, head up the main highway another half a mile to the **Beaver Creek Lodge** (a total of 27 miles up Logan Canyon), which offers more typical guest lodging. This log structure fits perfectly in the Rocky Mountain forest. The simple, handsome rooms keep in theme with log furniture and quilts—but the building is modern and spacious and offers guests plenty of light. Popular in all seasons, this is a snowmobiler's delight in winter and a horseback-riding haven during snow-free seasons. Oops! Forgot the snowmobile or horse? Rentals are available at the lodge itself. Optional packages include lodging, equipment (or animals) appropriate for the season, and meals. It may be worth considering hiring a snowmobile, as approximately 300 miles of groomed trails in the vicinity of the lodge make this one of the nation's top ten "sledding" destinations.

The next major pullout is for **Swan Flat** on the left side of the road. This road system, departing to the north (left), sends dirt spurs up toward the

Jim Bridger

In his day, Jim Bridger traveled a remarkable amount. A well-respected leader wherever he went, Bridger spread his name everywhere, especially in the Rocky Mountains, where he became a legend. Born March 17, 1804, in Richmond, Virginia, he became the ultimate mountain Renaissance man, founding fur-trading businesses and acting as a leading guide, scout, trapper, and explorer in a huge territory. In his prime (roughly from 1820 to 1850), he sometimes served as an intermediary between native tribes and white government and settlers. In the winter of 1824–1825, he may have become the first European to see the Great Salt Lake. (Now most believe it was likely Étienne Provost, but Bridger did carry that honor for a while.)

He was known not only for his accomplishments, skills, and experience, but also for his tall tales and his overall charm. During his lifetime he married two Native American women—one Flathead with whom he had three children and, after her death, the daughter of a Shoshone chief. He was conversant in many native languages, as well as English, Spanish, and French. He led troops in various Indian wars and discovered ways to improve and shorten the Oregon Trail. Suffering from numerous ailments, Bridger peaced out July 17, 1881, near Kansas City, Missouri. Amazingly, this man traveled more in the 1800s than most people travel today, even with our access to modern planes, trains, and automobiles.

Idaho border. As is obvious from its appearance, this area is a gateway to undeveloped outdoor recreation. Nearing the highest, broadest part of Logan Canyon, these roads can be snowmobiled or cross-country skied in winter and ATVed, biked, run, or hiked in the summertime.

A trail departing from the road (about 3.5 miles north of US-89, and almost in Idaho) leads to **Mount Bridger**. Named for Jim Bridger, a legendary mountain man of the 1800s—as are many other mountains and towns, from Montana and Idaho to Wyoming and Utah (see sidebar on page 61)—this peak is the tallest in **Rich County**. The trail to it begins as an ATV path, but it eventually thins. To reach the actual peak itself, hikers must use their judgment and depart from the trail, following the final ridge to the peak. A cairn and summit register mark the spot.

During the 1990s, the *Salt Lake Tribune* was penning an article about the tallest mountains in each of Utah's 29 counties. At that time, the 9,255-foot-tall Mount Bridger was unnamed, and it only received its moniker for the sake of the article. Though it is the shortest of all the counties' high peaks in Utah, it is still (here comes some trivia) the highest of all the shortest county high points per state in the United States . . . if that makes any sense!

Speaking of Rich County, it should be noted that this is quite a peculiar section of Utah. This area is the home of some strangely cool weather—as well as the spot where Utah's all-time low temperature was recorded. On February 1, 1985, Peter Sinks posted a low of -69°F—actually the lowest temperature ever measured in the continental United States. Even in the summer, it is rare that **Peter Sinks** experiences more than 3 consecutive days

Sinks Are Tubs

Peter Sinks is just one of the many sinks in this potholed region—sinks are actually a fairly common geological phenomenon along fault lines. Near the top of Logan Canyon, there is a double-fault system where the limestone-rich crust has been exposed to water seepage. As limestone is soluble in water, vast cave systems form in this rock over time. These caves grow so much that they collapse, creating what are today called sinks.

Peter Sinks, the chilliest spot in Utah, is one such basin; it is almost a full square mile in size. The shape of this basin and the physics of air densities keep the tub dramatically cooler than anything nearby. First, cold air is much denser than hot air and therefore settles to the bottom of any container; this land depression is the perfect catcher's mitt for such a cold lump of air. Second, in addition to the basin holding the cold air, it also blocks any wind, which might possibly churn the cold out of its resting spot. Visitors will notice an extreme temperature difference within just a few steps; be careful traipsing around the sinks, though, as drop-offs can sometimes be abrupt.

Bear Lake, Times Two

Salt Lake Valley isn't the only spot that was underwater during the most recent ice ages. During the time that **Lake Bonneville** filled the Salt Lake Valley (up until about 12,000 years ago), Bear Lake's waters, too, were way above the current shoreline, and it was about twice its current size. Though the two ancient lakes were not connected, the Bear River actually flowed into Lake Bonneville at its largest point, and this is thought to have been responsible for Lake Bonneville's final demise.

Lake Bonneville, a massive prehistoric body of water, had actually filled and drained many times during the ice ages. On its last time around, Bonneville was growing and growing, fed by a moist climate and trapped in the **Great Basin**. At a certain point, it became large enough to accept the **Bear River**. This river drained a huge basin centered on the far northeastern corner of Utah's panhandle, and must have significantly increased the volume in Lake Bonneville.

When Bonneville acquired the Bear River's inflow, the lake began filling much more rapidly than before. The land at **Red Rock Pass** (near I-15 and the Utah-Idaho border) suddenly gave way, sending a catastrophic flood of truly epic proportions across **Idaho** and through the **Snake River Valley**. This wall of water was more than 400 feet tall, traveled at more than 70 miles per hour, and had a flow of 15 million cubic feet per second. This flood is responsible for many features of southern Idaho's Snake River Plain, including the seemingly out-of-place rounded boulders now scattered across it.

without the thermometer dipping below freezing. Not the only sink around, Peter Sinks is part of a broader geological phenomenon (see sidebar, below).

Moving farther along US-89, the road swoops back toward the south. Just under 30 miles from Logan, **Bear Lake** suddenly comes into view on the left-hand side of the road. This massive, cyan-colored, Caribbean-looking body of water occupies a huge portion of the valley below. Bear Lake, the second-largest freshwater lake in the state (behind Utah Lake, near Provo), is an elongated body of water, 18 miles long and 7 miles at its widest point. It almost equally straddles Idaho and Utah. The original name, Black Bear Lake, given by its first European "discoverer," Donald Mackenzie of the North West Company (a fur-trading outfit), was later shortened.

In the 1820s and '30s, this huge body of freshwater was a common meeting place for mountain men such as Jim Bridger and Jedediah Smith, who traded goods among themselves and with Native Americans. Today this heritage is still remembered with the annual **Mountain Man Rendezvous**. Taking place in the middle of every September at **Rendezvous Beach**, this extended weekend festival is quite a spectacle, with reenactments in period dress, as well as food and crafts made in the spirit of those days.

Garden City's outskirts immediately begin to dot US-89 as it makes its long descent into **Bear Lake Valley.** This town is rather famous for its raspberries. And it's got it all: raspberry baked goods, confections, and even a festival—the **Bear Lake Raspberry Days.** Though many, many restaurants serve raspberry shakes all year long, anyone visiting the first weekend of August (Thursday through Saturday) should take advantage of the chance to experience this celebration of the annual, usually 3-week-long harvest. In addition to special food treats, there is a parade, a rodeo, a beauty pageant, craft booths, music, and fireworks.

Garden City marks the end of this drive. The easiest way to return to the Salt Lake City area is to retrace the route, back along US-89, through Logan, and on US-89/US-91 to I-15. Those with a bit more time (or aiming for a northern destination) should consider making a loop up into Idaho. Continuing north on US-89 leads to ID-36. This scenic byway ascends back west into mountain canyons that lead toward **Preston, Idaho**—the filming location of the popular 2004 movie *Napoleon Dynamite*. Similar in scenery to the Logan Canyon drive, this route heads through much less developed land, on a smaller highway. Preston sits right on US-91; this north–south running highway either leads straight back south toward Logan, Utah, or meets up with I-15, north of Preston and fairly close to **Pocatello, Idaho.**

IN THE AREA

Accommodations

BEAVER CREEK LODGE, 12800 US-89, Garden City. Moderate to expensive— rates vary significantly per season, length of stay, and activities. Call 435-946-3400 or 1-800-946-4485. Website: www.beavercreeklodge.com.

UNIVERSITY INN, 650 North 875 East, Logan. Moderately priced. Historic, downtown hotel-style lodging. Call 435-797-0017 or 800-231-5634. Website: www.uicc.usu.edu.

Attractions and Recreation

BEAR LAKE STATE PARK. Administering the public beaches, picnic areas, campsites, and general recreation at Bear Lake. Day-use and camping fees collected. Call 435-946-3343 or 1-877-887-2757. Website: www.stateparks .utah.gov.

BEAVER MOUNTAIN, 1351 East 700 North, Logan. Winter and summer resort. Call 435-753-0921. Website: www.skithebeav.com.

Dining

INDIAN OVEN, 130 North Main, Logan. Moderately priced. Casual but pleasant atmosphere; authentic Indian cuisine. Extensive menu with vegetarian options. Open for lunch and dinner, Monday through Saturday; closed Sunday. Call 435-787-1757.

LE NONNE, 129 North 100 East, Logan. Moderate to expensive. Formal, upscale restaurant in renovated historic home; traditional Italian cuisine. Lunch Thursday and Friday only; dinner Monday through Saturday; closed between meals (call for hours). Reservations recommended. Call 435-752-9577. Website: www.lenonne.com.

Other Contacts

BEAR LAKE RASPBERRY DAYS, downtown Garden City. Taking place the first weekend of August (Thursday through Saturday). A 3-day festival with parade, rodeo, crafts, music, fireworks, and more. Call the Bear Lake Convention and Visitors Bureau: 1-800-448-2327. Website: www.bearlake.org.

CACHE VALLEY VISITORS BUREAU (inside the Cache County Courthouse), 199 Main Street, Logan. Call 435-755-1890 or 1-800-882-4433. Website: www.explorelogan.com.

MOUNTAIN MAN RENDEZVOUS, at Bear Lake's Rendezvous Beach, 2 miles north of Laketown, off UT-30. A one-weekend event in the middle of every September. Call Bear Lake State Park: 435-946-3343 or 1-877-887-2757. Website: www.stateparks.utah.gov.

STOKES NATURE CENTER, 2696 East US-89, Logan. Open Wednesday through Saturday 10 AM–4 PM, or by appointment. Check ahead for holiday and seasonal closures. Call 435-755-3239. Website: www.logannature.org.

LOGAN RANGER DISTRICT VISITOR CENTER, 1500 East US-89, Logan. Open Monday through Friday 8 AM–4:30 PM, all year. Call 435-755-3620.

TOP OF UTAH MARATHON. Taking place each year in the middle of September, on a Saturday. Website: www.topofutahmarathon.com.

UTAH STATE UNIVERSITY, 1400 Old Main Hill, Logan. Call 435-797-1000. Website: www.usu.edu.

5

MIRROR LAKE SCENIC BYWAY

ESTIMATED LENGTH: Roughly 77 miles from Kamas, Utah, to Evanston, Wyoming

ESTIMATED TIME: Half day (with return trip)

HIGHLIGHTS: The **Uinta Mountains** are the tallest range in Utah. Over 100 miles long, they have more than ten peaks taller than 13,000 feet and, aside from Alaska's Brooks Range, are the most outstanding east–west running range in the nation. And, in a state with some of the nation's most notable scenery, UT-150 is a unique drive. On a drive just 77 miles from Kamas to Evanston, visitors climb more than 4,200 vertical feet from Kamas to an elevation of 10,715 feet at Bald Mountain Pass without ever leaving the main road. As the terrain gains height and loses heat, the ground cover transforms dramatically from grassy valley floor to thick forest to above-tree-line talus.

As this is clearly a high-elevation mountain road, it is most certainly closed in winter—and can remain buried under snow until well into June. During summer, these mountains can endure some of the wintriest storms— at the same time that Salt Lake City and Moab are experiencing three-digit highs. Even in August, when the snow has left the range, thunderstorms occur almost like clockwork every afternoon; hiking and other activities are best done in the morning.

GETTING THERE: Kamas, Utah, is a pretty straightforward town to reach. If coming from Salt Lake City, take I-80 east to its junction with US-40, just east of Park City. Head south a little more than 3 miles on US-40, taking Exit 4 onto eastbound UT-248 toward Kamas. Travel a little over 11 miles on this state highway, passing Jordanelle Reservoir to the south. Once in Kamas, a 0.2-mile dogleg to the north leads immediately to the well-signed Mirror Lake Highway (UT-150) that departs eastwardly from the center of town.

Those coming from the north or east also arrive via I-80. Begin by traveling south-southwest along I-80, taking Exit 155 for Wanship/UT-32. Follow

LEFT: HORSEBACK RIDING IN THE CHURCH MEADOWS OF THE UINTA MOUNTAINS

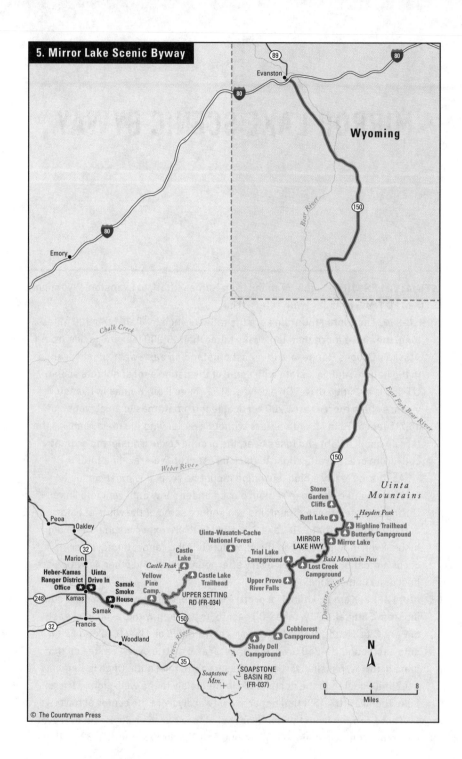

5. Mirror Lake Scenic Byway

Evanston

Wyoming

Emory

Chalk Creek

Bear River

East Fork Bear River

Weber River

Uinta Mountains

Stone Garden Cliffs

Hayden Peak

Ruth Lake

Highline Trailhead

Butterfly Campground

Peoa

Oakley

Uinta-Wasatch-Cache National Forest

MIRROR LAKE HWY

Mirror Lake

Marion

Castle Lake

Trial Lake Campground

Bald Mountain Pass

Heber-Kamas Ranger District Office

Uinta Drive In

Castle Peak

Castle Lake Trailhead

Lost Creek Campground

Samak Smoke House

Yellow Pine Camp.

Upper Provo River Falls

Kamas

UPPER SETTING RD (FR-034)

Duchesne River

Samak

Francis

Woodland

Cobblerest Campground

Shady Dell Campground

N

Soapstone Mtn.

Provo River

SOAPSTONE BASIN RD (FR-037)

0   4   8
Miles

© The Countryman Press

signs through this small town for UT-32, and continue onward about 16 miles southeast toward Kamas. The Mirror Lake Highway departs in an easterly direction from town and is an extension of East Center Street.

The Mirror Lake Highway (UT-150) begins in Kamas and cuts a crescent-shaped route northeast through the western corner of the Uinta Mountains, arriving at Evanston, just north of the Utah-Wyoming border. On its 56-mile journey, UT-150 ascends into Utah's tallest range, the Uinta Mountains, and then turns into WYO-150 for another 21 miles before arriving in Evanston.

Uintah County, where the range sits, got its name from the resident tribe, the Utes. Though Kamas is less than an hour from Salt Lake City—about as far away as Provo—this region remains largely unpopulated and is characterized by Indian reservations, one-stoplight towns, and ranches. Even if they wanted to, people couldn't feasibly live in the Uinta mountains year-round, as the range sits under thick snowpack sometimes as much as nine or ten months a year. The highest peaks in this range stand more than 1.5 miles higher than the valleys below them.

Geologically speaking, the Uinta Range belongs to the Colorado Plateau. This tectonically textured and extremely colorful landmass occupies a Montana-sized region centered on the junction of Colorado, Utah, Arizona, and New Mexico, and its watersheds feed the Colorado River. Quite

Exploring the Uintas Away from UT-150

As mentioned before, this mountain range extends well beyond the Mirror Lake Scenic Byway—which merely teases at the northwestern portion of the massive mountain chain. Though only one road penetrates the high mountains, many skirt its slopes. Opposite UT-150, in the northeastern corner of the Uintas, stands the **Flaming Gorge Reservoir**. This dammed section of the **Green River** is popular for boating and other types of water recreation—but the real gem exists just downstream from the dam. Here beneath the spillways can be found some of the best fly fishing in Utah.

Downstream of the reservoir is the **Uintah and Ouray Reservation**. This largely occupies the southern slopes of the Uintas, and contains a speckling of small townships along US-191 and US-40. The largest of these, **Vernal**, has a population just over 9,000, and from there, the town sizes fall off rapidly—with **Fort Duchesne** coming in at around 600.

The northern slopes of the range, in Wyoming, hold a lonely collection of tiny towns—by and large farming and ranching communities. Well off any kind of beaten path, these offer almost no amenities to tourists.

senior to mountain ranges in the south of Utah—such as the volcanic, 24-million-year-old Henry and La Sal Mountains—the Uintas are estimated to be roughly 60 million years old, created by tectonic uplift. The fundamental rocks found in this range—slate, shale, and most visibly, quartzite—are dated at 700 to 800 million years of age.

The region's human history begins in the valleys at the skirts of this giant range. With an elevation roughly in the 5,000-to-6,500-foot range, these relative lowlands are predictably more temperate than the peaks above. Atmospherically, they are actually quite dry, receiving less than 10 inches of precipitation annually. However, these valleys do receive massive amounts of runoff from the Uinta Mountains, as well as from the Wasatch Range to the west—runoff fed by snowmelt and plentiful summer thunderstorms.

Because of the relative livability of the region's valleys, people have occupied the area for as long as twelve millennia. The Fremont were a northern offshoot of the Anasazi; a subgroup of the Fremont, called the Uinta Fremont (ancestors to the more modern Ute tribe), occupied this region initially. This hunter-gatherer people flourished with access to the area's abundant resources, particularly streams and lakes. With plentiful water flow comes many other things: elevated plant and animal life as well as bountiful fishing. In addition to the copious springs and streams is a natural abundance of glacial lakes—more than a thousand. During the cool, high-elevation summer conditions, these have always been great fisheries—then and today.

Fishing is far from the only recreational activity in these peaks. Also popular in modern times are camping, backpacking, road biking, and rock climbing. Though much too cold and snowy for the bulk of the year, these mountains provide a fabulous summer retreat from the Utah inferno—one of the only places within a day's drive of Salt Lake City where a sweatshirt can actually be worn in August!

High Uintas Classic: "No Wimps and No Whiners!"

Every year during the middle of June, this 2-day stage race draws in a few hundred road bikers. Since 1989, this summer solstice event has taken place almost immediately after UT-150 has been cleared of snow, with a sizeable cash purse available for licensed racers. One of the longest continuously held races in the United States, the race—just like this drive—begins in Kamas and ends in Evanston, going right up and over Bald Mountain Pass, at more than 10,700 feet elevation, requiring an aggregate climb of nearly a vertical mile. Whether you're a cyclist or not, it's interesting to tour this route on a bike. Use caution when driving this road, as this beautiful ribbon of pavement attracts many cyclists throughout the summer, whether or not it's race weekend.

Into the entire range protrudes but one major road—and this is the **Mirror Lake Scenic Byway** or UT-150, which makes a sickle-shaped sojourn through the Uintas' upper northwestern corner. Undeniably one of Utah's most scenic, this road offers quite a change of pace from the plentiful red rock routes in the southern end of the state. The gateway to Utah's best summer escape, this highway can become inundated with vehicles during July and August. If the option exists, weekdays are a better choice for peaceful recreation. But if weekdays must be spent at work, crowds can be avoided by simply heading deeper into the backcountry.

A CLASSIC MEADOW HIKE IN THE HIGH UINTAS

If you are hungry in Kamas, consider a stop at **Uinta Drive In** (formerly Dick's Drive In) before heading into the mountains. This retro burger joint is one of the most beloved in town, serving juicy grilled patties and thick shakes. If burgers don't sound appetizing, or if vegetarian options are a must, check out the **Summit Inn** for home-style pizza of generous proportions. For dessert, they serve ice cream as well.

Leaving Kamas, the highway begins climbing immediately; after all, it has no choice if it is to gain so much elevation in its finite length. Before driving out of the valley and into the mountains, consider a stop at the **Kamas Ranger District Office**. In such a mountainous region, up-to-date information on road and trail conditions, as well as other updates pertaining to Mother Nature's alterations, can be quite helpful.

Just less than 5 miles east of Kamas is the small town of **Samak**, elevation 6,949 feet. Just 4.7 square miles and 287 residents, its most noticeable feature is a big, bright sign advertising BEAVER CREEK NUDIST RANCH. This alleged colony is named after the stream running alongside the road until beyond the **Beaver Creek**, **Taylors Fork**, and **Shingle Creek Campgrounds**. (After these, the road passes the Beaver Creek headwaters and moves into the **Provo River** basin.) Though this sign doesn't actually mark the location of a nudist ranch, it is a great, long-standing prank (of more than three decades!) on passersby. In a generally conservative state, this definitely causes people to pull over, and look more than once for the ranch. Many people even get out of the car and pose next to the sign along the way.

More than the home of a fake nudist colony, Samak is also the location of the **Samak Smoke House & Country Store**. A quintessential smokehouse indeed, this produces some fantastic, all-natural jerky made of turkey and beef. Its country store sells gift baskets with edible treats and goods made in

2010 Helicopter Crash, No Casualties

Soapstone Basin was the location of a Coast Guard helicopter crash on March 3, 2010. Of five people on board the MH-60T Jayhawk, none were killed. The chopper was returning home after a security detail at the 2010 Winter Olympic Games in Vancouver, British Columbia. Blizzardy conditions at the time of the crash were reported and are suspected to have been the cause of the accident.

the kitchen: biscotti, cookies, various coffees, nuts, and the like. These provide good finger food for camping trips, as well as gifts to bring back after a trip.

Heading northeast and upward, it is not even a mile before UT-150 leads into the **Uinta-Wasatch-Cache National Forest**. As national forests usually are, this one is filled with campgrounds, picnic areas, and trailheads. Along the way, drivers pass dozens of major pullouts and numerous other access points in the Ashley and Uinta-Wasatch-Cache National Forest. In order to maintain these recreational sites, the Forest Service collects a $6 day fee from anyone who parks anywhere along UT-150 (or its side roads), payable at the ranger booth east of Kamas. The passes are also good for the **Alpine Loop** (chapter 3), east of Provo. Week and year passes are available as well.

Immediately, campground access roads begin passing by. For those planning to tent here in shoulder seasons or chilly weather, these low-elevation sites present the warmest options, as they are literally thousands of feet lower in elevation than many of the upcoming campgrounds. The first of these, **Yellow Pine Campground**, is also the location of a trailhead. Named for the creek it follows, the **Yellow Pine Trail** leads up quite high into the mountains, eventually reaching **Castle Peak**. Because of its elevation gain (more than 3,000 feet), it passes through a number of different ecosystems—but due to its long length (just over 5 miles each way), the trail enjoys moderate grade.

About 8.5 miles east of Kamas, Upper Setting Road (Forest Service Road 034) intersects with UT-150. This high-quality, graded dirt road heads north and up along **Co-op Creek** toward **Castle Lake**. This road is actually one of the only means in the area to access this western Uinta high country without hiking the entire distance. From the terminus of the road, a trail heads west and joins up with the Yellow Pine Trail, mentioned above.

Soapstone Basin Road comes up just under 6 miles later, this time heading south into the range. Located here is yet another campground, as well as another trailhead, whose path branches into a spiderweb of options that trace along the bottom of **Soapstone Creek** and the base of **Soapstone Mountain**. Hiking to the south, then east, and over a pass will take hikers into **Mill Hollow**, and onto Mill Hollow Road (map recommended). This road parallels the south fork of the Provo River and heads northwest (parallel to UT-150) toward the towns of **Francis** and **Woodland**. For long-distance hikers or mountain

Gold Diggin'

It's a rare spot in the Rocky Mountains that wasn't affected by the nineteenth-century gold rush. Once the '49ers had scoured and all but extinguished the veins and streams of California, remaining prospectors turned inland to the mountains of Idaho, Colorado, Utah, and Montana—anywhere precious minerals and metals could possibly be found.

Legend has it that as far back as the 1500s, gold was brought to the Uinta Mountains on behalf of Montezuma and hidden for safekeeping. Mixed fables hold that secret caves, rich with this precious metal, were scattered throughout the Uintas. Lore even tells that outlaws from Butch Cassidy's Wild Bunch era stashed stolen gold bricks in **Nine Mile Canyon**. It is also believed—and backed by archaeological evidence—that Spanish miners operated outfits powered by enslaved Utes in the 1700s.

These tantalizing rumors have long sent prospectors and treasure hunters into the Uinta Mountains seeking the alleged veins and secret stashes—but with such a massive, rugged piece of land to cover, these searches were understandably almost always fruitless. Dark rumors have it that not only do dense deposits and rich stashes of hidden gold exist in these hills, but that a curse strikes down anyone attempting to access or carry away the riches. Though evidence is generally lacking, many people have reportedly vanished or suffered terrible deaths in their quest for Uinta gold.

One of the most famous and corroborated stories is that of Kentucky-born California mining magnate Thomas Rhoads. During a life that progressed generally westward, this man joined the LDS Church in Illinois in 1835. Before the official Brigham Young–led migration to the Salt Lake Valley, Rhoads went on a church-sponsored reconnaissance mission west of the Rocky Mountains. His party made it all the way to California, actually just ahead of the famously ill-fated Donner Party. In California, they had great luck as some of the first to take part in California's gold rush. But in 1849, Brigham Young summoned this party to come to Utah, the Mormons' newly founded Zion.

Rhoades came to Utah and, with his four wives and three dozen children, enjoyed wealth several times greater than most pioneers did, building a massive home immediately south of Temple Square in Salt Lake City. About this time, Brigham Young, then president of the LDS Church, appointed Rhoades to the duty of recovering gold from hidden mines in the Uintas.

Under control of the Ute tribe, these mines had apparently been in operation since the eighteenth century, when pre–Escalante and Dominguez Spanish had been running them with Ute slave labor. With the Spanish now gone, the Utes, who had little use for the metal, agreed to allow just one person access to these mines. That person was to remove only as much from the mine as he could carry each day. If anyone else tried to enter, or if that per-

(continued on next page)

son attempted to remove more gold than this, he should be executed. Chief Walker (or Wakara) approved this agreement, but under the condition that the gold be used exclusively for LDS Church purposes.

Allegedly, Thomas Rhoades made regular trips to the mine. Each lasted about two weeks, and would yield just over sixty pounds of the metal. When serious illness rendered Thomas incapable of this duty, he was replaced by his son, Caleb. This agreement continued until after Chief Walker and his successor, Arapeen, died; Chief Tabby allegedly discontinued the agreement, forbidding Mormons to access the mine.

Caleb reportedly made a few stealth missions to the mine, but he wanted support from the US government. He attempted to get rights to the land, claiming he could settle the national debt in exchange for these privileges. But the US government undoubtedly viewed this as a crackpot deal and sent their own companies in to search the land. Though they indeed found evidence of the old Spanish mining operations, they reportedly never found the mother lode and, to this day, its location remains a mystery.

Today still, the Rhoades family asserts that much of the gold on the Salt Lake Temple's Angel Moroni, as well as interior plating of the temple, was from Thomas Rhoades's Uinta trips. And many still believe in a lingering curse on the mine; people who have ventured into the hills in search of it have reportedly disappeared or perished. In any case, many historians believe that Mormon wealth is directly linked to this vanished Rhoades mine.

bikers, this very gentle 10.5-mile loop (with optional 3-mile-long dogleg) requires only about 1,500 feet of climbing on soft-packed soil—providing a very pleasant opportunity for extended exercise.

Continuing along UT-150, the elevation rises to 8,280 feet as the highway passes a few more campgrounds, **Shady Dell** and **Cobblerest**. Past these, UT-150 climbs quite a lot and enters a region visibly carved by bygone glaciers. As the road bends around an abrupt 90-degree turn (from north to east), it finally reaches **Bald Mountain Pass** at elevation 10,715 feet—just 29 miles northeast of Kamas. Despite the impressive elevation of these mountains, the roundness and smoothness of their basins and saddles is somewhat surprising. The environs rather feel like a safe, sculpted perch high in the sky.

The following section of road contains the densest collection of campgrounds, side roads, lakes, and trails. Look for several lakes—**Trial**, **Lilly**, **Lost**, **Buckeye**, **Blue**, and **Wall**—as well as many campgrounds, at **Lost Creek**, **Trial Lake**, and **Lilly Lake**. On the eastern side of the road are some of the most popular attractions of their kind, the **Upper Provo River Falls** and **Campground**, roughly 24 miles after Kamas and just before **Washington Lake**. Best steer clear of these on any normal summer weekend.

Continuing along, the road begins to descend slowly, though it lingers for a while on this vast promontory. As it passes Mirror Lake, trails popular for horseback riding and backpacking depart from either side of the road. Some campgrounds, like **Butterfly Lake**, and the **Highline** trailhead, exist in the area, as well as numerous rock climbing crags, including the more popular **Ruth Lake** and **Stone Garden** cliffs, both of which can be found by hiking from the left of the road.

STREAM MEANDERING THROUGH A MEADOW BENEATH RUTH LAKE

The road continues its descent, passing tall peaks on either side—including **Hayden Peak** to the east at 12,475 feet. Along the way, six more campgrounds line the pathway in the **Hayden Fork** drainage down and toward the **Bear River**. Numerous small lakes exist mostly on the western slope, accessible by trails only. Many paths depart from the highway, or from dirt spur roads, leading to the backcountry. If roadside attractions earlier along the route were too mobbed, consider turning off onto a random road at this point in the drive and begin exploring by foot.

As the mountains here were sculpted by glaciers, many of these hiking trails trace along the bottom of high meadows, making for beautiful walks

Rock Climbing: High-Altitude Cragging

Reputed among rock climbers as having one of the most active climbing communities in the nation, Salt Lake City is indeed home to an avid population of climbers. Though the dry, warm climate allows for great spring and autumn climbing (and even passable winter conditions), the summers are simply too hot for the sport in the lower-altitude canyons.

The Uintas have presented a perfect escape from the summer heat since route development skyrocketed here in the late 1990s. Though an occasional technical climb has been established here and there since the 1960s, routes were generally few and far between—and often not very difficult. However, 1995 saw the first major developments for rock climbing in the Uintas, with traditional and sport climbing lines going up rapidly in the mountains' quartzite. The number of routes quickly went from fewer than twenty to over four hundred—in little more than a decade. Today these climbs are spread among twenty main areas, and are detailed in Nathan Smith and Paul Tusting's guidebook *Uinta Rock*.

AFTERNOON THUNDERSTORMS VIEWED FROM AMETHYST LAKE TRAIL

without strenuous elevation gain. Though the trails are often beneath the ridgeline, lightning hazards do exist. Storms occur virtually every summer day in these mountains. Despite clear morning skies, clouds move in like clockwork in the afternoon and can present a dangerous threat to hikers exposed on higher terrain.

About 4 miles south of the Wyoming border, this road leaves the national forest and the campgrounds behind. Evanston, Wyoming, marks the "end" of the route. At this point, two options exist: backtracking on WYO-150/ UT-150, or taking a more expedited trip. The quickest way back south is via I-80 West, heading back toward **Park City** and **Salt Lake City.** Along the way, I-80 runs though **Echo Canyon**—the weakness in the Rocky Mountains through which the First Transcontinental Railroad ran. From Evanston, the highway miles back to Salt Lake City amount to about 80, requiring a bit more than an hour's drive.

IN THE AREA

Dining

UINTA DRIVE IN, 235 Center St, Kamas. Very affordable, very casual American cuisine. Call 435-783-4312.

SAMAK SMOKE HOUSE & COUNTRY STORE, 1937 East UT-150, Samak. Name says it all. Call 435-783-4880. Website: www.samaksmokehouse.com.

SUMMIT INN, 80 South Main Street, Kamas. Affordable, casual, family-friendly pizza restaurant. Call 435-783-4453. Website: www.summitinnpizza .com.

Other Contacts

ASHLEY NATIONAL FOREST REGIONAL OFFICE, 355 North Vernal Avenue, Vernal. This national forest presides over nearly 1.4 million acres in Utah and Wyoming, 180,000 of which are wilderness acres in the Uinta region. Call 435-789-1181. Website: www.fs.fed.us/r4/ashley.

BUREAU OF LAND MANAGEMENT SALT LAKE: Northern Uintas Office, 440 West 200 South, Suite 500, Salt Lake City. Call 801-539-4001. Website: www.blm.gov/utah.

BUREAU OF LAND MANAGEMENT VERNAL: Southern Uintas and Uinta Basin Office, 170 South 500 East, Vernal. Call 435-781-4400. Website: www .blm.gov/utah.

DINOSAURLAND TRAVEL BOARD, 152 East 100 North, Vernal. Regional visitor information; online listings for dining, recreation, lodging. Call 1-800-477-5558. Website: www.dinoland.com.

HIGH UINTAS CLASSIC, bicycle race. Website: www.evanstoncycling.org.

KAMAS RANGER DISTRICT OFFICE, 50 East Center Street, Kamas. Open Monday through Friday. Call 435-783-4338. Website: www.fs.fed.us/r4/uwc.

NATIONAL SCENIC BYWAYS PROGRAM. Call 1-800-429-9297. Website: www.byways.org.

UINTA-WASATCH-CACHE NATIONAL FOREST OFFICE, 6944 South 3000 East, Salt Lake City. A recently united Forest Service office, now overseeing 2.1 million acres of land; website updated with alerts. Call 801-733-2660. Website: www.fs.fed.us.

6

MOAB TO ARCHES

ESTIMATED LENGTH: About 25 miles from Moab to the northernmost part of Arches (Devil's Garden); 65 miles round-trip to drive each of the park's major, paved roads

ESTIMATED TIME: Half a day for a car tour; a full day if taking a hike or two

HIGHLIGHTS: Though it's difficult to imagine when driving US-191, **Arches National Park** sits immediately off this highway—not even 5 minutes north of Moab. Immediately after the fee station, the park road winds steeply up, away from the valley floor, and into one of the country's most remarkable natural rock gardens. Though named for its most notable feature, the arches, this park actually has several different regions, each with its own flavor. Even if you never leave the car, it is possible to see spires, fins, arches, and even petrified sand dunes. When in the **visitor center** near the park's entrance, pick up a free map; this will give an overview of the park's simple road system and the relative locations of the major attractions.

GETTING THERE: Start by finding Moab. (More information on getting to Moab is in the "Getting there" section of chapter 8, "Moab to Canyonlands' Needles.") Once you are there, the route to Arches couldn't be simpler. Head out of town in a northerly direction on US-191/Main Street, about 4.5 miles from the center of Moab. A well-signed right-hand turn for Arches National Park departs from the highway to the east. Shortly after this turn comes the fee station, visitor center, and park entrance.

There is a weekly fee to enter the park; America the Beautiful annual passes are accepted. A Southeast Utah Parks Pass can be purchased here for regional parks and monuments: Canyonlands, Natural Bridges, and Hovenweep.

LEFT: DELICATE ARCH AS SEEN FROM VIEW TRAIL IN ARCHES NATIONAL PARK

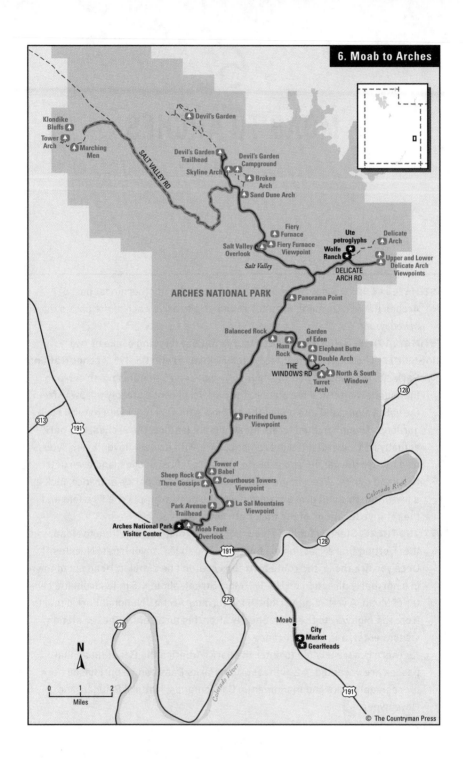

6. Moab to Arches

Klondike Bluffs
Tower Arch
Marching Men
SALT VALLEY RD
Devil's Garden
Devil's Garden Trailhead
Devil's Garden Campground
Skyline Arch
Broken Arch
Sand Dune Arch
Fiery Furnace
Fiery Furnace Viewpoint
Salt Valley Overlook
Ute petroglyphs
Wolfe Ranch
Delicate Arch
Upper and Lower Delicate Arch Viewpoints
Salt Valley
DELICATE ARCH RD
ARCHES NATIONAL PARK
Panorama Point
Balanced Rock
Garden of Eden
Ham Rock
Elephant Butte
Double Arch
THE WINDOWS RD
North & South Window
Turret Arch
128
Petrified Dunes Viewpoint
313
191
Tower of Babel
Sheep Rock
Three Gossips
Courthouse Towers Viewpoint
Park Avenue Trailhead
La Sal Mountains Viewpoint
Colorado River
Arches National Park Visitor Center
Moab Fault Overlook
191
128
279
Moab
City Market
GearHeads
279
Colorado River
191

N

0   1   2
Miles

© The Countryman Press

Highs In the 90S, Lows Below Freezing

Arches has a quintessential desert climate. This translates to dominant sunshine, bone-dry air, and huge daily temperature swings. By day, the ground bakes in radiant heat, supplied by uninterrupted solar rays. But as soon as the sun goes down, the arid, thin air does very little to retain any of this heat, allowing the temperatures to plunge.

Summer highs typically reach easily into the mid-90s, with overnight lows near 60°F. Winter afternoons reach the low to mid-60s, with nights getting down below 20°F. Late November through mid-February are typically the cloudiest months, rendering spring and autumn the most pleasant times here for heat-sensitive humans.

Arches National Park has more than 2,000 natural rock windows, giving it the densest concentration of such features in the world. In addition to that obvious attraction, there are all kinds of unusual rock shapes: from hoodoos to spires, from sheer cliffs to globular fins. Within the park you can find fifty-two known species of mammals, 186 species of birds, and over 480 types of plants.

People first passed through this region roughly 10,000 years ago. These migratory hunter-gatherer societies appeared first at the end of the last ice age. Within 2,000 years ago, the ancestors of the Fremont and Pueblo Indians made a part-time home here. The Ute Indians were present in the area when the first Europeans began their exploration of it. Contact with the Utes was documented by these early European explorers—but the Utes also left their own stories in the forms of pictographs and petroglyphs.

For obvious climatic reasons, however, these peoples were only able to live here during select times of year, when water was naturally supplied by rain and snow. During summer, the region was largely uninhabitable, as nearly all streams ran dry. On your drive, try to imagine what the area would have been like without roads, water lines, or infrastructure of any kind—and you'll probably feel a great deal of respect for those who were able to live on this pre-"civilized" land.

The first permanent resident of the area, John Wesley Wolfe, brought his son along and built a cabin in 1889. They lived in this cabin alone until 1910. The remains of this structure are visible at the **Wolfe Ranch** today (located at the trailhead for the **Delicate Arch Trail**). But the first person to take a specific interest in promoting the area's peculiar beauty was Alexander Ringhoffer, a prospector and miner. He summoned sufficient interest, and it was designated Arches National Monument by the federal government in 1929.

The main out-of-car activity in Arches is hiking; in fact, to even see the park's most famous landmark, **Delicate Arch**, a short hike is required. Numerous hiking trails in the park range from very easy to strenuous. As this is a national park, trails are typically very well maintained; however, severe weather may sometimes damage trails more quickly than the park service can rebuild them. Regardless of whether visitors intend to leave their cars or stay in them, everyone should arrive supplied with plenty of water, food, clothing, and sunblock—best stocked up on while still in **Moab**. (Outside of Moab, the last structure in the park is the visitor center, where very limited supplies are available.)

The largest store in Moab supplying groceries and beverages is the **City Market**. In addition to the obvious wares, it also has a small lunch bar, stocks premade sandwiches, and carries firewood bundles and ice. For those requiring outdoor-specific gear, **GearHeads** has the most general selection, ranging from rock climbing to camping. One critical item to carry in the desert is sunblock. The park's elevation is roughly between 4,100 and 5,700 feet, and fewer than a third of its days each year are cloudy. Lightweight, light-colored, loose-fitting clothing helps a lot, too. Before departing on any kind of hike, be absolutely sure to have plenty of water or electrolyte beverage. Some hikers suggest 1 liter per person per hour of activity, but it doesn't hurt to have (a lot) more in case of an injury or unforeseen delay.

Heading north from Moab is simple and uneventful. Restaurant and hotel signs lining the roadside thin as US-191 leads out of town. The highway crosses over the historic Colorado River. Taking a right turn here would lead east on UT-128, and on to chapter 7's tour of the Moab–Colorado River–Castle Valley–La Sal Mountain Loop Road tour.

Peculiar Geology

Roughly 300 million years ago, seas covered the area where Arches is today. Over time the waters retreated, then returned, then retreated and returned—multiple times—thus leaving behind significant salt deposits. Eventually the seawater left for good, and the residual thick salt layer was gradually covered in other sediments: mud and sand. This would eventually become sandstone layers—primarily Navajo and Entrada Sandstone—resting atop the solidified salt beneath.

Naturally the salt, under that much pressure, destabilized and could no longer support the layers above. The sandstone began slipping and sliding, over the millennia, rising and falling on top of the uneven salt layer. As it did this, it splintered all over the place. Some pieces dipped low and some remained high. All of this tilting and fracturing, dipping and doming, left the rock vulnerable to some strange weathering patterns. Natural unevenness in the rock's density and solubility allowed for arches and hoodoos to form—as the softer rock beneath sturdier rock wore away more quickly. Water, ice, and wind all played their parts in taking the weaker rock material, yielding the spires, fins, and rounded shapes remaining today.

PETRIFIED SAND DUNES

Four and a half miles from the center of Moab comes the obvious right-hand turnoff for Arches, and just over 0.5 mile beyond that comes the park entrance and fee station where all must pay $25 or present a national parks pass. As long as the vehicle is stopped here, it's worth taking a left and checking out the **visitor center**. In keeping with tradition, this is where the Park Service distributes all kinds of free and not-free literature: maps, books, guides. This is also the last outpost of civilization inside the park. Though Arches is stuffed with rangers and other visitors, none of these people will be selling water or food.

As the road ascends steeply away from the visitor center, keep an eye out for a small pullout and placard on the right-hand side of the road (just before the road curves to the left). Those interested in the area's geology will get a clear visual explanation of one of the primary causes for the park's strange formations. The **Moab Fault**, along which US-191 sits (between Moab and Arches), formed roughly 6 million years ago. When tectonic movements became too much for the earth's crust to handle, it cracked. Subsequently, the eastern (Arches) side of the fault ended up half a mile lower than the western side. This major vertical shift and ensuing rock fracturing is one of the contributing factors to the strange erosion patterns that have occurred in the park (as described in the "Peculiar Geology" sidebar, above).

About 2 miles beyond this sign (and 2.5 miles uphill from the visitor center), the road comes to **Park Avenue**, a trailhead and viewpoint. From the parking lot, the namesake feature is visible. This collection of tall, thin, dead-vertical fins stands clustered together to resemble a sandstone version of Manhattan. From here, it is possible to hike a 1-mile trail that descends down into the canyon beneath these fins, eventually leading to the **Courthouse Towers** parking area. The trail loses about 300 feet in elevation as it descends to the wash beneath the towers (almost always dry). People hiking to the towers experience a particularly impressive view, being dwarfed by the tall, clustered fins in a way that would be impossible from the road.

On the way to the **Courthouse Towers** pullout, notice the **La Sal Mountains Viewpoint** on the right side of the road. The **La Sal Mountains** are a commanding range that soars far above Moab. (For a closer look, consider taking the Moab–Colorado River–Castle Valley–La Sal Mountain Loop Ride, chapter 7.) These mountains rise much higher than anything around, topping out at 12,721 feet, at the peak of **Mount Peale**—almost 8,700 feet higher than Moab. An artistic contrast to the desert's oranges and reds, these deep blue peaks hold snow into the summer season, while the valleys below bake at triple-digit temperatures.

From the Courthouse Towers parking just down the road, sturdy, tall fins dominate the view. Thick and imposing, these are quite different from the arches coming up farther along. Rising hundreds of feet above the flat, broad valley below, they are an obvious high-rise simulacrum. Signs indicate **Sheep Rock, the Organ, Tower of Babel**, and **Three Gossips**. Looking closely, anyone should be able to spot Sheep Rock and the Three Gossips without any help. The Organ and Tower of Babel are not quite as intuitively recognized, but roadside placards help.

Leaving this tower metropolis, sit back and enjoy the general scenery, as the only official viewpoint in the next 4 miles is for the **Petrified Dunes**. Though not as visually striking as many of the park's features, the dunes are still worth a visit. Bona fide sand dunes, these were covered over time by other layers of sediment and compressed into solid rock. Later these overlay-

Cryptobiotic What?

People unfamiliar with the desert may not be aware that it is critical for hikers to stay on established trails—inside or outside of the park. Unlike in more lush environments, the desert's fragile ecosystem can literally be damaged by one person's footprints! As hot and dry climate cannot possibly support widespread vegetation, there are no root structures to hold everything in place. Rather, the soil itself is alive.

Cryptobiotic soil, as it's called, is a fragile mixture of lichens, mosses, and cyanobacteria—often invisible. This delicate carpet is extremely slow growing, and in some places represents 70 percent of the desert's living surface. These organisms play many roles in keeping the ecosystems healthy, from maintaining a chemical balance in the soil to preventing devastating water and wind erosion. Without it, the desert could quite literally blow away. Do your part to preserve it by staying on established paths.

Sister Ranges

Anyone who's seen the **Abajo** or **Henry Mountains** (also in southeastern Utah) has noticed an immediate resemblance to the La Sals. All impressively tall and distinct ranges, they rise high and solitary above the surrounding Colorado Plateau desert. All were formed roughly 25 million years ago by igneous intrusion. Magma forced itself high into the upper strata of earth's crust, cooling slowly beneath the surface. Covering layers of sandstone eroded away over time, exposing rock generally classified as porphyry—characterized by large crystals formed during the gradual subterranean cooling of magma.

ing rock types eroded, leaving the dunes exposed. They can be recognized as the pale rock mounds poking out between clumps of low vegetation.

Motoring along, the next distinctive attraction is **Balanced Rock**—just 0.2 mile before the road splits in twain. It will be a sight to see when this unlikely formation finally topples! This vaguely egg-shaped boulder, roughly the size of three buses, rests atop a tapered, slanted rock pillar. The total height of this feature is 128 feet, 55 of which come from the showpiece itself. This suspicious-looking feature is not a strange man-made prank; rather, it is a classic example of softer bedrock eroding beneath harder capstone. A short, paved path leads directly to the base. Worth noting: The trail to Balanced Rock and the viewpoint trail for Delicate Arch are the only two handicapped-accessible trails in Arches National Park.

Just a few seconds' driving leads to the turnoff for the **Windows** section of the park. This 2.5-mile road heads east through **Ham Rock, the Garden of Eden**, and **Covert Arch** to reach a parking area and viewpoint for the **North and South Windows, Turret Arch, Cove of Caves**, and **Double Arch**.

WINDOWS ROAD

Though it's a bit of a stretch to call it **Ham Rock**, this first formation you see after taking the turnoff is one of the most easily visible in the park—viewable from many vantage points. Roughly shaped like a ham (or egg . . . or avocado), it is perched high upon a Navajo Sandstone dome, making it easy to spot. Just after Ham Rock is a turnoff to the left. This overlooks the **Garden of Eden** and **Elephant Butte**, which stands 5,653 feet above sea level.

The end of this road is clearly marked with a turnaround and a large parking area. From here, a generally flat, 0.4-mile trail heads from the northern end of the parking lot to **Double Arch**, providing a leg-stretcher/vista combination. Though Double Arch is plainly visible from the road, the broad

BALANCED ROCK

trail leads almost directly to the base of this remarkable feature, providing a much more impressive view. Those planning to get out for photographs or a hike should respect Arches' requirement that all cars park in the designated areas, lest traffic accumulate at this popular viewpoint and trailhead.

Departing eastwardly from the same parking area is a 0.5-mile-long trail to the **Windows and Turret Arches**. Though visible from the road, these reward hikers with a much better view than that had from pavement. The **North and South Windows** arches are actually two twin-like windows in the same rock fin. **Turret Arch**, though relatively small, has a fairly unique look, with one primary arch reaching to the ground and a secondary, smaller hole resembling a window. Taken in view with the host rock formation and the trail steps leading up to it, it indeed resembles a house with a turret. To return to the main road, do an about-face and head back west 2.5 miles.

Hang a right and continue northeast along the main road, stopping at **Panorama Point**. From here, the landscape scoops down and away to reveal gently sweeping sagebrush-covered hills in the foreground with a backdrop of globular pinnacles and domes. From a distance, it is much easier to see the clear bands of pale yellow and rust-orange sandstone that had once been continuous strata—before wild tectonic uplift and subsequent erosive forces sculpted them into the distinctive art of southeastern Utah.

DELICATE ARCH ROAD

Two and a half miles after returning to the main road, make a right-hand turn if you want to see the most famous arch in the state, **Delicate Arch**. Though not the largest, this showpiece arch seen on the Utah license plate is arguably the most aesthetic. It stands alone atop an expansive buffed sandstone dome devoid of vegetation and is a freestanding arch of more than 180 degrees. At one point, government officials even considered varnishing this arch to prevent further erosion and the arch's eventual demise—but the plan was deemed contrary to the mission of national parks and eventually forgotten.

To see this arch, some walking is unavoidable. A couple options exist: Hike to the arch itself, or view it from afar. To see it from a distance, two separate viewpoints can be reached via quick and easy hikes. These yield somewhat distant, though strikingly scenic, vistas. On the other hand, a proper hike takes you directly to the arch itself. For those with the time to hike directly to the arch, the 1.5-mile journey would be worth the effort even if it didn't lead to the Delicate Arch. Along the way, this path gains a bit of elevation, but as it passes through brush, across slickrock, and in washes, the effort is hardly noticeable. Finally, Delicate Arch appears, having been hidden from view until the very end of the hike. Its absence along the way is perhaps what allows visitors to truly enjoy the surrounding geology and wildlife for their own sake. (To pick up this trail, head to the **Wolfe Ranch**.)

If, however, there is not enough time to complete this trek, simply drive to the terminus of the Delicate Arch Road, from which two short viewpoint access trails depart. Both are casual (one is just 150 feet; the other is 0.5 mile). The lesser trail is one of just two handicapped-accessible trails in the park (the other one being for Balanced Rock). Both viewpoints are separated from the arch and its rounded sandstone base by a deep and narrow canyon. This dramatic relief makes for quite a view, and renders Delicate Arch rather impressive in appearance.

Leave the Delicate Arch spur of the road and regain the main road again. To see the rest of the park, make a right-hand turn and head north. This portion of the park is much more hiking oriented than the previously described car-friendly sections. Though two roadside viewpoints come up quickly, the bulk of the attractions ahead must be accessed on foot. That is not to say

TRAIL TO DOUBLE ARCH AT THE END OF THE WINDOWS ROAD

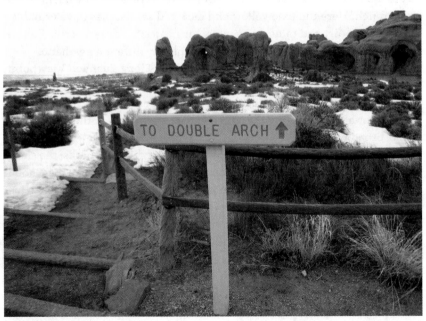

Wolfe Ranch

In 1898, John Wesley Wolfe and his son, Fred, relocated from Ohio to Utah. Prior to the move, John had sustained a serious leg injury during his service in the Civil War. Seeking a warm, dry climate to soothe his persistent aches, he and his son set up shop on one hundred acres at this location in the Salt Valley Wash. Here there was just enough of a water supply and corresponding grasslands to establish a very modest ranch.

John and Fred remained at that spot until returning to Etna, Ohio, shortly before John's death in 1913. To this day, the original log cabin, wooden fences, root cellar, corral, and other wooden structures remain—largely thanks to the arid climate in which decay progresses at an extremely slow rate. Today, these structures are open for viewing.

Those up for a 5-minute hike can take a walk to view even older human artifacts in the same locale. A fairly dense collection of **Ute petroglyphs** remain etched on boulders located in a wash, well signed from the same parking area as for the Wolfe Ranch. Depicted are several riders on horseback, as well as bighorn sheep and a few smaller animals.

that the roadside scenery will disappoint; just that many of the arches must require some effort to peep—a bonus for some!

This next section of Arches is called the **Fiery Furnace**. Just over a mile from the junction with Delicate Arch Road comes the **Salt Valley Overlook** on the right. Salt Valley is the place in which John Wesley Wolfe ran his small cattle ranch. Here the pale yellow and dark red sandstones have crumbled into buttes of dirt and talus, upon which grow twisted desert scrub. Take in this view, because the next vista has a completely different aesthetic.

Almost immediately after this pullout is the **Fiery Furnace Viewpoint**, showcasing a comical-looking collection of bubbly, knobby spires. The predominant rock color here is a deep red, and there are rows and rows of these pillars—not a stretch to say that it resembles an inferno in the belly of this round, broad valley.

Sand Dune Arch can be reached by a couple of different paths; the shortest trail to it departs from a pullout on the right-hand side of the road, about 4.5 miles past the Windows Road junction. This trail reaches the arch in just a quarter of a mile. Surrounded by other rocks, sheltered, and often shady, this has a much different feel than many of the other arches. Sand Dune Arch rises out of a bed of deep sand (hence the name) and has an almost jungle-gym feel. Kids particularly enjoy this one, as they feel like they're in a larger-than-life sandbox.

For more of a hike, continue along this same trail. It leads out of the rock fin maze, through sagebrush, and to **Broken Arch** in just another mile. (This trail system is also accessible by a shorter approach from Devil's Garden Campground site 40; the route is easily seen by looking at the Arches National Park map, available in the visitor center.) Broken Arch isn't actually broken at all, but it looks as if two arms of rock have leaned over to meet each other.

DIRT ROAD SPUR

The next turnoff (on the left-hand side) is to a dirt road forking off to the left (just a mile before the terminus of the main road). This spur tours the Salt Valley before forking in two. Continue straight all the way to the park's border (and beyond), or to see more arches, hang a left and drive another 1.1 miles to a pit toilet at the **Klondike Bluffs** area. From this parking area, a pedestrian path leads to **Marching Men** and **Tower Arch**.

Petroglyphs or Pictograms?

These two words are often thrown around interchangeably. And they're used all the time in southern Utah, where abundant rock provided pristine tablets for the artists of earlier eras, and where the dry climate has preserved these works for thousands of years. Visible in Arches National Park is the work of the **Ute** and **ancestral Pueblo** tribes. Some of southwest Utah's rock art dates back roughly 2,000 years, spanning many different eras of these peoples. Much of the work can be attributed to shamans. After self-inducing hallucinogenic states, they were able to communicate with the spirit world. These experiences would then be recorded on the rock.

There is a simple difference between petroglyphs and pictograms, worth learning: A **pictogram** (also called **pictograph**) is an image painted on the rock with any number of available dyes and pigments. Back in the days before latex paint and Red 40, other coloring agents were used, such as animal blood and plant pigments.

A **petroglyph** (examples of which can be accessed by a trail at the Wolfe Ranch) is an image pecked or carved into the stone's surface. On Utah's sandstone, this renders a striking visual effect, as the deep red varnish on the rock's surface has been chipped away to expose much lighter, less oxidized rock below. Over the centuries, artists used antlers, bones, harder stones, and later metal tools to create these images.

One rough relative age indicator of petroglyphs is the etching's coloring. The newer images of a set will be much lighter than the older ones, as the manually exposed rock has simply had less exposure to the elements and therefore less time to oxidize. Depending on the climate, petroglyphs have the potential to remain visible for much longer than pictographs.

This section of park is the sweet spot for four-wheel-drive high-clearance vehicles. From the main dirt road, an 11-mile strip of much rougher road works back south toward Balanced Rock and a few other points of interest. Before attempting these roads, it is best you consult with a good map, a weather report, and a park ranger to be sure there are no park-enforced closures or nature-induced impasses.

Back on the main road, a quick drive to the north delivers the **Skyline Arch** pullout. A hiking trail does lead to the base of this arch, but unlike most, this one is actually better viewed from the road. From afar, it appears most impressive, as it crowns a tall rock fin. But due to topography, it all but disappears from view to those standing directly beneath. A massive rock fall in 1940 roughly doubled its size to its current span of 69 feet.

The **Devil's Garden** trailhead area is the very last stop on the road. From this little hub are many attractions. There is the **Devil's Garden Trail** itself, a dirt road leading to a campground, and yet another trailhead leading out from the campground. There is even potable water available at the campground—so don't be shy about refilling.

The **Devil's Garden Campground** is the only campground within the park, and quite a pleasant one. Surrounded by a cluster of house-sized rock

CLIMB FROM VISITORS CENTER INTO THE PARK

domes and filled with juniper, it has a cozy feel. It is much more sheltered than other sections of the park—the ideal location for Arches' only campground. The setup here is semiprimitive, with groomed sites, picnic tables, grills, and toilets. Though drinking water is available, there are no showers; a few sites are large enough to accommodate RVs. There is an extra fee per night, on top of the entrance fee to the park, to camp here. Reservations are possible online or by telephone, March through October, for an additional charge. To hike from the campground, find site 40 and depart to the south, traveling along a loop-and-hook-shaped trail past **Broken Arch** and **Sand Dune Arch**. (This is the same trail as is accessed by the Sand Dune Arch pullout on the main road, above.)

IN THE AREA

ARCHES NATIONAL PARK, P.O. Box 907, Moab. Call 435-719-2299. Website: www.nps.gov/arch.

CITY MARKET, 425 South Main Street, Moab. Open daily. Call 435-259-5181. Website: www.citymarket.com.

DEVIL'S GARDEN CAMPGROUND RESERVATIONS. Extra fee required to reserve a campsite in advance. Call 1-877-444-6777 or 1-877-833-6777 (Telecommunication Device for the Deaf). Website: www.recreation.gov.

GEARHEADS, 471 South Main Street, Moab. Open daily. Call 435-259-4327. Website: www.moabgear.com.

ASCENDING INTO THE LA SAL MOUNTAINS ON THE LA SAL MOUNTAIN LOOP ROAD

7

MOAB, COLORADO RIVER, CASTLE VALLEY, LA SAL MOUNTAIN LOOP

ESTIMATED LENGTH: About 63 miles (or 75 miles with the Fisher Towers detour)

ESTIMATED TIME: A short half day unless stopping to hike, wine taste, or rock climb

HIGHLIGHTS: This loop drive departs from the world-famous outdoorsy town of **Moab**, tours along the **Colorado River**, past a winery, past the famous sandstone towers of **Castle Valley**, and eventually up and into the subalpine, too-fun-to-drive **La Sal Mountain Loop**. This route starts and finishes right in Moab, and is a succinct way to tour some of the area's more diverse terrain.

GETTING THERE: To get to Moab, take I-70 to Exit 182, turning south on US-191. Thirty-two miles later, this turns seamlessly into Moab's Main Street. (For more specific instructions on how to come from Salt Lake City, see the "Getting There" section in chapter 8.)

As always when leaving town in the desert, be sure to do a quick inventory of water, food, and gas. Though this route never gets terribly far from Moab, it has virtually no services along the way. Once you're satisfied with the trip's rations, point your wheels north and leave **Moab** by heading north on Main Street/US-191. Just 3.5 miles from the center of Moab (and hardly a mile from the outskirts), make a right onto UT-128, just before the bridge over the Colorado River. When making this turn, reset the trip odometer. In the twists and turns of this narrow canyon, hiking trails, pullouts, and other features pop up rapidly and are often hard to spot, even by those who know the stops' locations along the roadside.

There is a freshwater spring running from a pipe fitted into the sandstone walls on the south side of this road, just a quarter mile past the turnoff. Called **Matrimony Spring**, it allegedly gives couples great marital luck. This water is untreated by any chemicals and flows around the clock—so it is an excellent water source for locals and campers, twenty-four seven. In recent years, the spring closed due to health concerns, but the efforts of local groups have brought it back into service.

Continuing roughly east, keep an eye peeled for **Updraft Arch**. A pullout just 0.3 mile past Matrimony Spring provides safe viewing of this window. This eye-shaped slit in the already-impressive Navajo Sandstone cliffs high above the road is located just to the east of the pullout.

Not even 2 miles after the start of UT-128 begins the **Colorado Riverway Recreation Area**. Operated by the Bureau of Land Management, the land features several riverside campgrounds and picnic areas, as well as trails for hiking, mountain biking, and off-roading, and open lands for wild camping.

Its developed campgrounds stretch quite a while along the banks of the Colorado River. Though sites are primitive (read: no electricity or running water), the campgrounds' views, aesthetic locations, and tidiness render them quite popular. Along UT-128 are seven such campgrounds, five of which are clustered around **Big Bend**, about 6.5 miles east of US-191. Together, these offer roughly one hundred sites. (An overview of the campgrounds is posted on a BLM kiosk just 1 mile onto UT-128.)

Over the years, many of the rivers and mountains in the United States have been renamed so as to be more respectful of historically oppressed

Elk Mountain Mission, William Granstaff, and the Sagebrush Rebellion

In May 1855, after a very rugged and topographically challenging journey from Salt Lake City (founded in 1848), a forty-one-man group of missionaries arrived in the Spanish Valley and began to set up shop. Their goal was to meet and convert local peoples to Mormonism.

They erected a stone fort called **Elk Mountain Mission** at the northern end of present-day Moab—actually where Moab's **Motel 6** parking lot is today. They planted crops and attempted to establish friendly contact with the local Ute tribe, who inhabited southern Utah at that time. These Mormons perceived their arrival as successful, as they had already baptized more than a dozen Utes by the middle of July.

The Utes, however, didn't like what they were smelling, and trouble between the two groups started to brew. The Utes grew mistrustful of the valley's new conversion-happy residents. According to the Mormons' September 20 journal entries, crops from the fort were being stolen at night by Utes. On September 23, one Mormon man was allegedly shot by a son of the Ute chief. This sparked a gun battle at the fort, where a handful of Ute attackers were killed—meanwhile, other ambushes in the vicinity knocked off a few Mormons. Finally, the Utes torched the Mormon crops, giving the fort residents the final ousting they needed. The following day, all surviving Mormons packed up what they could carry and headed north, shy a few dozen cattle and five horses.

This fort would remain abandoned for more than twenty years until a trapper and cattle driver, William Granstaff, and another trapper known only as "Frenchie" would come to occupy it. William came to the region in the 1870s as a prospecting and cattle-running cowboy. The namesake of Negro Bill Canyon, Granstaff grazed his cattle there regularly. In 1877 he and Frenchie helped themselves to residence of the Elk Mountain Mission Fort in Spanish Valley—where Moab is today. But their residence wouldn't last long; Frenchie disappeared from records and in 1881, Granstaff was accused of bootlegging booze and hightailed it out of the area.

VIEW FROM CASTLE CREEK WINERY

groups. Well—this one still hasn't been: **Negro Bill Canyon**. Named after William Granstaff, this shady, narrow canyon is one of the few around with a perennial stream. The running water is usually a bit high in the early spring, with the flow dipping a bit lower during the late spring and early summer months. Even on warmer days it still refrigerates the already-cool canyon.

A 2.5-mile hike along the canyon bottom leads to the **Morning Glory Natural Bridge**. Though the terrain is relatively flat, running water can require some skilled stone stepping, making the round-trip journey take up to 2 or 3 hours. Because stream crossing is required, it's not unreasonable to consider doing the walk in some beefy sandals, lest the water wet and stink up a pair of good shoes and create blisters. Along the way, a handful of side canyons branch off—watch for a small sign about 2 miles from the trailhead that points to Morning Glory Natural Bridge. In about half a mile, the path leads directly to this 243-foot-wide arch.

Back on UT-128, the next 9 miles of driving lead past several campgrounds and day-use areas: picnic grounds, boat ramps. Many are concentrated around the Big Bend portion of this river where the Colorado makes a sweeping S-curve. At this location is a smattering of obvious boulders on which rock climbers will be playing in good weather. It might be possible to spot climbers higher up, on the canyon rim walls, as a few multipitch rock climbs ascend these cliffs.

Just before turning off UT-128, into Castle Valley, look to the north for the obvious **Castle Creek Winery** and adjacent **Red Cliffs Lodge**. Together the two operations occupy a spacious and green campus on the northern side of the Colorado River. Castle Creek, Utah's first and largest commercial winery, was opened in 2002. Now offering three whites and four reds, it produces more than eight thousand cases of the goodness each year. It planted its own cabernet sauvignon and syrah in 2006, and the winery was able to harvest and press some of its own grapes in 2008. Castle Creek has won multiple awards for several of its wines, from the Finger Lakes and Pacific Rim international competitions to the Utah Best of State Award. Today it offers indoor and outdoor dining, tours, and wine tasting to anyone passing through.

Red Cliffs Lodge features guest beds as well as on-site and backcountry recreational opportunities—somewhat like summer camp for the whole family. Choices for accommodations include twenty cabins and eighty rooms, all overlooking the Colorado River. Packages include river rafting, horseback riding, scenic flights, golfing, jet boat rides, off-roading, mountain biking, and hiking. Just on the grounds, guests have access to a swimming pool, a fitness facility, tennis courts, and a small museum (see sidebar, below). Ideal for special occasions and team-building activities, this lodge can attract large groups, so those wishing to avoid the company of wedding parties should inquire when making reservations.

Very shortly after Castle Creek and the Red Cliffs Lodge (and about 15.5

Moab Museum of Film and Western Heritage

Even those visiting this area for the first time will surely recognize a number of Moab's vistas simply from the many famous photographs and films shot on location here. Castle Valley and the Colorado River's iconic scenery have long represented the Wild West—the days of cowboys and sharpshooters romanticized by Hollywood.

In the late 1940s, John Ford started a rich tradition of filming here when he chose Moab as the location for several of his movies—many of which actually were shot on the grounds of the Red Cliffs Lodge. The roster of stars who appeared in these pictures includes **John Wayne**, **Henry Fonda**, **Anthony Quinn**, **Ben Johnson**, and **Maureen O'Hara**.

The portrayal of the Wild West on the banks of the Colorado River actually wasn't stretching the truth too much. Butch Cassidy and his famous Wild Bunch often rode through the region on the way to a heist or away from the law. The Red Cliffs Lodge itself was settled in the late 1800s and has been in continuous operation as a working ranch ever since.

miles east of US-191), make a right turn and head south into Castle Valley onto Castle Valley Drive. This road is actually rather easy to miss, so keep a sharp eye out. A map on the right-hand side of Castle Valley Drive, just after the turn, confirms correct navigation.

Entering Castle Valley, it doesn't take long to understand what the fuss is about. To the immediate east of the road is the ultraclassic vista of **Castleton Tower** and **the Rectory**. Castleton is the thinnest, fingerlike spire on the southern side of the formation; the Rectory is the elongated one to its north. From the valley, elevation 4,500 feet, to the tops of the towers at roughly 6,660 feet, there is just over 2,000 vertical feet of relief. Each of these towers has perfect "splitter" cracks running more or less from the base to the summit—and the rocks are therefore home to several three- to four-pitch rock climbing routes. The summit of each of these towers, as one could easily imagine from the ground, is almost perfectly flat and quite interesting to sit atop.

Those who feel the desire can hike to the base of these towers. At a normal to brisk pace, the hike to the main saddle between Castleton and the Rectory takes just over an hour. Though most people hiking this path are climbers en route to the base of the climbs, the walk itself is quite worth the effort. The

Fisher Towers: Utah's Coolest Mud Pile

For those not in a rush, this is a small and worthwhile detour—requiring an extra 5.5 miles on UT-128 beyond the Castle Valley Drive. A total of 21 miles east of US-191, look for a right-hand turnoff for **Fisher Towers Road**. Here stands a small (five-site) campground and 2.2-mile foot trail leading to the base of this formation.

Named for a resident miner in the 1880s, these unlikely fins look more like upside-down mud drippings than stone towers hundreds of feet tall. Made of Moenkopi-topped Cutler sandstone, these have been naturally stuccoed with mud. These towers extend from a parent butte (to the north) that has gradually eroded away to expose three main fins and other smaller features. It is not difficult to imagine that over time, the mesa will continue to erode, exposing more similar formations as it goes.

The towers have earned notoriety among rock climbers for their world-famous routes, particularly the Ancient Arts, which finishes atop the most precarious-looking corkscrew summit. Anyone visiting the towers will understand immediately, though, that these routes have been deemed classic for their distinctiveness—and most certainly not for high-quality rock climbing. This trail is on the eastern side of Castle Valley, so visitors to the towers will also get to enjoy views of **Castleton** and **Rectory** (or the "Priest" and "Nuns") towers, standing more than 2,000 feet above the valley floor.

Zac Robinson

CLIMBERS APPROACHING THE RECTORY

trail pleasantly gains elevation on gradually pitched switchbacks, picking its way up the talus and boulders beneath the formations.

The most easily reached trailhead for this hike is found by taking a left onto a dirt road roughly 4.7 miles south of UT-128. Drive along this to the obvious parking area and impromptu campground. The journey begins by scampering up a wash (requiring some agility and scrambling skills) until you reach a dirt road and plateau. As there are no signs, intuition will have to point the way to the main trail. However, because there are no trees on these talus slopes, route finding will not be difficult. A high-quality path leads all the way to the towers—once found, this should lead directly to the saddle. Occasionally, a storm will wash away sections of this unvegetated trail—but, barring any severe weather, it should still be passable. Near the top, however, there is a particularly exposed section of trail. Though the walking there is not at all technical, a misstep could send the misstepper down a steep, steep mountainside. Keep your eyes forward and your balance in check.

Heading south in the Castle Valley, no turns are necessary to reach the **La Sal National Forest**, as Castleton Road turns naturally into the **La Sal Mountain Loop Road**. As the road winds up and out of Castle Valley, be sure

FRAGILE DESERT SOIL BENEATH CASTLETON

Moab Century Tour

If this route seems stimulating by car, imagine doing it on a bike! During the middle of September each year, a fully supported road ride takes place roughly along this drive. Distances range from 38 to 102 miles, and route options include out-and-back journeys on UT-128 along the Colorado River or the burlier La Sal Mountain Loop Road in a counterclockwise direction. For those who are in town and want to participate, many bike shops offer high-end rental fleets right on Main Street in Moab.

to turn around and take in the increasingly panoramic views below. Though its towers are impressive when viewed from below, its integrated features are quite noteworthy from this retracted and elevated perspective. If you didn't have time to make the detour to the Fisher Towers, try to spot them now in the far backdrop (northeast side of the Castle Valley).

Several Forest Service dirt roads branch off of this main road, but the main route should be quite easy to follow. As it climbs, this road makes sweeping, dramatic turns along the foothills and plateaus of the striking **La Sal Mountains**. From north to south, the major peaks are as follows: **Grand View Mountain** (10,905 feet), **Horse Mountain** (11,150 feet), **Mount Waas** (12,331 feet), **Manns Peak** (12,273 feet), and **Haystack Mountain** (11,634 feet), with **Mount Tomasaki** (12,230 feet), rather hidden behind Haystack, to the east. As the road whirls around the skirts of this range, it might be difficult for the driver to keep track of each peak.

Almost the entirety of the La Sal Mountain Loop Road is in the **Manti–La Sal National Forest**. Because of this, camping is permitted at almost any reasonable spot away from the road. A few official campgrounds do exist—one at the end of Forest Service Road 063 (nearest the base of Mount Waas), and another at the end of Forest Service Road 076 (on Boren Mesa)—both short doglegs from the east of the La Sal Mountain Loop Road.

As the road makes one of its deepest bends toward the east and into a forested fold of mountainside, it passes over **Mill Creek** and **Mill Creek Canyon**. This canyon, though mostly hidden from view from the road above, is lined with more excellent sandstone walls—perfect for rock climbing. There is no published guidebook to the area, so if you want to check it out, be prepared for adventure. Even attempting to descend into the canyon requires route finding, as rope ladders and the like are the way in.

Hang on for the turns and curves in the road ahead, and the road will eventually head back downhill to join Spanish Valley Drive. To reconnect with US-191, stay on this road as it heads north and roughly parallel to US-191. Take a left on County Road/Old Airport Road for 0.6 mile, and then a right on US-191. Moab is just under 8 miles north.

MILL CREEK CANYON IN THE HIGH LA SAL FOOTHILLS

Though a short and unpopulated loop, this route toured many natural points of interest. The road passed through desert, slickrock, high alpine terrain, low canyon floors, and by a giant laccolith—or igneous intrusion between two sedimentary strata—in the La Sal Mountains. In addition, it passed one of Utah's most famous wineries, as well as one of its most photographed and filmed valleys. Once back in Moab, consider checking out chapters 6 and 8 for two other suggested drives that depart from this town.

IN THE AREA

Accommodations

RED CLIFFS LODGE, Milepost 14 UT-128, Moab. Moderately priced. Cabins and guest rooms to rent overlooking the Colorado River; many other activities available by appointment. Call 1-866-812-2002. Website: www. redcliffslodge.com.

Dining

CASTLE CREEK WINERY, Milepost 14 UT-128, Moab. Tours, wine tasting, and even dining available. Open year-round. Call 435-259-3332. Website: www.castlecreekwinery.com.

Other Contacts

COLORADO RIVERWAY RECREATION AREA, Bureau of Land Management Office, 82 East Dogwood, Moab. Call 435-259-2100.

FISHER TOWERS RECREATION AREA, Bureau of Land Management Office, 82 East Dogwood, Moab. Call 435-259-2100.

MOAB CENTURY TOUR. A 3-day cycling event in the middle of September with rides and other events. Website: www.skinnytireevents.com.

THE NAMESAKE "NEEDLES"

8

MOAB TO CANYONLANDS' NEEDLES

ESTIMATED LENGTH: 80 miles each way

ESTIMATED TIME: Half a day

HIGHLIGHTS: Moab is southern Utah's most famous tourist destination, surrounded by unique and dramatic geology. Not just pleasant to look at, the
surrounding environs also serve as an excellent and accessible playground
for all kinds of invigorating recreation, such as river rafting, mountain biking,
rock climbing, and hiking.

GETTING THERE: Moab is within reasonable driving distance from three major cities: Salt Lake City, Denver, and Las Vegas. Salt Lake City is the closest, about
five hours away. Those arriving from the east or west should simply come via
I-70, turning south on US-191 at Exit 182. After 32 miles, this highway turns
into Moab's Main Street.

  To get to Moab from Salt Lake City, head south on I-15 for roughly 50 miles.
Leave the interstate via Exit 258 in Spanish Fork, heading southeast on US-6.
This "shortcut" between I-15 and I-70 saves about an hour of driving and is
actually quite scenic. Beware, though: The time-saving nature of this route
makes it popular with every type of through-driver, from passenger cars to RVs
and tractor trailers. Be alert to other drivers' mistakes. US-6 dumps directly
onto I-70. Head 23 miles east on this interstate, also using Exit 182 for US-191.

This particular drive alone is scenic enough to offer a half day's entertainment just by sightseeing from pavement. On the way, though, it leads to
numerous outdoorsy opportunities. En route, it passes arguably the world's
best sandstone crack climbing area, **Indian Creek**, and ends up in the southeastern portion of **Canyonlands National Park**—perched above deep, steep
canyons at the edge of the **Colorado River**. Here, trails lead down toward
the rivers and smaller hikes afford views of ruins and geological spectacles.

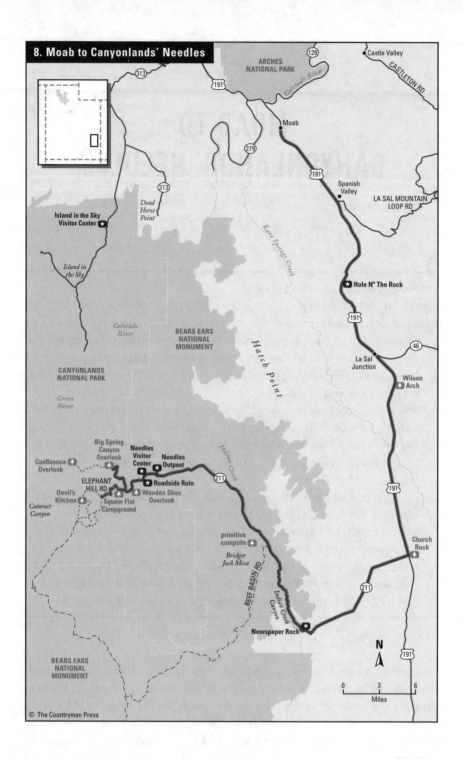

8. Moab to Canyonlands' Needles

ARCHES NATIONAL PARK

Castle Valley

CASTLETON RD

Colorado River

313

191

128

Moab

279

191

Spanish Valley

LA SAL MOUNTAIN LOOP RD

313

Dead Horse Point

Island in the Sky Visitor Center ★

Kane Spring Creek

Island in the Sky

★ Hole N" The Rock

191

Colorado River

BEARS EARS NATIONAL MONUMENT

Hatch Point

La Sal Junction

46

Wilson Arch

CANYONLANDS NATIONAL PARK

Green River

Confluence Overlook

Big Spring Canyon Overlook

Needles Visitor Center ★

Needles Outpost ★

Indian Creek

211

ELEPHANT HILL RD

★ Roadside Ruin

Devil's Kitchen

Squaw Flat Campground

Wooden Shoe Overlook

191

Cataract Canyon

primitive campsite

Bridger Jack Mesa

Church Rock

BEEF BASIN RD

211

Indian Creek Canyon

Newspaper Rock ★

BEARS EARS NATIONAL MONUMENT

N

0   3   6
Miles

211

191

© The Countryman Press

Into the "Wild"

On this drive, don't expect to encounter anything resembling civilization. With the exception of the **Hole N" the Rock** (a touristy gift shop) and **Needles Outpost** (with a small, seasonally open gas station just east of the Canyonlands National Park border), there are no on-route services beyond the southern end of Moab.

This journey is purely a sightseeing wilderness drive with opportunities to hike and explore the off-pavement environment. So before hitting the road, be sure to fill up the tank and pack a lunch, extra water, and sunscreen. A heads-up: Cell phones typically don't work beyond US-191, and any car that breaks down has to rely on the mercy of other passersby. If you are short on gas and unable to return all the way to Moab, you can head farther south along US-191 to **Monticello**. Though small, this town has multiple service stations and shops. It's out of the way, but it is about 20 miles closer to Canyonlands than Moab is—and sometimes 20 miles can make a difference.

Almost all features of this route are natural; don't expect towns, restaurants, hotels, or even reliable gas stations. The biggest man-made structure along the way is the **Canyonlands Visitor Center**, just inside the park.

This particular route begins in the outdoorsy tourist town of **Moab**. To those who haven't yet been, you may imagine that the environs surrounding Moab are all the same—desert, sandstone, and sagebrush—but in fact, this area has a surprising amount of diversity and natural depth. The groundcover morphs quickly and visibly with the slightest changes in elevation, nearness to a river, and hillside aspect. Each stratum of sandstone varies dramatically from one to the next in terms of color, texture, and thickness. And though the oranges, reds, and yellows of sandstone—the region's predominant rock type—dominate the foreground, the imposing **La Sal Mountains** provide a deep blue backdrop. Evergreen forests, sagebrush, cottonwood trees, and cryptobiotic soil cover this impressive eruption above the skyline east of Moab.

This drive aims for the Wingate Sandstone cliffs, fins, and towers sprouting out of broad canyons. Along the way, though, it must first ascend onto a high desert plateau as it passes the **La Sal Mountains**. It then plunges into the depths of **Indian Creek Canyon**, past sheer cliffs and steep talus piles, and arrives in the **Needles** area of **Canyonlands National Park**.

To begin this route from Moab, head dead south on Main Street. As it leaves town, Main changes its name to US-191. The first 40 miles of the drive are the least scenic or exciting, though they do pass quickly and include a few points of interest. Look around and enjoy the stark natural surroundings and the subtle changes from one vista to the next. The only major north–south

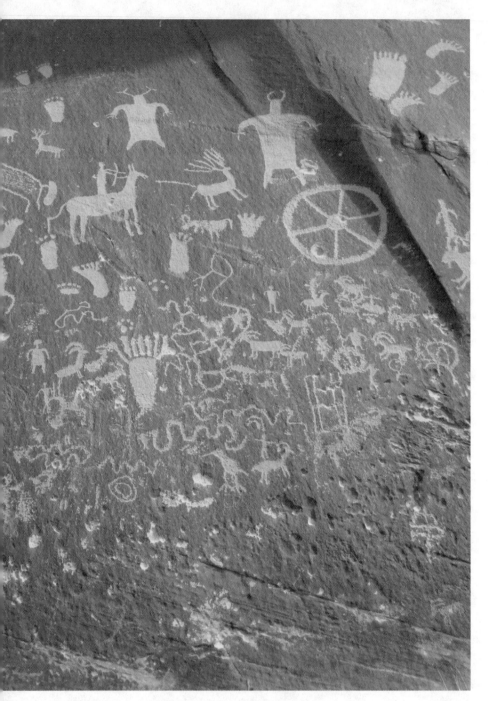

NEWSPAPER ROCK, AT THE TOP OF INDIAN CREEK CANYON

highway in the area, US-191 can sometimes get busy. Though this highway is predominantly two lanes, it does have semiregular passing lanes—there's no need to overtake other vehicles impatiently. If stuck in a line of traffic, just wait a few miles, and a chance to safely pass will come soon.

About 8 miles south of Moab, the **La Sal Mountain Loop** (Old Airport Road) departs from the highway to the east. Detailed in chapter 7, this commences a 60-mile loop that ascends the rising base of these impressive mountains, and ends by winding down through **Castle Valley** and along the shores of the **Colorado River**.

Continuing south, the road dips steeply down and heads directly to **Hole N" the Rock**, about 16 miles south of town. This bizarre little shop is housed in none other than a rock—a massive outcrop of red sandstone. In addition to a kitschy retail store, there is also a zoo with zebras, buffalo, and camels, among other creatures—open throughout the year. The total in-rock space measures 5,000 square feet and includes a gift shop and residence, adornments and furniture of which are carved directly into the rock. Over twelve years, this cavernous home was created by Albert Christensen, who removed 50,000 cubic feet from its parent rock. After his death in 1957, his wife, Gladys, transformed it into a public attraction, charging a small fee for tours of the residence.

Another 10 miles down the road (still on US-191) stands the obvious **Wilson Arch**, named for Joe Wilson—an early settler and resident in the area. This robust-looking Entrada Sandstone formation has a width of 91 feet and a height of 46 feet. As with other natural arches in the area, this was formed by the continuous freeze-thaw cycle in the desert, whereby seeping water exploits cracks and weaknesses in rock as it freezes and expands. Pullouts exist on either side of the road and provide for safe viewing out of highway traffic.

About 14 miles farther along (roughly 40 miles from the southern end of Moab), keep a sharp eye out for the large yellow sandstone "submarine" approaching on your left. Officially labeled **Church Rock** on maps, this natural road marker signals the junction with UT-210. Slow down and prepare to turn right, or west, toward Indian Creek and Canyonlands National Park. The next few miles of driving uneventfully lead over high desert plains. Climbing slightly through sagebrush toward small, juniper-covered hills, be sure to keep a sharp eye out for deer and free-range cattle. Especially near dawn and dusk, hundreds of deer can line the road on this stretch.

After miles of straights with almost no turns at all, the pavement suddenly plunges into the upper reaches of **Indian Creek Canyon** by way of very sharp, serpentine curves. Just before the road descends, the speed limit changes to 40 miles per hour and curving-road advisory signs pop up. Beware—the bottommost S-curve is very severe and intimately adjacent to a very steep drop-off! Once at the canyon bottom, the road winds along a riverbed lined with cottonwood trees and growing sandstone cliffs. At the top of this creek basin, the canyon is narrow and cozy, and the surrounding cliffs are still short.

Quickly after you arrive at the canyon floor, **Newspaper Rock** pops up on the right-hand side of the road. Pull into the parking lot to view an incredibly dense collection of petroglyphs. Carved onto a darkly varnished vertical slab, hundreds of figures have been protected from precipitation by a natural rock ceiling. The oldest of these rock etchings were created as early as two thousand years ago by the Basketmaker, Pueblo, and Fremont peoples. Newspaper Rock was designated a Utah State Historical Monument in 1961. Today a protective fence stands around it, but all the rock art is clearly visible for no charge.

After leaving Newspaper Rock, UT-210 continues to wind gradually downhill through tight curves for another 5 minutes or so. As the creek eats deeper into the bedrock, the yellow, domed sandstone yields to incredibly sheer Wingate Sandstone deeper down. As the miles tick by, the canyon broadens markedly into a gaping valley, and the rock band's full height becomes exposed. These cliffs on either side of the road comprise one of the world's premier destinations for rock climbers interested in crack climbing. Keep an

BRIDGER JACK MESA VIEWED ACROSS THE CREEK AT BEEF BASIN ROAD ON A COLD MORNING

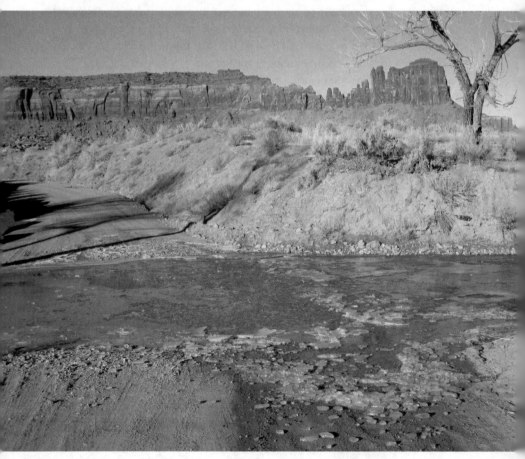

Canyonlands in Thirds

Though more or less one continuous landmass, Canyonlands consists of three geographically separate entities. The **Green River** flows into the park from its northwestern corner, and the **Colorado River** enters from the northeast. They join in the center of the park, forming a Y and effectively dividing the park into three regions. This southeastern portion, the Needles, is named for its predominant filamentous rock formations. Though other parts of the park must be accessed by long, circuitous drives, viewpoints from the Needles offer expansive vistas of the other regions of the park, particularly the northernmost region, **Island in the Sky**. When viewed from the Needles, the name's inspiration is obvious. To the west sits **the Maze**, the park's most wild portion, access to which is achieved primarily by high-clearance four-wheel-drive vehicles and foot travel.

eye out for pullouts (especially on the northern side of the road); slow down, and on nice days, climbers will be scattered about the crags above.

The next few miles provide "nothing" but increasingly dramatic scenery as the basin expands even more. Multiple other drainages join together to form an ever-broadening valley surrounded by high talus piles crowned by sheer buttes. To the south, the **Bridger Jack Mesa** can be recognized as a peninsula of rock that has been worn particularly thin. The pillars of Wingate that comprise it resemble a set of jagged teeth, and predict the future of today's thicker mesas. It is possible to get a closer look at this formation and even camp near the base; take a left at the signed **Beef Basin Road** (8 miles after Newspaper Rock), noticeable by the outhouse at the turnoff. A very rugged dirt-and-rock road winds toward the formation and to primitive camping very near its base. Those driving passenger cars should maneuver this road very carefully, lest your oil pan be sacrificed. Though it is not steep, this road's surface is embedded with many tall rocks.

If you are not taking the Bridger Jack detour, continue westward as the road straightens somewhat and ascends slightly out of this valley. This is the final approach to **Canyonlands National Park**. Seventy-two miles outside of Moab, signs mark the park boundary. Just after you cross into Canyonlands, the turnout to **Needles Outpost** appears on the northern side of the road. This is a very small gas station/convenience store affair that is indeed an outpost. Despite its remote location, this joint still stocks a respectable spectrum of goods, from maps and camping supplies to basic groceries. There is also a grill-style simple restaurant and a campground with showers and drinking water. Check ahead to be sure they are actually open for the season. Located so far from any town or highway, this shop has very limited deliveries, so prices are elevated and availability is not guaranteed. (Note: This business closed briefly in the summer of 2015 but reopened in September of that year under new ownership.)

Forge on into Canyonlands. Just over 3 miles into the park comes the fee station, where fees are collected (America the Beautiful passes accepted). Half a mile later you will find the **Needles Visitor Center**. Inside is a miniature museum giving an easily digested overview of the park (with a

RUINS IN INDIAN CREEK'S BEEF BASIN

Mike Schenk

THE LA SAL MOUNTAINS AS A BACKDROP OVER CANYLONLANDS

three-dimensional relief map), as well as a handful of brochures, books, maps, and basic supplies for purchase. The rangers are quite willing to recommend hikes and drives, and talk about current trail conditions. From here, one main, 10-mile-long paved road stretches in a southwesterly direction into the park. A few looping and dead-end side spurs depart from this road.

One of the first striking views is that of **Junction Butte** and the **Grand View Point Overlook**, to the northwest. Located across the Colorado River, in the Island in the Sky section of the park, these prominent buttes soar over the surrounding landscape.

Not even half a mile past the visitor center you will find the pullout for **Roadside Ruin** on the left side of the road. This stone-and-mud cylindrical grain silo was built under a rock overhang by ancestors of the Pueblo people between AD 1270 and 1295. The natural shelter, as well as the very dry climate, has allowed this structure to remain preserved almost perfectly for hundreds of years after its creation. A 0.3-mile loop trail leads from the parking to the silo.

The next major roadside point of interest is the **Wooden Shoe Arch**. This natural Cedar Mesa Sandstone arch was formed by rock of uneven strength. Millions of years ago, it was submerged under sea. Salt deposits from the ocean waters filled fissures in the rock that were later weathered away by aboveground erosive elements. Left behind is this wooden-clog-shaped arch. The pullout for this is 1.3 miles past the Roadside Ruin parking.

Just after the overlook, there is the option to turn left toward **Squaw Flat Campground** and **Elephant Hill Road**. This scenic jeep and hiking loop winds down into some of the more colorful rock formations of the Needles District, including the **Devil's Kitchen**. The road itself was built by a bulldozer operator employed at a nearby cattle ranch in the 1940s. At that time, cattle ranching in the area was hot, and this road serviced small airstrips used by planes delivering supplies to the ranches. Today, this dirt 4x4 road is popular for jeepers. The first stretch is drivable in a "normal" car, but the second portion, a loop, is considered to be a challenging jeep road and is not passable in ordinary vehicles. Dogs are actually allowed on the first portion of this road—however, caution is advised for pedestrians, as the road's twists and turns severely limit visibility.

Following the main road to its terminus, it bends almost due north and begins to wind more deeply into the desert sandstone strata. Look to the northeast to see a spectacular backdrop of the **La Sal Mountains**—the range you passed on your way out of Moab. Especially when this range is covered in snow, the La Sals and desert contrast quite powerfully. These deep blue slopes, often patched with white snowfields, form a striking backdrop for the red and yellow desertscape, dotted with light green sagebrush.

A small roundabout at the **Big Spring Canyon Overlook** clearly marks the terminus of the road (and the official end of this one-way drive). From here the **Confluence Overlook Trail** leads to a view of the confluence of the Green and Colorado Rivers. To reach the overlook, the hike is 5.2 miles each way. Though easy in terms of elevation loss (only descending about 200 vertical feet), it is long; be sure to bring plenty of water and sunscreen, as it requires up to several hours to make the round-trip.

Worth seeing, these two powerful rivers flow together right in the center of Canyonlands—the Green from the northwest and the Colorado from the northeast. Some of the most important bodies of water in the history of the American West, these were famously navigated and meticulously charted by John Wesley Powell in 1869 and again in 1871. From the confluence, one can easily understand Green River's name; in contrast with the muddy, brown Colorado, this river appears to be nearly the color of emerald.

Just downstream of this junction is the famous **Cataract Canyon**, through which only knowledgeable rafters (holding a permit) or guided clients may pass. This short and fierce stretch of river is the last, most exciting leg of a longer raft trip. Aptly named, the sheer walls of this canyon dramatically squeeze down the Colorado River—now also with the waters of the Green—just before pouring into Lake Powell. This sudden narrowing of the channel, as well as a very steep gradient, creates enormous and turbulent rapids that are highly unforgiving to all but the most experienced boaters.

At the end of the route, all that is left is to return to Moab, assuming the gas tank is full enough to make it. If in doubt, consider turning south on US-191 and driving to Monticello. Though not on the way for those wishing to return to I-70, its gas stations are 20 miles closer to Canyonlands than Moab is.

IN THE AREA

CANYONLANDS NATIONAL PARK OFFICE, 2282 Resource Boulevard, Moab. Call 435-719-2313. Website: www.nps.gov/cany.

CANYONLANDS NEEDLES OUTPOST, UT-211, Needles District, Canyonlands National Park, Moab. Open seasonally only; call for hours regarding specific services. Call 435-979-4007. Website: www.needlesoutpost.com.

HOLE N" THE ROCK, 11037 South US-191, Moab. Open daily. Call 435-686-2250. Website: www.theholeintherock.com.

THE KAYENTA HILLS START TO GIVE WAY TO TOWERS

David Sjöquist

9

MONUMENT VALLEY

ESTIMATED LENGTH: 163 miles from Kayenta to Moab; 230 miles taking all suggested side trips

ESTIMATED TIME: A full day with side trips; up to three days with stops for hikes, museums, and photographs

HIGHLIGHTS: Though this drive actually starts in Arizona—oops!—it would be a scam to write a book on Utah's scenic drives and not include **Monument Valley**, one of the most photographed and iconic routes in the American Southwest. The nearby, under-the-radar scenery between **Mexican Hat** and **Blanding** includes ruins, museums, state parks, and national monuments of great scenery and complementary solitude.

This route begins **Kayenta**, in the **Navajo Nation**, among tombstone-like towers 1,000 feet tall, and continues across desert planes, over the **San Juan River** to the many state parks and natural attractions between Mexican Hat and Blanding—**Goosenecks State Park, Natural Bridges National Monument, Valley of the Gods**—and eventually into **Moab**. The drive through the valley itself is almost completely devoid of human infrastructure, save for the road itself.

GETTING THERE: Kayenta is located in the northeastern corner of Arizona, on US-160, about 100 miles east of Page and about 40 miles west of the US-160/US-191 Junction.

Kayenta, Arizona (or **Tó Dinéeshzhee**, in Navajo) is part of the **Navajo Nation (Diné Bikéyah)**, a 17-million-acre state occupying the northeastern part of Arizona, southeastern portion of Utah, and northwestern corner of New Mexico. Kayenta itself was settled in 1910 as **Oljeto**, first as a trading post, later fueled by uranium mining activities. Today it is a small and dusty town that offers a spread of basic services for tourists—from an auto mechanic to restaurants and hotels. Among a majority of national fast food

9. Monument Valley

NATURAL BRIDGES
NATIONAL MONUMENT

Sipapu
Bridge

★ Natural Bridges
Visitor Center

Edge of the Cedars
State Park Museum ★

Dinosaur Museum ★ Blanding

191

275

Kachina
Bridge

Owachomo
Bridge

Mule Canyon
★ Ruin

95

95

Kane Gulch
★ Ranger Station

276

261

262

Grand Gulch
Primitive Area

BEARS EARS
NATIONAL MONUMENT

191

GLEN CANYON NATIONAL
RECREATION AREA

San Juan River

VALLEY OF THE GODS
RD (FR-242)

Cedar
Mesa

Valley of
the Gods

162

Bluff

MULEY
POINT RD

★ B&B

Muley
Point

Moki
Dugway

Valley of
the Gods

163

San Juan River

261

316

Goosenecks
State Park

San Juan Inn/Trading Post
★ Olde Bridge Grille

191

Alhambra Rock

Mexican Hat

163

Navajo Nation
Indian Reservation

Oljato-
Monument
Valley

MONUMENT VALLEY RD

Wildcat Trail/
West Mitten Butte

160

Vis.
Center ★

Monument Valley Navajo Tribal Park

Elephant Butte

The View Hotel/
Trading Post

Rain God
Mesa

Mexican
Water

163

Navajo Nation
Indian Reservation

Dennehotso

191

160

Arizona

N

Kayenta

Amigo
Cafe

★ ★

0   5   10

Blue
Coffee Pot

Miles

© The Countryman Press

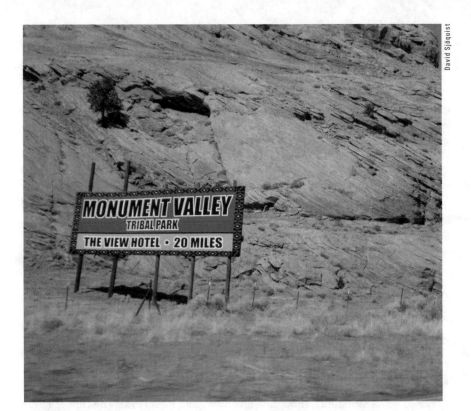

LEAVING KAYENTA, ARIZONA

chains and motels, a few local restaurants and one hotel north of town present alternative choices.

For Southwestern/Mexican cuisine with a Navajo influence, stop by the **Amigo Cafe**. Standard fare of combination platters, burritos, and enchiladas is joined by the very popular Navajo taco. This restaurant is visibly a favorite in town among locals and tourists. Make sure to have cash in the wallet, as it is the only accepted method of payment. You won't need much, though—a small amount of money purchases large portions. The **Blue Coffee**

Kayenta Fourth of July Rodeo

The Kayenta Fourth of July Rodeo takes place every year July 2–4. Much more than a quick-and-dirty rodeo, this 4-day, town-wide celebration includes an all-Indian rodeo, youth rodeo, team roping, barrel racing, bull riding, a pancake breakfast, a massive fireworks finale on the Fourth of July, and a special event featuring prized livestock called the "Best of the Best." The rodeo has won many awards, including several Rodeo of the Year and Outstanding Rodeo designations.

The Monument Valley Film Festival

Founded in 2007, this takes place in Kayenta around the third weekend of September each year. After the completion of their debut full-length film, *Mile Post 398*, Shonie and Andee De La Rosa established this—the Navajo Nation's only film festival at present. All films are written, directed, or produced by Native Americans. *Mile Post 398*, released in 2007 by Sheephead Films, tells the story of a Navajo man facing drug and alcohol problems, his decision to quit, and his resulting struggle to make amends with family.

Pot offers a menu heavier in Navajo cuisine. A tip: Order within the Navajo selections, as they are the kitchen's strength. Fry bread, Navajo tacos, and stews beat the alternative fare.

National midlevel and budget chains supply the guest beds in town. While these ensure a familiar style and level of quality, **The View Hotel** in Monument Valley Navajo Tribal Park (described below) offers vastly more local flavor. This hotel stands just south of the Utah-Arizona border, so it's not too far from town.

To embark on the drive, take US-163 north directly out of Kayenta's center. Climbing slightly on the way out of town, it seems unlikely this should be the correct route. Suddenly, though, a few turns and dips reveal the immediately familiar and awe-inspiring view of Monument Valley. One of the most barren yet striking pieces of desert stretches into view. In the whole valley, it seems the only man-made intrusion is the highway. To either side rise pillars of sheer Wingate Sandstone, atop islands of red talus. Everyone has seen images of this valley, though offhand, it's hard to know where. The first film shot here, *The Vanishing American*, in 1925, began a list of scores of titles. Among the most famous are the 1939 *Stagecoach* with John Wayne, *Easy Rider* (1969), and *Forrest Gump* (1994). In more recent times, over a dozen video games have been set here.

About 21 miles north of Kayenta (halfway to **Mexican Hat**), US-163 crosses into Utah. Just after this, look out for a right-hand turn to **Monument Valley Navajo Tribal Park**. Though this famous valley can be viewed fairly adequately from US-163, this park offers a relaxed and picturesque detour. It is open 365 days a year, barring extreme weather; the route adds a few hours to the trip. In the park wait a visitor center, scenic drive, and campground, just as there would be in a National Park Service–operated affair. Stop in at the visitor center to learn a bit about the religious and cultural significance of this valley. Additionally, there is a gift shop and **The View Hotel** (see sidebar). The tribe collects an entrance fee (America the Beautiful passes not accepted), and hours are roughly confined to daylight hours.

The only hiking trail in the park not requiring an authorized Navajo guide, the **Wildcat Trail**, departs from the campground just inside the park boundary. A 3.2-mile loop with a bit of elevation change, this requires some effort but is still moderate in distance and elevation gain. The journey begins with a descent into the valley and proceeds to make a loop around the **West Mitten Butte**. (From this trail, its partner, **East Mitten**, is also readily visible.) Navajo take this path in a clockwise direction, just as they would walk in a hogan—the traditional rounded permanent home sacred in the Navajo religion.

Those sticking to the road will embark upon a 17-mile high-grade dirt road loop among the towers. Self-guided tours are free beyond the entrance fee, but paid tours are also an option, costing roughly $50 to $100 per person, depending the route. Various portions of the park, however, like **Hunts Mesa** and **Mystery Valley,** may only be accessed by way of guided tours. If interested, inquire at the visitor center or call the park.

Pavement extends east beyond the visitor center for another few miles before turning to dirt. Around this transition, the **West and East Mitten Buttes**, whose shapes should make their identity obvious, rise out of the desert floor to the left (north). More than a dozen other named buttes will be visible on this drive, so those interested in pinning down their identities should pick up a brochure labeling them.

Continuing along, the road dips subtly toward the south and heads into the main thicket of towers. Just after passing **Elephant Butte** on the left, the road

The View Hotel

Located adjacent to the tribal park's visitor center, this hotel warrants a stop, even for those not requiring a place to bed down. The young owner, a sixth-generation Navajo in a family with long-standing stewardship of the Southwest Native American arts, has saturated the entire facility with this legacy. The hotel showcases contemporary Native American arts and jewelry as well as recent and ancient historical artifacts from the valley. On display are photographs from Hollywood pictures filmed in Monument Valley and tribal memorabilia.

The on-premises **Trading Post** offers wares for sale, the showpiece of which is its Navajo woven rug collection, the largest within 250 miles. Additionally, there are hats, pottery, jewelry, and other art pieces. This is no rinky-dink souvenir shop; most of the goods for purchase would sooner be called art than trinkets (though less serious crafts are sold here, too).

That said, The View Hotel also represents the only in-park accommodations, and likely the finest for miles and miles around. Opened December 2008, this 95-room, eco-friendly establishment was built by, and is today still owned and operated by, Navajo. Be sure to make reservations (particularly during the summer), as the hotel has no peer in the area. No alcohol is served here, as it is forbidden by the Navajo Nation.

enters its loop portion, encircling **Rain God Mesa**. Around this formation stand several others in the foreground, their relative positions ever changing when passed on this curving road. Don't expect to see much wildlife—populations of all kinds are tempered by the extremely dry climate—but do notice the purple sage and junipers that contrast strikingly with the deep red desert soil and rock. Soon the loop ends and dumps onto the same road you drove into the park. Do not attempt to depart onto side roads; these are closed to parties unaccompanied by an authorized Navajo guide.

Leaving the park, head back to US-163, turn right, and continue farther north into Utah. Up next is perhaps the nation's most famous single stretch of road—and perhaps one of the few instances in which a highway itself is an exciting attraction. Finally, the towers of Monument Valley fade in the rearview mirror. Crossing over the **San Juan River**, the pavement comes into **Mexican Hat**, about 20 miles beyond the park turnoff. For the passerby, this tiny town serves as little more than a junction on the way to and from the surrounding state, national, and tribal parks. The town is named for a rock formation, a 60-foot-wide capstone disk atop a much smaller cylinder—the "Mexican Hat" properly resembles an upside-down sombrero. As of the 2010 Census, this town had a whopping thirty-one residents.

CROSSING THE SAN JUAN RIVER

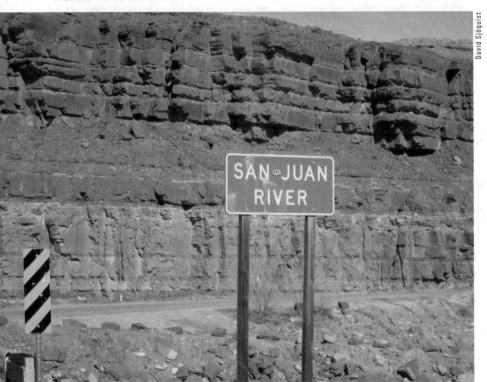

David Sjöquist

Navajo Nation

As of the 2010 Census, there were roughly 300,000 Navajo living in the United States, and about 60 percent of them resided in the Navajo Nation itself. This enormous tract of land is, at 17 million acres, larger than Lithuania. In the 1920s, oil deposits were discovered on Navajo land, and in 1923 an official tribal government was formed to help organize the leasing of this land by American oil corporations. Since then, this administration has grown to cover the general needs of the nation and people, and today's Navajo Nation Council has eighty-eight delegates representing 110 chapters.

Though small and shrinking, Mexican Hat does offer some amenities. Travelers wanting to spend more than a day casing the area can stop here and rest up at the **San Juan Inn**. Possibly one of the more unique lodging options around, this inn offers guest rooms in the hotel, as well as yurts. From the outside, the yurts appear primitive, but these private structures actually have modernized, simple interiors. The hotel itself directly abuts the cliff edge above the San Juan, affording exposed views of the water below. As with any desirable lodging options in the area, be sure to call for reservations in peak season.

In addition to beds, the San Juan Inn runs a restaurant and **Trading Post** (read: convenience store) on the premises. The **Olde Bridge Grille**, open daily and year-round, serves an American menu supplemented with a few classic Navajo dishes. Since it is outside of the Navajo Nation, this establishment can legally serve liquor, wine, and beer. This is an ultra-casual western joint with pool tables. The **San Juan Trading Post** carries basic wares: beer, snacks, maps, and books. Its main focus, however, is on Navajo and other Native American arts: rugs, pottery, clothing, and jewelry.

Leaving Mexican Hat, prepare for a desolate stretch of road! Though the scenery is beautiful, almost no infrastructure interferes with viewing it in near-perfect solitude. The next destination is **Goosenecks State Park**, which you will reach shortly by driving north of town on US-163 East and taking a quick left on UT-261/UT-316. (The state park sits at the terminus of 316.) From the center of town, the total drive is just 5 or 10 minutes. This state park overlooks a severely curvy section the San Juan River. About 1,500 feet lower than the desert surface, more than 6 miles of river wind across a linear distance of just 1.5 miles. A 300-million-year erosion process has gently revealed a fine brown, gold, tan, and orange rainbow of horizontal rock strata. These generous river loops create a maze of interlocking, finger-like peninsulas. In the distance are **Monument Valley** and **Alhambra Rock**, an exposed volcanic intrusion of dark rock. The park functions primarily as an overlook point, with very simple infrastructure, and the principle activities here are gawking and photography. No drinking water is available here, but picnic tables are provided and primitive camping permitted; no entrance fee is required.

After Goosenecks, the next stop is **Valley of the Gods**, a very Monument Valley-esque area. A collection of scattered rock pinnacles in a flat valley, this is home to smaller but often more peculiar spires than those of Monument. Valley of the Gods can either be seen by driving through it (another 17-mile dirt loop, but this time free of charge) or bypassing it and viewing it from the top of **Cedar Mesa** after ascending the **Moki Dugway**. To tour this valley, take UT-316/UT-261 back south to US-163. Take a left to head northeast on this highway, watching for a dirt road, UT-242, on the left (in about 4 miles). Head north into the Valley of the Gods here. This road follows **Lime Creek**, a wash usually only flowing in spring, and then snakes around the rock formations in a westerly direction before popping out on UT-261, just south of the Moki Dugway. Though this is a short loop, it wouldn't hurt to carry a map.

The Valley of the Gods is, but for the road, entirely undeveloped and offers much more solitude than the already-quiet Monument Valley. Entirely on BLM land, all camping here is free and unregulated. Though no official trails exist, overland desert-floor wandering is permitted—best done in dry washes, so as to avoid walking on and destroying cryptobiotic soil. Bring a detailed topographic map along to assist with identifying formations whose names range from **Rooster Butte** to **Lady in the Bathtub, Rudolph,** and **Santa Claus.**

Among 360,000 acres in the **Cedar Mesa, Valley of the Gods Bed-and-Breakfast** is the only house! Solar- and wind-powered and fire-heated, this self-sustaining building requires no outside power source, and its owners must manually haul water from Mexican Hat. Originally built in 1933, the structure has seen serious restorative renovations, but it only became a B&B in 1993. The unique rooms are lit by oil lamps in the evening, and beds and walls are covered with Southwestern and Navajo rugs. Construction is of 2-foot-thick sandstone and limestone block walls, with sturdy beam work crafted of recycled timbers. Breakfast here is almost always held outside, except when the weather fails to cooperate. The bed-and-breakfast is located just east of UT-261 on Valley of the Gods Road/UT-242. To preserve the solitude for other guests, pets and children must be accepted by prior approval. Call ahead for reservations, as rooms are very limited.

Moki Dugway is a 3-mile section of UT-261 just north of the Valley of the Gods B&B. A stretch of road that would never be cut in modern times, this switchbacking dirt road was built for uranium mining trucks in 1958. Sustained sections of 10 percent grade aggressively ascend the steep side of **Cedar Mesa**, climbing more than 1,100 feet to an elevation of 6,424 feet. Many signs announce the meanders as they approach, warning off heavy vehicles. Soon the two-lane highway shrinks to a one-lane paved street, and eventually a graded dirt road. As traffic is still two-way, the grade so steep, and the switchbacks so dramatic, the recommended speed is just 5 miles per hour. At the top of the ascent, be sure to look back south over Valley of the Gods and Monument Valley for a scene of almost completely undisturbed landscape.

Continuing north on UT-261, look for the signed turnoff (very soon after Moki Dugway) to **Muley Point**. Five dirt road miles lead back to the edge of Cedar Mesa once again. This truly spectacular cliff-edge viewpoint offers a 360-degree panorama that summarizes the entire drive so far. From atop strewn boulders and fractured sandstone, you can see all of the "valleys," the Goosenecks, Alhambra Rock, and Navajo Mountain to the south and west. Because of the dramatic relief and steepness of the canyon walls, the San Juan River remains out of sight. West of Muley Point, the San Juan River flows into the Glen Canyon National Recreation Area, as the easternmost tributary for **Lake Powell.**

OK, hikers—here's another chance to get out and super-stretch the legs. The **Grand Gulch Primitive Area** is a 35-mile-long gulch that, rarely visited, is lined with undisturbed petroglyphs and pictograms. Leaving on foot from Kane Springs actually involves quite a hike just to access the gulch: up to five hours each direction. The BLM requires visitors to preregister, which is a good idea anyway when visiting such a wilderness area. As this is a delicate archaeological area, all pets must be on leashes at all times. For directions and permits, visit the **Kane Gulch Ranger Station**, about 4 miles south of UT-95 on UT-261. This ranger station holds limited operational periods (March 1–June 15 and September 1–October 31; permits must be obtained between 8 AM and 12 PM).

Finish out UT-261 by heading north to **UT-95**. A very quick jaunt to the west and then a turn to the north on UT-275 leads directly to **Natural Bridges National Monument**. With just three arches in the area, this is like a small, concise version of Arches National Park. In a place with only a few arches, visitors can pay more attention to the area's human history than to holes in rock. Three primary hiking trails, one each for **Sipapu Bridge**, **Kachina Bridge**, and **Owachomo Bridge**, lead away from the pavement and tour the backcountry. Petroglyphs, pictograms, ruins, and other artifacts have been left behind here by the Hisatsinom (a people often included under the "ancestral Pueblo" blanket term), ancestors to the Hopi. These people occupied the area during three distinct and separate eras, each time returning with much different tools and agricultural technology. The earliest occupation was around AD 200, and the latest ended around 1270.

One of the last stops on the way into Blanding via UT-95 is **Mule Canyon Ruin** on the north side of the road, roughly 12 miles east of UT-261 (and 19 west of Blanding). This complex of above- and belowground structures dates back to around AD 750. Archaeological evidence suggests that these people were predominantly Mesa Verde Anasazi, with some Kayenta Anasazi influences. The ruins consist of twelve rooms that were used as living and storage space, a kiva (or center of ceremonies), and a tower. This is located about 0.25 mile north from the UT-95 turnoff; park and walk into the canyon to the west. Operated by the BLM, this area has no entrance fee.

Nobody would guess it at first glance, but Blanding is actually home to a few museums. The **Edge of the Cedars State Park Museum**, right in town, is situated around an actual village that was built and inhabited by the ancestral Pueblo from roughly AD 825 to 1125. Visitors, if physically able, can climb down a ladder into one of the original structures. A walking trail tours the ruin, and the grounds have been landscaped with native plant species. The museum itself hosts traveling and permanent exhibits pertaining to art and human history, and it showcases artifacts such as pottery and historical and contemporary photography. This museum holds the region's largest collection of Anasazi pottery. Every May (on the first Saturday of the month), an annual Indian art market takes place here.

Also in the town of Blanding is the **Dinosaur Museum**. Paleontology is an especially active science in the Four Corners region as the lands are richly littered with fossils. This museum draws from the work of locally active scientists but also includes dinosaur remains from around the world. Here, history is explained through plate tectonics, showing where the different continents of land have been located at different points throughout history, how this dictated where certain fossils are found today, and why different mountain ranges formed. A genuine meteorite is even on display in the museum.

After Blanding, the drive is pretty much done. The most direct route back to Kayenta is via US-191 and US-160. To get to Moab, head north on US-191 about 75 miles; I-70 is just another 30 miles north of Moab. If you are staying in Moab, check out the three Moab-based drives in chapters 6, 7, and 8 of this book.

IN THE AREA

Accommodations

VALLEY OF THE GODS BED-AND-BREAKFAST, on Valley of the Gods Road (UT-242), just east of UT-261. On the pricey side. Eco-friendly, off-the-grid historic home. Call Gary or Claire Dorgan, 970-749-1164. Website: www .valleyofthegodsbandb.com.

THE VIEW HOTEL, Monument Valley Navajo Tribal Park, Monument Valley. Somewhat pricey. Modern hotel embellished with Navajo culture. Call 435-727-5555. Website: www.monumentvalleyview.com.

SAN JUAN INN, US-163 and the San Juan River, Mexican Hat. Moderately priced. Hotel rooms and yurts for rent; general store and restaurant on-site. Call 1-800-447-2022. Website: www.sanjuaninn.net.

Attractions and Recreation

DINOSAUR MUSEUM, 754 South 200 West, Blanding. Open April 15 to October 15 only, Monday through Saturday. Very modest admission fee. Call 435-678-3454. Website: www.dinosaur-museum.org.

EDGE OF THE CEDARS STATE PARK MUSEUM, 660 West 400 North, Blanding. Open year-round. Small admission fee. Call 435-678-2238. Website: www.stateparks.utah.gov/parks/edge-of-the-cedars.

GOOSENECKS STATE PARK, northwest of Mexican Hat, at the terminus of US-316, Mexican Hat. Call 435-678-2238. Website: www.stateparks.utah .gov/parks/goosenecks.

CLASSIC MONUMENT VALLEY VIEW IN REAR VIEW MIRROR

GRAND GULCH PRIMITIVE AREA, Kane Gulch Ranger Station, about 4 miles south of UT-95 on UT-261. Permits required to enter; contact the BLM for directions. Call 801-587-1500.

MONUMENT VALLEY NAVAJO TRIBAL PARK AND VISITOR CENTER, Monument Valley. Fee required to enter; America the Beautiful passes not accepted. Open year-round; visitor center closed Thanksgiving and Christmas. Scenic drive open 365 days a year, barring severe weather. Call 435-727-5874, 435-727-5879, or 435-727-5870. Website: www.navajonationparks .org.

MULE CANYON RUIN, Bureau of Land Management, San Juan Field Office, 435 North Main, Monticello. Call 435-587-2144.

NATURAL BRIDGES NATIONAL MONUMENT, HC-60 Box 1, Lake Powell. Call 435-692-1234. $3 individual entry, $6 per vehicle; all federal lands passes accepted. Website: www.nps.gov/nabr.

Dining

AMIGO CAFE, US-163, Kayenta, AZ. Affordable. Open daily for breakfast, lunch, and dinner. Mexican and Navajo cuisine. Cash only. Call 928-697-8448.

BLUE COFFEE POT, US-163 and US-160, Kayenta, AZ. Affordable. Open Monday through Saturday for breakfast, lunch, and dinner. Navajo cuisine. Call 928-697-3396.

OLDE BRIDGE GRILL, see San Juan Inn, above. Very affordable. American and Navajo cuisine; casual. Open daily, year-round. Call 435-683-2322. Website: www.sanjuaninn.net/restaurant.

Other Contacts

KANE GULCH RANGER STATION, about 4 miles south of UT-95 on UT-261. Call 435-587-1500.

KAYENTA FOURTH OF JULY RODEO. Annual four-day celebration in Kayenta. Call the Kayenta Township, 928-697-8451. Website: www .kayentatownship-nsn.gov/blog/.

MONUMENT VALLEY FILM FESTIVAL. Website: www.kayentatownship -nsn.gov/.

SAN JUAN TRADING POST, see San Juan Inn, above. Open daily, year-round.

CIRQUE IN THE HENRY MOUNTAINS

10

HENRY MOUNTAINS AND
THE BURR TRAIL

ESTIMATED LENGTH: 170 miles without side trips

ESTIMATED TIME: Nearly a full day with sightseeing stops

HIGHLIGHTS: The southern **San Rafael Swell** and **Henry Mountains** are in a wonderfully remote region of south-central Utah. Neither near Moab nor Zion National Park, they remain largely vacant, with miles of uncluttered scenery and rare solitude. A geologically spectacular journey, this route heads south along the eastern front of the Henry Mountains to the northern shore of **Lake Powell,** then loops west on the historic **Burr Trail,** and traverses the **Grand Staircase-Escalante** region.

GETTING THERE: This suggested route begins in the town of Green River and ends in Boulder (Utah). Green River is located just north of Moab, right on I-70 between Exits 160 and 164. From Salt Lake City (or any northern point of origin), the best approach is via I-15 South, and then US-6 and US-191 South. This diagonal cut-across saves more than 100 miles—though it's a high mountain pass and should be taken in good weather only. From the east or west, simply arrive by way of I-70. Almost no one arrives from the south, as the towns in that direction are small and distant and Lake Powell essentially barricades any potential approach paths.

NOTE: The Burr Trail, a key component of this drive (from Bullfrog to Boulder), contains a very steep dirt section and should be taken in good weather only. Though the road is primarily chipsealed, a 17-mile stretch (though **Capitol Reef National Park**) remains grated dirt. It is not recommended for RVs or vehicles towing trailers, regardless of conditions; the dirt surface is typically all right, but the sharp twists and steep grade render it inappropriate for heavy, long vehicles.

Green River exemplifies the classic interstate town. Big truck stops, dreary landscape, desolate feeling. This comes as a surprising fact, as Green River

10. Henry Mountains and the Burr Trail

10

Moore

John Wesley Powell
River History Museum
Ray's
Tavern ⭐

6

70

Green
River

Green
River

Fremont
Junction

70

24

72

TEMPLE
MOUNTAIN RD

GOBLIN
VALLEY RD

*San Rafael
Desert*

Muddy Creek

Goblin Valley
State Park

24

CANYONLANDS
NATIONAL PARK

CAPITOL REEF
NATIONAL
PARK

Hanksville-Burpee
Dinosaur Quarry ⭐

COW DUNG RD

Caineville

Bull Mountain
Market Pizza and Deli ⭐
⭐ Blondie's
Hanksville Eatery & Gift

*Fremont
River*

24

Torrey

24

Robbers Roost
Canyon

Grover

95

*Dirty
Devil
River*

GLEN CANYON NATIONAL
RECREATION AREA

12

*Mount
Ellen*
+

Colorado River

H e n r y   M o u n t a i n s

Boulder

slot
canyon

*Long
Canyon*

BURR TRAIL

*Circle
Cliffs*

12

GRAND STAIRCASE-
ESCALANTE NATIONAL
MONUMENT

W a t e r p o c k e t   F o l d

95

95

Old Hite
Marina ⭐

BEARS EARS
NATIONAL
MONUMENT

276

BURR TRAIL

Escalante River

Ticaboo

*Lake
Powell*

BEARS EARS
NATIONAL
MONUMENT

GLEN CANYON NATIONAL
RECREATION AREA

Bullfrog

Bullfrog Visitor Center ⭐

CHARLES HALL FERRY

Halls
Crossing

276

N

0   5   10

Miles

© The Countryman Press

Major John Wesley Powell

Powell was one of the earliest and most influential explorers of the Intermountain West. A true renaissance man, he was considered an expert in botany, ethnology, history, surveying, geology, and more. Born in 1834 in Mount Morris, New York, John Wesley Powell was a largely self-educated man who fought in the Civil War for the Union Army. During the war, John lost his arm in battle, making him an unlikely candidate for what would later become a career in rugged river exploration.

Prior to the late 1860s, the interior of the west was all but completely untamed and uncharted. Though occasional trappers and traders had penetrated the region, there were no reliable maps or records of the area, and the US government wished to know more. In 1869 (and again in 1871), Powell traversed the entirety of the Green and Colorado Rivers from Green River, Wyoming, to the Gulf of California. Along the way, he made scrupulous notes and drawings of everything pertaining to weather, wildlife, geology, and native peoples.

The immensity and strangeness of his expedition required a bravery that likely cannot be understood today. Not only were the lands, wildlife, and indigenous people completely unknown, Powell's mode of travel was new and quite dangerous. White-water boating was unheard of—and some of the biggest drops in North America are found along his route. Powell described this strange phenomenon in his journals, detailing his strategies for passage as well as accidents and equipment losses incurred on the way. Losses notwithstanding, his crews were mainly successful—led by their one-armed captain.

must be passed by those traveling en route from Salt Lake City to Moab, Zion to Denver, and Grand Staircase-Escalante National Monument to Arches and Canyonlands National Parks. The impersonal façade, though, is a bit misleading, as this town sits at the gateway to much of Utah's best canoeing, kayaking, and white-water rafting (on the Green River).

Because of its location on the Green River, and because of this river's significance in the history of the west, the town has erected the **John Wesley Powell River History Museum**, named after the river's famous explorer. In a small, unimpressive town, this museum is a refreshing and educational surprise. Though it passes quietly through town, the Green River holds value in United States history. This museum communicates this, as well as the stories of the people who explored its waters.

For a quick meal to start the trip, **Ray's Tavern** is the best bet for those seeking something other than fast food or a truck stop diner. Reputed among tourists statewide, this place serves a good burger and cold beer. Its petite structure can get crowded, but the tavern offers bar seating in addition to tables. In this small joint with a rustic atmosphere, it's OK to come dressed

A BETTER-THAN-NORMAL DIRT ROAD IN THE HENRYS

in Wranglers or in bike shorts. As of the time this book was written, Ray's Tavern had begun opening for business on Sundays—a new development.

To begin the drive, head west just briefly on I-70, watching the miles count down to Exit 149. Take this and drive south (the only option) into the San Rafael Swell. Continue along UT-24 about 23 miles until you see a sign to the right for Goblin Valley Road and **Goblin Valley State Park**. Make this turn to the west, following signs (and two more left-hand turns) to head south on UT-303 and into the park. Though it might sound complicated, this detour requires only 10 to 15 minutes and is well signed.

Aptly named, this valley appears to be filled with sandstone monsters—quite a sci-fi look, with thousands of rounded statuettes standing shoulder to shoulder. For a $13 day-use fee, visitors have access to a visitor center and some of the most peculiar rock formations in existence. Though these hoodoos are not necessarily unique to this valley, they are nevertheless in extremely high concentration here. These mushroom-shaped figures are formed when an erosion-resistant rock layer sits atop a weaker stratum. As time passes, the bottoms layer erodes more quickly, leaving a rounded capstone resting atop a thinner base.

As with any natural phenomenon of such distinctive character, this was a compelling place to indigenous tribes as well as to early cowboys and pioneers. The Ute, Paiute, and Fremont left significant rock art in the form of pictographs and petroglyphs. Cowboys and pioneers used it as a place of reference for travel and occasionally as a hideout. In 1964, this was designated a state park to help protect it from vandalism. Visitors today are welcome to hike among the goblins.

Return to UT-24 and head south to **Hanksville**. As the road approaches this small town, the **Henry Mountains** will become unmistakably visible to the south. As with the La Sal Mountains near Moab and the Abajo Mountains, these isolated peaks rise high above their surroundings, standing alone. Roughly 25 million years old, all three of these ranges were formed by magma forcing itself high into earth's crust. The magma cooled gradually while still underground. Over time, the sedimentary layers atop these intrusions eroded away, exposing rock classified as porphyry. This volcanic rock has large crystals formed by the slow subterranean cooling of the mountain-forming magma.

Because of its height, this range visibly creates its own weather system, col-

Butch Cassidy's Watering Hole

Hanksville, a tiny mining and agricultural town, is the last stop before the Henry Mountains and the general wilds beyond. It also serves as a filling station for passersby, as it sits directly on the route to the Henry Mountains, Goblin Valley State Park, Capitol Reef National Park, the Grand Staircase-Escalante National Monument, the boat takeout for Cataract Canyon on the Colorado River, and the northern tip of Lake Powell.

Actually, in times past, it served the same purpose as a filling station. During their outlaw tour of the Old West, the legendary Butch Cassidy (Robert LeRoy Parker) and the Sundance Kid (Harry Longabaugh) regularly hid out in the Robber's Roost, just to the southeast of Hanksville, beginning in the 1880s. They made sure to establish friendly connections with the people of Hanksville so that they could be resupplied with beer, food, and other wares without having to surface in the face of the law.

With extremely rugged, mazelike terrain and natural lookout towers, this "roost" provided the gang with shelter from the law, as they could easily see parties approaching and defend their post. Here they stashed weapons, ammunition, and other restorative supplies. Today **Robbers Roost Canyon**, a tributary canyon to the **Dirty Devil River**, is named after this hideout. Additionally, the original Wild Bunch corral, various carvings, and a stone chimney still stand. Here there have been established many moderate to technical slot canyon routes. Any visitor to the Robbers Roost Canyon today will understand how the law never managed to penetrate.

lecting clouds that then drain their precipitation onto the slopes below. Even if the weather in Hanksville is sunny and warm, storms can be unleashing on the Henrys. Because of this heightened rainfall, be exceedingly cautious if entering the range on dirt roads. This soil will clump and gather on wheels while wet.

Before heading into this range, be absolutely sure to refill the car with all necessary fluids, the bottles with water, and the bellies with food.

Blondie's Eatery & Gift is a diner-type affair where you can order at the

Lake Powell's Bathtub Ring

Lake Powell is a massive reservoir, and the Glen Canyon Dam is one of man's greatest architectural accomplishments. Built over the course of ten years—from 1956 to 1966—this 710-foot-tall dam has the capacity to store 30 cubic kilometers of water between the walls of the Glen Canyon. Today it is responsible for up to 13 percent of power production in Utah and 6 percent in Arizona, as well as the supply of more than 10 million cubic kilometers of water to Arizona, California, New Mexico, and Nevada.

However, not all reports on this reservoir are positive. In addition to the massive environmental disruption it has caused upstream and downstream of the dam, the reservoir itself has faced serious logistical problems.

In 1983, following a very snowy winter, a warm and wet spring fell swiftly upon the area surrounding Glen Canyon. The above-average rainfall and rapid temperature increase conspired to pump the Colorado River full of water and inundate the reservoir with a sustained river flow of more than 100,000 cubic feet per second—a veritable deluge. By necessity, the spillways were very cautiously opened for the first time in the dam's employment and, due to the incredible flow of water, were indeed damaged. Massive chunks of sandstone were ripped from the spillways, and there was even concern that the entire dam might fail—but strategic operation kept damage in check. During this time, however, the water level rose to within 6 feet of the dam's crest.

Fast-forward almost twenty years to one of the most severe and prolonged droughts in the history of the southwestern United States. In 1999 the water levels were relatively high, stable, and under control. Enter a multiyear drought. Over the next few years, the water began to recede dramatically. As this happened, white rock was exposed on the sheer lakeside canyon walls, and what was formerly reservoir returned to river at the inlet tips of the lake. New miles of river rafting formed on the Colorado River beneath Cataract Canyon. Reservoir-bed sediment was exposed and turned suddenly into rapids-causing boulders. By 2005, water levels dropped to record lows—at which time the reservoir was filled to only one-third capacity. As of 2017, the waterline oscillates at a slightly higher level but still reflects the ongoing water scarcity afflicting the southwestern United States.

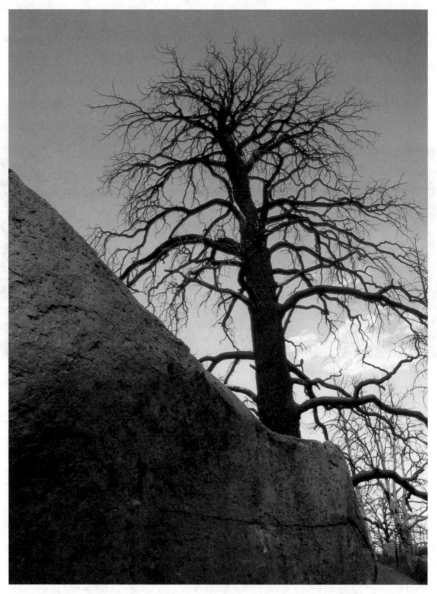

VICTIM OF MASSIVE WILDFIRE

counter and don't have to mess with table service. On the menu: burgers, chicken, salads, sandwiches, and espresso. A big stone sign out front makes it hard to miss. Call ahead for takeout from **Bull Mountain Market Pizza and Deli**. Enjoy food outdoors or take it to the campsite or hotel; this restaurant has no dining room.

Curious about paleontology? Just dying to know more about the late Jurassic period? On the way out of town, hit the **Hanksville-Burpee Quarry**,

VIEW OF THE HORN, BETWEEN MT. ELLEN AND MT. PENELLEN

a 150-by-600-foot dig into the Morrison Formation. Part of the late Jurassic Period and roughly 145 to 150 million years old, this site has been long known to locals for its richness in fossils. But it wasn't until 2007 that the Rockford, Illinois, Burpee Museum of Natural History applied for digging permission and learned of the region's true wealth. They began excavating in the summer of 2008. Only three weeks into the dig, the site yielded a possible stegosaurus, two unknown carnivorous dinosaurs, and multiple sauropods. The Burpee Museum provides a public tour detailing and demystifying the site's science.

Now begins the wilderness! Head south from town on UT-95. Though our drive turns west onto UT-276 about 30 minutes south of town, UT-95 leads directly to the northern tip of Lake Powell. Those interested may take this detour, but the Hite Marina, located there, is now out of commission. Hite was once the northernmost marina in the lake. It sits exactly where the Colorado River joins the reservoir and slows down—immediately after one of the most turbulent stretches of white water in the United States: Cataract Canyon. In the last few decades, however, Lake Powell has been evaporating at a rate faster than its tributaries can fill it, and the water level has fallen more than 120 feet. Beneath the natural red sandstone, a giant bathtub ring of white rock encircles the entire lake—readily visible in this area. As the waterline dropped, the shoreline receded. Hite tried to stay in business by extending its boat ramp several times. Now defunct, the Hite Marina looks much more like a landing strip for jet planes than for boats.

Those not taking the Lake Powell detour should look for a right-hand turn onto UT-276, about 30 minutes south of Hanksville (and long before Hite Marina). From the valley (elevation 4,300 feet), consider the Henry Mountains, and try to guess which peak is Mount Ellen, the highest in the range at 11,506 feet.

The Henrys can be accessed by a number of dirt roads heading up through washes and foothills and eventually to the mountain saddles. This range is altogether wild, and aside from the roads, there have been no "improvements" made to the mountains—not even trails. However, as almost nobody drives here, any kind of hiking desired can be accomplished right along the roads. As of my visit, this network of roads was altogether unsigned. People with a specific peak in mind should take a good guess at which road will lead to it, and follow the eye. In June 2003, a 34,000-acre wildfire consumed much of the vegetation here—the burnt trees are still quite visible today. This blaze yielded high visibility across much of the range.

Many, many dozens of miles of dirt road exist in this weather-battered range, and rain and snow can wash out roads and expose oil-pan-eating rocks much more quickly than these mountain lanes can be repaired. If entering this range, it would be wise to do so in good weather only, with high clearance

American Bison

A herd of roughly 250 to 400 bison live in the Henry Mountains. This special group is one of only four genetically pure (i.e., no cattle genes) free-roaming (i.e., noncaptive) herds in North America. The other three are found in Wind Cave National Park, South Dakota; Elk Island, Alberta; and the famous Yellowstone National Park, Wyoming and Montana.

Prior to Europeans arriving permanently in North America, bison traveled in massive herds across the continent, from near central Mexico to the upper northwestern section of Canada. Populations at that time have been estimated to be in excess of 50 million; today, with the aid of preserves, the count is somewhat less than 500,000—with the majority living as "owned" animals.

This herd hasn't simply survived to the present day in the Henrys; it was intentionally seeded there in 1941 by the transplant of 18 bison from Yellowstone Park to the southeast of Hanksville. As the herd grew naturally, it shifted its home to the Henry Mountains.

The herd grew to as many as 500 animals; biologists today believe the ideal population size to be 325 adults—so since the 1960s, the group has been monitored via helicopter census and kept at appropriate numbers by lottery-style, once-in-a-lifetime hunting permits granted annually.

and a four-wheel drive. The clays in the soil here make the mud extremely tacky and can create major problems for a vehicle.

The range spans an elevation rise of roughly 1.5 vertical miles, with correspondingly diverse fauna. Lower yucca, cactus, and sage—characteristic of warm, dry deserts—blend into rabbit brush, scrub oak, juniper, and pinyon pine, which eventually fade into tender alpine fauna like moss and lichens above the tree line. As with many places in the west, overgrazing has forced the plant life to almost entirely repopulate, driving old species away and allowing new species to therefore emerge dominant.

Continuing south and past the Henry Mountains, UT-276 passes through

John Atlantic Burr: Namesake of the Burr Trail

From Bullfrog Marina to Boulder, Utah, the **Burr Trail** is a 66-mile scenic byway that passes though the **Waterpocket Fold**, **Capitol Reef National Park** (no fee to cross through; there are no park facilities here), and **Long Canyon**. This route is named after pioneer John Atlantic Burr, a homesteader who built a 3-mile stretch of this road, the most unlikely part of today's current thruway. Born in 1846 on the Atlantic Ocean (hence the middle name), aboard the SS *Brooklyn*, John moved west and eventually made a life for himself driving cattle between Bullfrog Basin and Boulder, Utah. Crossing through the Waterpocket Fold—a 100-mile-long, formidable rock wall—required the construction of a path through a weakness. Needing a passageway through which to drive his cattle, this is what John Burr created, earning a legacy for his name.

THE MULEY TWIST SECTION OF THE BURR TRAIL

Waterpocket Fold

Yet another of Utah's kooky and unique geological freak shows, this is the defining feature of Capitol Reef National Park. A hundred miles long, this sandstone reef is actually a massive fold in the earth's crust, also called a monocline, or a "step up" in rock strata. About 60 million years ago, massive tectonic activity in the area released movement in an older fault, allowing the rocks around it to shift. This movement resulted in the west side of the fault being lifted 7,000 feet higher than the east side, and the earth on that side folding over the fault itself.

All of this occurred underground, but as the Colorado Plateau was lifted higher and higher in the last 20 million years, the ground layers atop this fold were finally washed and blown away. Subsequent weathering has revealed many colorful layers of stone. The name "waterpocket" refers to dips and basins in the rock that are eroded by water—a similar idea to the water tanks in Hueco Tanks State Park, Texas.

Ticaboo. Ticaboo is an unincorporated town with little more than a post office—so don't expect any kind of resupply here, fuel or otherwise. This highway then approaches the northern edge of **Lake Powell** at **Bullfrog.** Those who desire to see the lake may head a few extra miles south along UT-276 to the water's edge and the visitor center. (And those wishing to bypass this stop may just turn west onto the Burr Trail, just past Ticaboo.) Bullfrog itself is a touristy, lake-oriented town whose primary economy is servicing those who require a boat rental or a marina for putting their own boat into the water. As boating here is a heavily seasonal activity, don't expect much at all to be open from late fall through early spring.

Those suddenly feeling the urge to be on the south side of Lake Powell can take the **Bullfrog Ferry** to Halls Crossing and to a continuation of UT-276. The ferry is only in regular service April 1 through October 31, save for winter maintenance runs. While operational, it runs four to five times a day, with the schedule likely to change without notice. No reservations are possible, but people planning to use the ferry should call ahead to check the schedule and arrive early to ensure themselves a spot. Warning: To enter the **Glen Canyon National Recreation Area**, a $15 toll must be paid (America the Beautiful passes are accepted).

As the Burr Trail heads west toward Boulder, it first winds and climbs gradually through natural drainages, nearing the **Waterpocket Fold.** As the road gets closer to this feature, it goes through a maze of buttes and washes, gradually climbing toward the centerpiece of the drive: 3 miles of road with switchbacks of incredible severity. As the road approaches the Waterpocket

Fold, it will become increasingly obvious why the Burr Trail—which navigates through this barrier—is a famous route. The notion of building a tunnel through any point of this feature seems impossible without massive blasting and modern construction—both of which were unavailable to John Burr. And though it is not recommended that RVs or vehicles with trailers pass through here, any normal passenger vehicle should be fine. Just shift into low gear so as not to burn out the transmission. Over the course of the drive, the road climbs in elevation from 3,900 feet to 6,600 feet above sea level.

After climbing to the top of the last switchback, the road becomes much tamer. Drivers will be able to relax, shift out of low gear, and take in the view. Look south (left) to see the Circle Cliffs in the distance. With an elevation up to 7,251 feet, they rise about 600 feet above the plateau at road level. From the right vantage point (looking back toward the east), the Henry Mountains form a deep blue backdrop behind this striking red cliff band.

The eastern front of the Waterpocket Fold marks the eastern border of **Capitol Reef National Park**. For the next stretch, this drive will traverse through an "unimproved" section of this park. Though signs alert passersby to the park boundaries, no fee must be paid. Drivers can pull off along the way and picnic at one of the roadside tables atop the plateau ascended by the Burr Trail.

The last major feature—and minor topographical obstacle for the car—is **Long Canyon**, which the road dips down into, then arrives out of, just east of Boulder. Very soon before the descent into Long Canyon, there is a good view of the Circle Cliffs amphitheater with the Henry Range as a backdrop. At this point, the road to Boulder is just under 18 miles long. The next bit of pavement meanders its way along the flat bottom of a very narrow, um . . . *long* canyon—about 7 miles in length. With shorter walls and a much more slender girth, this somewhat resembles the Colorado River east of Moab, with its sheer, smoothly sculpted Navajo Sandstone walls—burnt red with black streaks. To the north is Rattlesnake Bench, and to the south is King Bench.

About 5.5 miles beyond the top of Long Canyon, look for a small side canyon to the right (north). This abrupt, nontechnical slot canyon gives observers a taste of such environs without the effort or technical gear required to access most in the area. Dark and usually a bit damp, this corridor is much cooler than its surroundings, so don't let ambient heat deter you from an opportunity to explore off-road. (However, be very careful to avoid such narrow canyons if there is any rain in the region; flash flooding can strike suddenly and be lethal.)

The mouth of Long Canyon is just more than 10 miles from the outskirts of Boulder. Boulder, a cute, artsy desert town, and Escalante are prime stops near the Grand Staircase-Escalante National Monument—replete with coffee shops, B&Bs, bookshops, galleries, and restaurants. Bustle on up to Boulder, take out this guidebook, and find a good place to cozy up for the night. (For more information on lodging, dining, recreation, and shopping in this area, check out pages 159–161.)

IN THE AREA

Attractions and Recreation

BULLFROG VISITOR CENTER, Lake Powell and UT-276, Bullfrog. Open irregularly, beginning in May. Call to inquire at 435-684-7423.

HANKSVILLE-BURPEE QUARRY, 380 South 100 West, Hanksville. Website: www.blm.gov/utah.

GLEN CANYON NATIONAL RECREATION AREA, P.O. Box 1507, Page, AZ. Call 928-608-6200. Website: www.nps.gov/glca.

GOBLIN VALLEY STATE PARK. Visitor center open 8 to 5 daily (sometimes closed for staff lunch breaks in the off-season). $13 day-use fee; $25 per campsite (which includes the park entrance fee). Campground reservations: 1-800-322-3770. Website: www.stateparks.utah.gov/parks/goblin-valley.

JOHN WESLEY POWELL RIVER HISTORY MUSEUM, 1765 East Main Street, Green River. Admission is $6 for adults 13 and up, $2 for children. Open Monday through Saturday 8–7 and Sunday 12–5 in summer; Tuesday through Saturday 9–5 in winter. Call 435-564-3427. Website: www.johnwesleypowell.com.

Dining

BLONDIE'S EATERY & GIFT, 40 North UT-95, Hanksville. Diner-style restaurant where customers order at the counter. Open daily 7–9. Call 435-542-3255.

BULL MOUNTAIN MARKET PIZZA AND DELI, 30 East UT-24, Hanksville. Take-out only; seasonal hours. Call 435-542-3249.

RAY'S TAVERN, 25 South Broadway, Green River. Call 435-564-3511. Website www.raystavern.com.

Other Contacts

BULLFROG FERRY, end of UT-276, Bullfrog. In regular operation April 1 through October 31; no reservations. Call 435-893-4747.

11
ESCALANTE TO CAPITOL REEF

ESTIMATED LENGTH: 72 miles from Escalante to Capitol Reef National Park. From there, another 37 miles to Hanksville (to join the Henry Mountains route, as detailed in chapter 10); or, alternately, another 73 miles to Richfield via UT-24, which brings the ride to a close at I-70. Extra detours suggested as well.

ESTIMATED TIME: Roughly 3 hours from Escalante to Hanksville, or 3.5 hours to get from Escalante to Richfield. With any sightseeing, this drive should take a day; many detours could occupy weeks.

HIGHLIGHTS: Along the way are two of Utah's coolest desert towns, **Escalante** and **Boulder**—gateways to the area's hiking, canyoneering, and mountain biking. Vibrant yet remote, these cater to visitors but have not yet been choked with tourism. The drive also passes multiple museums and state parks that illustrate the history of the **Grand Staircase-Escalante National Monument**. The final destination on the route is the famous **Capitol Reef National Park**.

GETTING THERE: This drive begins in Escalante—the endpoint for chapter 12's route from Parowan to Escalante. That drive (along UT-12) is the fastest and best way to approach from the south; if coming from the north, arrive by way of UT-24, which connects to I-70 in Sigurd and west of Green River.

Any drive that begins in **Escalante** is off to a good start. This little oasis of fun and artsy-ness barely occupies a dot on the map, yet for a town with a population of fewer than 900, it has a rich concentration of inviting cafés, restaurants, and guest beds. Though modern-day Escalante is a fun stop along a great highway, it hasn't always been so accessible; UT-12 was built only in the 1950s, replacing the notoriously hairy Hell's Backbone road.

Even in Utah, this particular region stands out as a less traveled cor-

LEFT: ESCALANTE RIVER

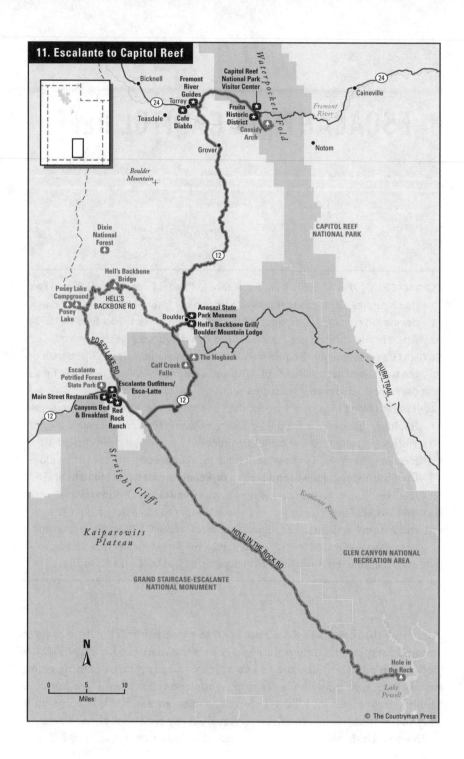

11. Escalante to Capitol Reef

Bicknell

Fremont River Guides

Capitol Reef National Park Visitor Center

Waterpocket Fold

24

Caineville

Torrey

24

Teasdale

Cafe Diablo

Fruita Historic District

Fremont River

Cassidy Arch

Notom

Grover

Boulder Mountain

CAPITOL REEF NATIONAL PARK

Dixie National Forest

12

Hell's Backbone Bridge

Posey Lake Campground

HELL'S BACKBONE RD

Posey Lake

Boulder

Anasazi State Park Museum

Hell's Backbone Grill/ Boulder Mountain Lodge

POSEY LAKE RD

Calf Creek Falls

The Hogback

BURR TRAIL

Escalante Petrified Forest State Park

Escalante Outfitters/ Esca-Latte

Main Street Restaurants

12

Canyons Bed & Breakfast

Red Rock Ranch

12

Straight Cliffs

Escalante River

HOLE IN THE ROCK RD

GLEN CANYON NATIONAL RECREATION AREA

Kaiparowits Plateau

GRAND STAIRCASE-ESCALANTE NATIONAL MONUMENT

N

Hole in the Rock

Lake Powell

0 5 10
Miles

© The Countryman Press

Hole In the Rock Road

In the fall of 1879, a group of colonizing Mormons set out from Salt Lake City en route to what would become Moab. Called the San Juan Mission, this expedition sought a route across Utah to its southeastern corner. Since they were moving to an unsettled region, they carried their many supplies in cumbersome wagons. Even today, with modern roads and vehicles, Utah's terrain is steep and difficult to cross. However, back in the 1870s, the region was almost entirely uncharted, and the group certainly had no access to modern roads or vehicles.

For the sake of taking the most direct route possible, the group traveled across the relatively flat **Kaiparowits Plateau** beneath the **Straight Cliffs**. This worked out well until they encountered what were then 1,200-foot-tall cliffs at the northern edge of **Glen Canyon**. Needless to say, this was a pretty "stopper" feature. Not to be turned away, scouts began exploring the canyon rim to find a weakness. Searching revealed the Hole in the Rock, an extremely narrow and steep slot cutting down through the cliffs and offering a glimpse of the **Colorado River** (now **Lake Powell**, penned behind the **Glen Canyon Dam**, with a much higher water level). Immediately across the river, they spotted the Cottonwood Canyon, leading back up and onto the **Wilson Mesa**. Convinced, they prepared to cross the river via these two features.

However, the Hole in the Rock needed alteration before it could provide adequate passageway for wagons, livestock, and people. Explosives widened the necessary parts of the slot, and wagon-lowering anchors were carved into the stone. The group implemented wooden tracks and sandstone slabs to smooth sections of the slot, enough that wagons and livestock could successfully arrive at the river, down grades as steep as 50 percent. In early 1880, they made it to the river, only to find the way up Cottonwood Canyon to be even more challenging.

Once atop Wilson Mesa, the group of 250 people, 1,000 animals, and 83 wagons traveled onward and established the town of Bluff in 1880. This Hole in the Rock route was used for just a year by incoming residents and suppliers before a much more reasonable route, passing through Halls Crossing, was discovered and put to use.

---

ner throughout history. In 1776, Franciscan explorer-priests Escalante and Dominguez engaged in a famous northward trek from present-day Santa Fe, New Mexico. They hoped to determine an overland route to Monterey, California. Though this mission failed under approaching winter in northern Utah, when the priests were forced to return home, they nevertheless accomplished the first major exploration of the continental interior.

Other Europeans subsequently entered the region in passing, making note of it. During the Black Hawk War of 1866, Captain James Andrus for

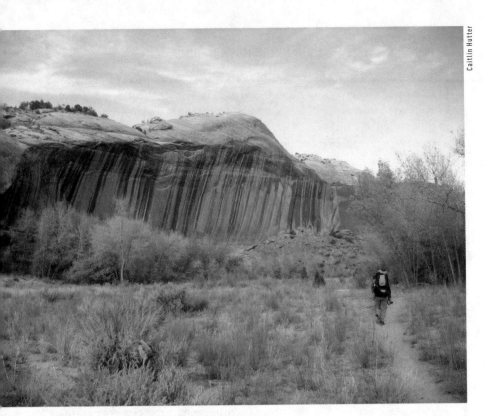

NAVAJO SANDSTONE BY THE ESCALANTE RIVER TRAIL

some reason named it Potato Valley. The famous Green River explorer Major John Wesley Powell and his head mapmaker, A. H. Thompson, visited the area in the 1870s, documenting its topography and ecology.

On one trip in 1875, Thompson encountered a group of Latter-day Saints attempting to establish a township there. As the story goes, he advised them to name the town Escalante after the early priests. And so it was done. Built by Mormons, this town indeed features the gridded and number-named streets that follow this religion's trademark "Zion plan" for city layout. Original brick homes from the late nineteenth century still stand on the noticeably wide streets.

Early area residents enjoyed mild winters and survivably hot summers. They made a living in cattle and sheep ranching, as well as mining and logging. Long growing seasons and endless sunshine allowed for irrigated crops to be plentiful. This town served as a crucial Mormon outpost for those coming from Salt Lake City en route to colonizing the surrounding area in the name of the Latter-day Saints Church. Even with the presence of towns such as Escalante, these groups still had their work cut out for them when it came to overland travel.

The town of Escalante has grown and shrunk—but its current population of 783 is just a few hundred less than its 1940s all-time high. Isolated from major cities and roadways, this town enjoys its prime location on the incredibly scenic **UT-12**. This highway streams a tourist population through Escalante during the summer, on the way to and from **Bryce Canyon** and **Capitol Reef National Parks**, the **Burr Trail** (in chapter 10 of this book), and many other state parks.

For grub in Escalante, look no further than UT-12, which swoops through town as **Main Street**. About half a dozen restaurants stand there, trying to lure in business with western-themed names and décor. **Cowboy Blues**, for example, serves ribs, steak, trout, pasta, pizza, burgers, soup, salad, wine, and draft beer—daily and all year. Casual and family friendly, they offer a special children's menu.

Circle D Eatery offers old-school breakfast, lunch, and dinner in a clean, brightly lit space; they have a huge variety of options and a great ability to satiate. Most items on the menu involve meat, but vegetarians will find a few options as well. The menu includes a creative selection of basic and gourmet local beef burgers, sandwiches, ribs, chicken, pasta, and fish. Circle D also has a beer and wine menu featuring local options as well as national favorites.

For coffee, pastries, sunscreen, fishing and hiking gear, guidebooks, a place to camp, or even a bed to sleep in, check out the **Escalante Outfitters/ Esca-Latte**. This cute little shop/café is like Escalante's clown car of services. Though the front building appears small, it's charmingly packed with a huge variety of retail and rental goods to match the vast number of recre-

SUNRISE ON THE HOGBACK OF UT-12 BETWEEN ESCALANTE AND BOULDER

Caitlin Hutter

ation options in the Grand Staircase-Escalante National Monument. Additionally, there's a restaurant that serves pizza, quiche, and more. Tucked behind and around the shop is the lodging and camping portion of the campus. The owners and staff here tend to be quite cheery and do everything, from cleaning the cabins to making espresso drinks! They're a hardworking crew—even offering guided fly fishing trips and informational hikes, as well as tips and recommendations for bike rides.

Cabins, bunks, and campsites are available for rent at Escalante Outfitters, but if they're full, several alternatives exist right in town—and, just as with the dining options, these are located primarily on Main Street. Large groups or families (up to twelve people) should consider staying at the **Red Rock Ranch**. This single 2,700-square-foot "cabin" sits at the southern end of town. With generous windows and a hilltop position, this two-story affair provides plenty of space for groups not wanting to split up. Originally a family home, this has all the amenities for a self-sufficient vacation, like a kitchen, fireplace, and lawn. It was built in 2000 and has a clean, modern interior.

For a couple, check out **Canyons Bed-and-Breakfast**. Lacking in the batty-old-grandmother feel that a lot of bed-and-breakfasts exude, this has no overstuffed beds, lace curtains, or Victorian anything. Instead, this 1905

CALF CREEK

Caitlin Hutter

PEEKABOO CANYON, HOLE IN THE ROCK ROAD

ranch-style house gives guests private room entry (with a covered porch) and modern yet simple, newly remodeled rooms. Breakfasts consist of well-balanced, home-cooked dishes, and include fresh fruit, eggs, and coffee. (For those wishing to get an early start to the day, continental breakfast is available before the official meal.) A limited number of rooms—just four— keeps the establishment uncrowded.

Those with a few spare hours to check out something beyond the hotel room should visit the **Escalante Petrified Forest State Park**. First, as the name would suggest, a sizeable petrified forest is the showpiece of this park. Two footpaths meander through the grounds, allowing visitors to get a closer look at fossilized tree remains, some of which are more than 4 feet wide. One, the Petrified Forest Trail, is roughly a mile long and climbs 200 feet; the other, Sleeping Rainbow Trail, is a quarter mile shorter and is an extension of the first. A third option, Bailey's Wash, can be walked—but it is not a developed trail; consult a ranger to find its location and get directions about the actual route.

In addition to the hiking trails and petrified forest there is . . . a lake? Yep, the **Wide Hollow Reservoir**. Created in the 1950s to provide irrigation for Escalante, it is presently stocked with rainbow trout and bluegill. To get there, head slightly west from downtown on UT-12/Main Street and then north on Reservoir Road. The on-site campground provides an alternative to in-town lodging.

Now comes the part where you must choose your own adventure: Either take UT-12 toward Boulder, checking out its attractions and detours on the way (**Hole** in the Rock and **Calf Creek Falls**), or head north out of Escalante toward **Posey Lake** and the famous **Hell's Backbone Road**. We'll start with the UT-12 version, but then come back and visit the Posey Lake/Hell's Backbone alternative.

ESCALANTE TO BOULDER VIA UT-12

Though the famous Hell's Backbone route certainly takes one's breath away, this trip to Boulder on UT-12 certainly isn't boring either—providing ridgeline driving and plenty of scenery along the way. A section of this route called the **Hogback**, about two-thirds of the way to Boulder, is a neatly curving section of UT-12 atop a ridge with steep drop-offs on either side that certainly encourage the driver to remain attentive. About 29 miles in length, it should take just less than 40 minutes to complete without detours.

Those interested in checking out some wild pioneer history should visit **Hole in the Rock** (see sidebar). This narrow notch was the passageway that allowed late nineteenth-century settlers to navigate the then-1,200-foot cliffs down to the shores of the Colorado River. (Today, the river is dammed and the water levels of Lake Powell are much higher than they were in the unaltered river.) Evidence of this early civil works project remains clearly visible to this day: blasting marks left by explosive powder, anchor points for lowering wagons on ropes, and even steps to smooth the way.

To visit this remarkable couloir, head east from Escalante (about 4.5 miles) on UT-12, turning right (southeast) on **Hole in the Rock Road**. This dirt lane leads to the national historical site after about 55 miles, passing through an explorer's paradise on the way. Though well maintained for about the first third, the road surface grows less and less smooth, eventually becoming impassible by non-off-road vehicles somewhere near the end (between 5 and 15 miles, depending on grading). Therefore, the last section of road makes for a great, low-skill mountain bike ride. Along the Hole in the Rock Road, many side roads branch out, offering hiking trails, wild camping spots, and picnic areas. If you're heading into this area, it's worth getting a somewhat detailed map, so as not to miss these lesser-known opportunities.

Back on the main road to Boulder, consider stopping at **Calf Creek Falls**, a popular attraction in the area. Accessible by hiking only, this 126-foot waterfall sits atop a trail whose starting point is the Calf Creek Campground (15 miles east of Escalante on UT-12). Campsites here cost little and come with pit toilets, picnic tables, and fire rings. The namesake attraction, Lower Calf Creek Falls, is reached by hiking just over 2.5 miles up a relatively flat yet sandy and narrow canyon. **Calf Creek** runs year-round with clear, cool water falling into a scenic pool in a cozy sandstone amphitheater. Even though the pool is cool and refreshing, the hike is, like the rest of the area, hot in summer and should be done with sufficient fluids and sun protection. (The Upper Calf Creek Falls, upstream from here, can also be accessed, but from a separate slickrock trail that departs from UT-12 5.5 miles north of the campground/main trailhead.)

ESCALANTE TO BOULDER VIA POSEY LAKE AND HELL'S BACKBONE

Posey Lake Road can be picked up easily in Escalante; it starts as 300 East Street (a north–south running lane) in the eastern side of town. Take this street north, following it as it doglegs east and then north again and out of

Grand Staircase-Escalante National Monument

This enormous monument occupies 1.9 million acres (nearly 3,000 square miles) of land. About 1.5 times the size of Delaware, it sits in the south-central portion of Utah. To the south, it is bordered approximately by US-89 and Lake Powell; on the east, it ends at Capitol Reef National Park; and on the west it stops roughly at Bryce Canyon National Park and the Dixie National Forest.

Spanning about 9,000 vertical feet and roughly two dozen major rock strata, this lifted and folded piece of crust has revealed some of the earth's most beautifully deposited rock layers as it has cracked and been eroded by wind and water. Forming the "staircase" are the Pink, Grey, White, Chocolate, and Vermilion cliffs, as they step from an altitude of 12,000 feet near Cedar Breaks and the Paunsaugunt Plateau down to 3,000 feet above sea level at the bottom of the Grand Canyon. Fissured and sculpted into its steps are Bryce Canyon, Zion and Kolob Canyons, the Sevier River, and the Coral Pink Sand Dunes.

This vast and wild landscape offers an incredible wealth of recreation and scenery, in addition to natural and human history. Unlike other national monuments, this is administered by the Bureau of Land Management instead of the National Park Service. Designated a national monument only in September 1996 by Bill Clinton, during his presidential reelection campaign, it has been speculated that this monument was created perhaps in an effort to gain votes. Some officials complained about the sudden allotment of such a vast portion of land, concerned with lost mining opportunities and access; others were glad—even though a national monument does not enjoy identical protection to wilderness lands, its sanctity is much more sheltered than it would be without national monument status.

To learn more about Grand Staircase-Escalante National Monument, stop by any of its offices or visitor centers, of which there are more than ten. See the website for more information. And be careful, as always, to check the weather before exploring slot canyons to be sure that there are no storm systems in the area; flash floods kill people every year in Utah.

town and turns into Posey Lake Road. Stay on this route for a total of about 18 miles and take a right on Hell's Backbone Road, for roughly 20.5 more miles of driving. This dumps directly onto UT-12 again, about 4.5 miles south of Boulder. The total route to Boulder is about 44 slow miles on dirt road suitable for any passenger vehicle (barring severe weather).

With the route plan sorted, get ready for one of Utah's more famous sections of driving. Posey Lake Road climbs north from Escalante and up into the high Dixie National Forest. **Posey Lake** itself, about 15 miles north of town, is enclosed by a mixed aspen and evergreen forest. At 8,600 feet above sea level, its campground provides a cool, shaded rest stop. Hiking trails departing from Posey Lake lead to Tule Lake and connect with segments of the Great Western Trail; numerous dirt roads crisscrossing the forest pass by other lakes and can be casually mountain biked. Though the elevation is quite high here, the topography is nevertheless pretty mellow. There is a small overnight fee for this campground, which features a boat ramp (for nonmotorized boats only) and pit toilets.

The **Hell's Backbone Road** itself was built by the Civilian Conservation Corps in 1935 and reaches an elevation of up to 9,000 feet above sea level. This high, exposed road thrills visitors as it traipses along crumbling forested ridges and spiny sandstone mountains. Snaking around, it gains popping vistas down and across the region. Along the way is the famous **Hell's Backbone Bridge**, which penalizes inattentive drivers with a 1,500-foot plummet if they err. Though a gravel road, it is a popular tourist attraction and therefore well maintained. People often describe the road as terrifying to drive—but it is truly a proper road, and it requires no special technical skills to navigate.

Arriving in Boulder—a nexus in the Grand Staircase-Escalante National Monument—requires visitors to regroup and decide where to go next. From here, many directions of travel are possible. But don't be too slow with decision-making, as the drive through town can nearly be missed in the blink of an eye. To take the **Burr Trail** (detailed in chapter 10 of this book), head east out of town on **Burr Trail Road**. Easily located, this road departs exactly where UT-12 makes a sharp 90-degree turn to the north (left) upon its entrance into Boulder. Taking this road commences a reverse-direction version of chapter 10's tour of the Burr Trail and the **Henry Mountains**.

However, remaining on this chapter's prescribed route, one of the first and most easily accessible attractions in town is the **Anasazi State Park Museum**. Here, a village dating from roughly AD 1050 to 1200 has been partially unearthed. The intactness of the structures allows one to easily imagine the lives of these ancestral Pueblo people who managed to forge a settlement here a thousand years ago. From the roughly 100 structures, a variety of artifacts have been recovered that suggest the type of lifestyle these folks had. These items can be seen on display in the museum, which

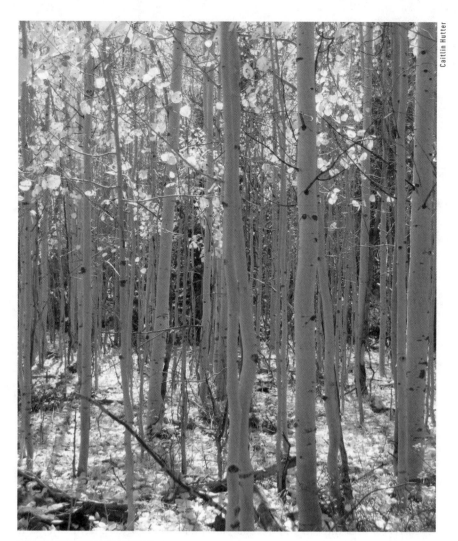

BOULDER MOUNTAIN QUAKING ASPEN

also serves as an **information center and permit vendor** for the Grand Staircase-Escalante National Monument.

Another immediately obvious attraction in Boulder is the **Hell's Backbone Grill**, the region's most acclaimed restaurant. Focusing on fresh cuisine, it serves homegrown vegetables whenever possible—which is usually the case, given the immense growing season that overlaps nicely with tourist season. When not grown on-site, the produce served is nonetheless organic, and the meats come from local sources. The grill is located on expansive, gardened grounds that pleasantly embellish the dining experience. Hell's Backbone Grill has claimed multiple Utah state best-of titles, as well as national awards and write-ups. Located in southern Utah, the atmosphere

here is semicasual. This restaurant closes during the winter months; call ahead if you're visiting during the shoulder seasons to be sure they're open.

For an equally soul-fulfilling slumber, make reservations to stay right here at the **Boulder Mountain Lodge**. Situated on the same green property as the Hell's Backbone Grill, this hotel maintains its space from the restaurant but enjoys the same environmentally conscious ownership and wholesome, relaxing surroundings. Spacious rooms with private balconies overlook the grounds and scenery beyond. Pets are actually welcome here. Due to the magnetic nature of both the restaurant and the lodge, would-be guests should be sure to lock down reservations well ahead of time.

For a fewer-frills, fewer-dollars (but equally raved-about) dinner, check out the **Burr Trail Grill**. This serves a selection of house entrees, sandwiches, burgers, salads, and soups, as well as beer and wine. Next to the grill and deli (in the same building) is the **Burr Trail Outpost**, which brews espresso drinks, sells guidebooks and gear, showcases local artwork, and arranges guide services. This restaurant is open seasonally for lunch and dinner only; call ahead if visiting during the shoulder season.

And for more affordable, just-want-to-sleep-in-a-bed lodgings, check out the **Circle Cliffs Motel**. Located right on Main Street (UT-12), toward the northern end of town, Circle Cliffs is definitely a no-frills motel. Rooms range from single bed to apartment. A place for those who'd rather invest their money in other parts of the trip.

Heading north from Boulder, visitors say goodbye to the Grand Staircase-Escalante National Monument and look forward to a 35-mile trip to **Torrey** and UT-24. Heading more or less due north, UT-12 enters the **Boulder Mountain** section of the drive. Occupying a sizable area on the map, this "land of a thousand lakes" offers itself up to hunters, fishers, hikers, campers, and backcountry explorers. This massive eminence, which tops out at 11,317 feet above sea level, is a wild area for a variety of recreation. Numerous forest roads reach west into the region, accessing lakes, campgrounds, and general wilderness. High aspen stands and deep green conifer forests contrast with red sandstone valleys of the surrounding area. Lakes here are often crowned with encircling cliff walls and forests, thinned somewhat by their high elevation. The best method for exploring Boulder Mountain begins with choosing the category of recreation. Then grab a detailed topographic map, stock up with supplies, and head into the wild.

Because of all the lakes and streams, fishing seems to be one of the most popular activities in the area. **Fremont River Guides** happily escorts those without their own equipment, know-how, or wherewithal in the region. These guys know the ins and outs of the area's streams and lakes and how they respond to season, time of day, and weather. In a region with so many bodies of water—literally thousands—including teeny, often unmapped lakes, beaver ponds, and small streams, this kind of expertise can be quite helpful.

All necessary gear will be provided (if needed). Everyone fishing in Utah is required to have a license; check on Fremont River Guides' website for a link to Utah's license vendors.

Time to boogie out of Boulder Mountain, up past the small town of Torrey, and onto UT-24, heading east to eventually reach Capitol Reef National Park. But those who missed out on dining in Boulder should try **Cafe Diablo** in Torrey. In a casual atmosphere, this restaurant serves a creative hybrid menu, including contemporary American, Southwestern, and South American dishes, with fish, poultry, steak, and even rattlesnake. Not just a meat-and-potatoes kind of place, Cafe Diablo excels in creativity, with homemade sauces and fresh, unique sides. Despite a laid-back dining room, the menu is high-end.

Just east of Torrey is **Capitol Reef National Park**, called a "reef" because its major feature—a 100-mile-long spine of rock—forms a veritable barrier against any east–west land travel. The **Waterpocket Fold**, a Navajo Sandstone ridge, is a huge uplift that when viewed aerially appears to be a stiffly pleated portion of the earth's crust, with parallel ridges of pale yellow and deep red sandstone. (If you're curious to know more about this feature, see "Waterpocket Fold" in Chapter 10.) From the ground, it is easy to see why early pioneers found it to be a legendary barricade to travel.

Two primary sections of the national park exist: Capitol Reef and Cathedral Valley. The **Capitol Reef** gets the "capitol" part of its name from the golden Navajo Sandstone domes that resemble government buildings. About 10,000 feet and 250 million years' worth of rock layers can be seen here. First lifted by the Waterpocket monocline and subsequently eroded over time, these strata are visible anywhere along this fold.

As any national park does, Capitol Reef includes a paved scenic drive that covers the visual highlights of the park without requiring one to exit from the car. This primary road departs from UT-24 and heads 10 miles south into the park.

It is advisable to stop in at the visitor center and pick up a park guide before embarking on this drive; as the road tours so many millions of years' worth of geological history, many interesting things can be seen in the rock that would go unnoticed without a few tips. With some simple education, the eye can pick out rock that was deposited by wind and water—and spot fossilized footprints as well.

The first sight along the way is **Fruita**, an abandoned settlement, in which a historic home, the **Gifford Homestead**, still stands, dating back to the early twentieth century. Here period artifacts are on display and lifestyle demonstrations take place.

Unlike in many parks, however, most of Capitol Reef's road miles remain unpaved—likely a reflection of this park's (refreshing) relative lack of crowding; beyond the asphalt scenic drive stretch many other long, looping dirt roads that should be driven with an accompanying gazetteer or park map.

Caitlin Hutter

MCGATH RESERVOIR ON BOULDER MOUNTAIN

About 4 miles south from UT-24, the dirt **Grand Wash Road** heads east from the pavement, twisting for a mile into the wash. Where the road ends, a trail begins, which leads deeper into more scenic stretches of Grand Wash. Along the walk, the trail passes **Cassidy Arch,** named after outlaw Butch Cassidy of Wild West fame, who occasionally sought refuge from the law here. This sturdy, round arch forms a window from a plateau above down to the narrow gulch below. Also along the gulch are small man-made caves; these tunnels in the rock are the remnants of defunct uranium mines from the early 1900s and are a very common sight around the desert Southwest. A word of caution: Stay away from this road and this hike altogether if there is any bad weather in the area; as a wash, this serves as a natural drainage way, and flash flooding can easily arise without warning. At the end of this 10-mile scenic drive, the pavement ends, and route must be retraced.

The northern region of Capitol Reef National Park, or **Cathedral Valley,** must be accessed by an entirely different road system to the north of the park's UT-12-accessible section. Located in the far northern corner of the Capitol Reef National Park, it can either be reached by dirt road heading northwest from Caineville or by heading east from UT-72, also via dirt road, into the park. The Cathedral Valley is often unvisited, but it contains some of the most beautiful features to be found within the park. Inside a broad, flat, green valley stands a city of red rock fins and spires quite resembling cathedrals. Before heading for a visit to this valley, call the park to determine the current road conditions; roads can become worn-out and very rocky, requiring high clearance. Also, wet conditions transform the dirt into a very slippery and sticky clay capable of miring vehicles.

After Capitol Reef National Park, the way out is up to the driver: Continuing east along UT-24 brings travelers directly to **Hanksville,** which sits near the beginning of the Henry Mountains/Burr Trail route (chapter 10 of this book); heading west on UT-24 leads toward I-70 near Richfield, and back onto fast roads that quickly access civilization.

IN THE AREA

Accommodations

BOULDER MOUNTAIN LODGE, 20 North UT-12, Boulder. Moderately priced (cheaper during the shoulder and off-seasons). Pets welcome. Open year-round. Call 435-335-7460 or 1-800-556-3446. Website: www.boulder -utah.com.

CANYONS BED-AND-BREAKFAST, 120 East Main Street, Escalante. Affordable. Open March through October only; closed in winter. No children under 12 permitted; pets not accepted; no smoking. Call 435-826-4747 or 1-866-526-9667. Website: www.canyonsbnb.com.

CIRCLE CLIFFS MOTEL, 225 North UT-12, Boulder. Relatively affordable. Open year-round. Call 435-335-7333.

RED ROCK RANCH, 450 East 300 South, Escalante. Moderate to pricey; pro-rated fees for longer stays. Single-home rental for large groups; five bedrooms. Call 435-703-9944 or 435-817-5157. Website: www.rrescalante.com.

Attractions and Recreation

ANASAZI STATE PARK MUSEUM, 460 North UT-12, Boulder. $5 day-use fee; $10 families. Open March 1 through October 31 daily 8–6; November 1 through February 28 daily 8–4; some holiday closures. Call 435-335-7308. Website: www.stateparks.utah.gov/parks/anasazi.

FREMONT RIVER GUIDES. 135 East Main Street, Torrey. Call 435-425-3999 to arrange trip and meeting place. Website: www.flyfishingsouthernutah .com.

CAPITOL REEF NATIONAL PARK, 11 miles east of Torrey on UT-24. 52 West Headquarters Drive, Torrey. $10 day-use fee. Call 435-425-3791. Website: www.nps.gov/care.

ESCALANTE PETRIFIED FOREST STATE PARK, 710 North Reservoir Road, Escalante. $8 day-use fee. Open year-round; some holiday closures. Camping available (for an extra fee). Call 435-826-4466. Website: http:// stateparks.utah.gov/parks/escalante-petrified-forest.

GRAND STAIRCASE-ESCALANTE NATIONAL MONUMENT, Kanab Headquarters, 669 South UT-89A, Kanab. Call 435-644-1200. Website: www.blm .gov/programs/national-conservation-lands/utah/grand-staircase-escalante -national-monument.

Dining

BURR TRAIL GRILL AND OUTPOST, 10 North UT-12, Boulder. Casual atmosphere, American and Southwestern cuisine. Call 435-335-7565. Website: www.burrtrailoutpost.com.

CAFE DIABLO, 599 West Main Street, Torrey. Moderately expensive. Indoor and outdoor seating; casual. Reservations recommended; open mid-April through mid-October nightly for dinner only. Call 435-425-3070. Website: www.cafediablo.net.

CIRCLE D EATERY, 475 West Main, Escalante. 7:30 AM–9 PM. Wednesday through Monday, 5 PM–9 PM. Tuesday. Call 435-826-4125. Website: www .escalantecircledeatery.com.

COWBOY BLUES RESTAURANT, 530 West Main Street, Escalante. Affordable. Western American cuisine. Open daily for lunch and dinner, year-round. Call 435-826-4577. Website: www.cowboyblues.net.

ESCALANTE OUTFITTERS/ESCA-LATTE CAFÉ, 310 West Main Street, Escalante. Gear retail, bike rentals, pizza restaurant, beer, espresso, and free Wi-Fi. Guided informational hikes and fly fishing trips. Cabins, bunks, and campsites for rent. Call 435-826-4266 or 1-866-455-0041. Website: www .escalanteoutfitters.com.

HELL'S BACKBONE GRILL, 20 North UT-12, Boulder. Moderately priced. Contemporary American cuisine crafted with organic and local produce and meats. Reservations strongly recommended. Open mid-March through Thanksgiving. Call 435-335-7464. Website: www.hellsbackbonegrill.com.

Other Contacts

DIXIE NATIONAL FOREST, presiding over the bulk of the land along this route. Call 435-826-5400. Website: www.fs.usda.gov/dixie.

ESCALANTE OUTFITTERS (see Escalante Outfitters/Esca-Latte Café, above)

INTERAGENCY VISITOR CENTER IN ESCALANTE, 755 West Main, Escalante. Information on the many nearby state and national parks, as well as Grand Staircase-Escalante National Monument. Call 435-826-5499.

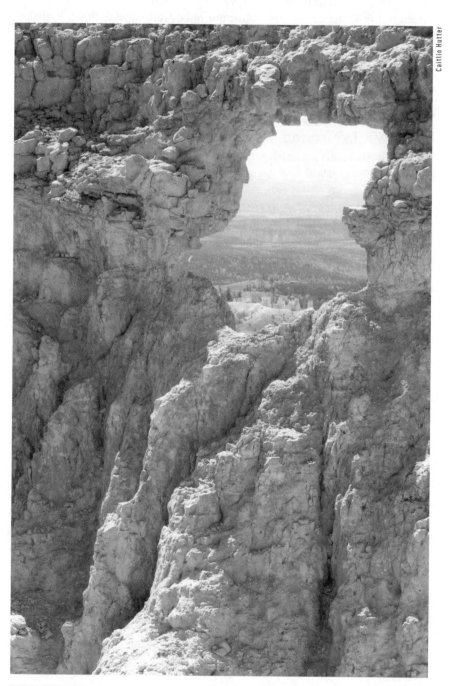

BRYCE CANYON ARCH

12

PAROWAN TO ESCALANTE

ESTIMATED LENGTH: 115 miles from Parowan to Escalante (plus 40 extra miles round-trip to include the Parowan Gap Petroglyphs and Grosvenor Arch detours)

ESTIMATED TIME: 2.5 hours driving; days or weeks with stops and exploration

HIGHLIGHTS: Look at the atlas and notice that this entire route is dotted with "scenic drive" markings—and it's no wonder why. Here the earth has been more uplifted, gnarled, colored, and scraped bare than almost any other place in the country. Over just 50 miles in the first section of this route, UT-143 ascends 4,500 feet (nearly one vertical mile) and through half a dozen major life zones. This pavement ribbon connects some of the state's most scenic areas as it enters the western rim of the glorious and sizeable **Grand Staircase-Escalante National Monument**. Along the way, it passes **Brian Head Resort, Cedar Breaks National Monument, Bryce Canyon National Park**, the turnoff for **Kodachrome Basin State Park**, and **Escalante Petrified Forest State Park** in the town of Escalante. Though this drive "ends" there, another (detailed in chapter 11 of this book) begins from the same point (and even connects into chapter 10's drive to the Henry Mountains).

GETTING THERE: This area is packed with about as much geological beauty as possible—from tall, evergreen-covered mountains to exposed red rock canyons. That said, there is no specific "best" way to get here. The main goal is to get into the vicinity of Parowan (Exit 75 off I-15), departing from the interstate north of Cedar City on UT-143. Those with extra time and arriving from the north should consider driving US-89 instead of I-15; this runs roughly parallel to the interstate but tours Circleville Canyon alongside the Sevier River.

Parowan, Utah, seems but a speck on the map, with a population of just over 2,790. Surprisingly, this was one of the first towns incorporated in Utah, and

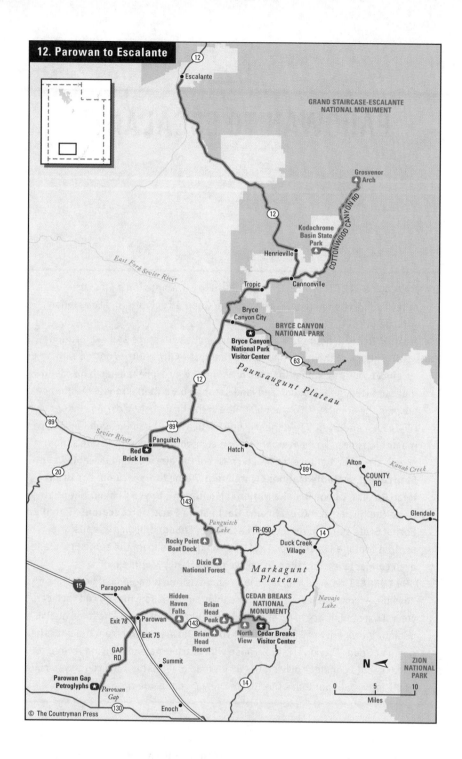

12. Parowan to Escalante

Escalante

GRAND STAIRCASE-ESCALANTE
NATIONAL MONUMENT

Grosvenor
Arch

COTTONWOOD CANYON RD

Kodachrome
Basin State
Park

Henrieville

Cannonville

East Fork Sevier River

Tropic

Bryce
Canyon City

BRYCE CANYON
NATIONAL PARK

Bryce Canyon
National Park
Visitor Center

63

12

Paunsaugunt Plateau

89

Sevier River

89

Panguitch

Hatch

Alton

Kanab Creek

Red
Brick Inn

COUNTY
RD

20

143

Glendale

Panguitch
Lake

FR-050

Rocky Point
Boat Dock

Duck Creek
Village

14

Dixie
National Forest

Markagunt
Plateau

15

Paragonah

Hidden
Haven
Falls

Brian
Head
Peak

CEDAR BREAKS
NATIONAL
MONUMENT

Navajo
Lake

Exit 78

Parowan

143

Exit 75

Brian
Head
Resort

North
View

Cedar Breaks
Visitor Center

GAP
RD

Summit

N

ZION
NATIONAL
PARK

Parowan Gap
Petroglyphs

Parowan
Gap

130

Enoch

14

0   5   10

Miles

© The Countryman Press

Parowan: World Record Lawn Mowin'

Most people in Utah don't know it, but this small town is home to a *Guinness Book of World Records* record holder for . . . the longest lawn mower ride. In 1997 resident Ryan Tripp saddled his riding lawn mower in Salt Lake City and set out east, driving 3,116 miles east to Washington, DC, raising $15,000 for the kidney transplant of a young girl. The kicker? Ryan was only 12 years old at the time of this journey. The lawn mower itself was not modified in any way; it was a quite wide, very normal sit-down lawn mower. Afterward, Ryan appeared on the *Late Show with David Letterman* and made a few other media appearances.

Two years later, he journeyed to each of the fifty state capitals in order to advocate for tissue and organ donation awareness. This time, he did not travel on his mower—but he did bring it with him, and he mowed the lawn at each state's governor's mansion.

the first in all of southern Utah. Founded in 1851—just 3 years after the Mormons' arrival in Salt Lake City—it hasn't grown much since.

The original inhabitants of the area are thought to have been the Fremont and Anasazi Indians, and petroglyphs dating from AD 750 to 1250 serve as evidence. To check out these very striking and detailed drawings, take a short detour to the **Parowan Gap Petroglyphs**, just northwest of town by way of **Gap Road**. Onto the faces of varnished sandstone boulders (on the gap's east side) have been etched many complex images. These drawings signify aspects of prehistoric life, from hunting to spiritual rituals.

Because of the illustrations' variety of age, style, and content, many scholars think these markings were the work of several different cultures, likely including the Fremont, the Southern Paiute, and more. In any case, dating shows these etchings to span roughly a thousand years, and they depict figures including snakes, lizards, mountain sheep, humans, and bear paws. The most famous and studied item, though, "the Zipper," is believed by many to represent a calendar that records the motion of the sun over time.

To get there, head north on Parowan's Main Street to 400 North Street. Turn left (west) and continue for 10.5 miles on a high-quality gravel road, parking near Milepost 19. **Nal Morris** is one of the primary researchers of the pictographs' cosmological significance; visit his website (www.parowangap.org) for some really interesting information.

Moving onto the route proper, leave Parowan (the town), heading south on UT-143. Roughly 8.5 miles south of town, look for a pullout (and wooden fence), as this denotes the trailhead for **Hidden Haven Falls**. This small interpretive trail leads into an ever-tightening, highly pleasant vegetated canyon. Nearly all of the 1.5-mile trail is user-friendly and hikeable by anyone; only the last 100 feet are rugged and difficult to pass. The first part of the trail heads through a wildlife study area and is consistently signed. Sharing the same parking area are the namesake falls, where a waterfall cascades roughly 200 feet. By winter, this freezes and is frequently visited by ice climbers.

Brian Head Resort is a little more than 4 miles beyond the falls. During the snowy months, this small resort has the best skiing in southern Utah. By summer it offers lift rides, disc golf, a hiking trail, and mountain biking. Mountain bikers can come with or without their own wheels; a shop right at the resort rents out a variety of bikes, including cross-country and downhill frames as well as children's bikes and accessories. Like the bicycle fleet, the mountain's selection of trails consists of cross-country and downhill options, intermediate to advanced trails, short rides and long, technical and (relatively) leisurely. Shuttle and lift services for bikers can be purchased. Helmets are required, and can also be rented, along with "armor." Disc golf equipment rentals are available as well.

About a mile south of Brian Head on UT-143 sits a forest service road heading east. Signed by the Dixie National Forest as Brian Head Peak 3, this road leads to a lookout point. A high-quality 2.5-mile dirt road climbs to the top of **Brian Head Peak,** 11,307 feet high. Despite the lofty elevation of this peak, its shape is quite rounded and gentle. Atop the mountain stands a small wood-and-stone hut, built by the Civilian Conservation Corps between 1935 and 1937. From the top of this mountain, several ranges can be spied. To the south stand Arizona's Navajo Mountain and Mount Trumbull; Nevada's Highland Peak and Wheeler Peak; and Utah's Tushar Mountains, Table Cliff Plateau, and the Paunsaugunt and Aquarius Plateaus; to the west are Utah's Wah Wah and Never Summer mountain ranges.

Hardly a few miles farther south on UT-143 (at its junction with UT-148) comes the next stop, **Cedar Breaks National Monument.** One of Utah's most

Parowan Gap

Looking to the west, one must wonder how there came to be such a distinctive notch in the Red Hills. Before the existence of this ridgeline, a stream ran through what was then a valley. Tectonic activity in the area, however, caused a long strip of sedimentary rock to cut free from the surrounding crust. Pressed between two parallel faults, it was lifted upward by squeezing. As this band of rock rose, the stream continued its course, cutting a gap through the rising earth faster than it could grow. Eventually the climate changed and the stream disappeared. Today wind continues to carve away at this weakness, rushing by as it funnels through this narrow gap. If you go to check out the petroglyphs, take notice of the elevated wind speeds in the 600-foot-tall notch.

Grand Staircase?

The so-called "Grand Staircase" is a geological set of steps set inside the huge—130,000 square miles—Colorado Plateau. This region of the South-west is centered on the Four Corners intersection of Arizona, New Mexico, Utah, and Colorado. Serious tectonic activity along the Hurricane fault (which trends east–west south of Cedar City) and the Sevier fault (another east–west fault north of Kanab) yielded this spectacular uplift with more than 6,000 vertical feet of relief. As this rapid uplift occurred, hundreds of millions of years of sedimentary deposits were revealed to expose sandstone that would oxidize to become deep and vibrant reds, oranges, and yellows.

The lowest step of the staircase lies in the south near Kanab, Utah, and Lake Powell, and ascends in major rock strata. These are the Chocolate, Vermilion, White, Grey, and Pink Cliffs. Here, Bryce Canyon has eroded into the topmost of these, the Paunsaugunt Plateau; Zion National Park, to the southwest, has been created by the Virgin River eroding steeply into a Navajo Sandstone layer sitting atop the White Cliffs.

remarkable natural excavations, this orange basin cuts deeply and abruptly into a high, green plateau. This bowl-shaped ring of brightly colored striated rock formed by steep erosion, leaving behind 2,000-foot curved walls of crumbly, fire-red earth. With its bold colors and peculiar weathering patterns, it undeniably bears a strong resemblance to Bryce Canyon National Park—but may even feature richer and more vibrant colors than its sister.

As long as 900 years ago, the Southern Paiute lived in this area. This tribe was based in southern Utah and lived somewhat nomadically. Planting valley crops in the spring, they would then climb high into the mountains in and around present-day Cedar Breaks to get some reprieve from the severe summer heat of lower elevations.

Within the monument are a handful of picnic areas, campsites, and three hiking trails for use by summer visitors. Despite being few in number, these trails cover a wide variety of terrain—from high alpine meadows to red rock overlooks and mountain creek washes—and offer a range of difficulty. The road, however, typically becomes impassable for the winter anywhere between October and December, depending on the year. Yet rather than shutting the park, the closure actually opens the road up for cross-country skiers, snowmobilers, and snowshoers. This is one of the most scenic spots for Nordic skiing in Utah, as the only thing that contrasts with the red walls more beautifully than green forests is winter's white snow.

A yurt ranger station stays open during the cold months and serves as an impromptu visitor center. The normal visitor center is open, and the fee

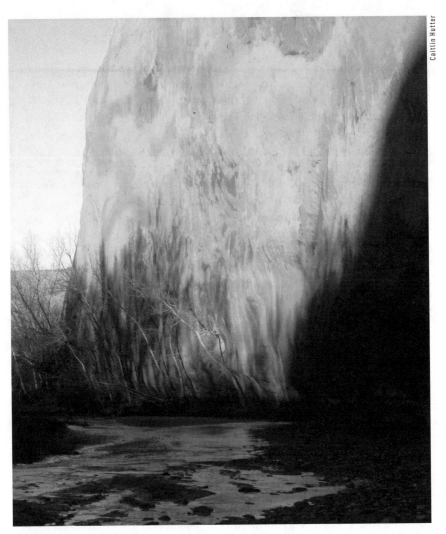

HARRIS WASH

booth active, only from roughly June 5 through the middle of October, but the scenic drive remains open as long as it stays free of deep snow. As when visiting any high-elevation locale around winter, check ahead to be sure that all roads are open; its 10,000-foot altitude makes Cedar Breaks a catcher and holder of deep snowpack.

Moving east along UT-143, keep an eye out for small, high mountain lakes. The next section of geology, vastly different from that of Cedar Breaks, features lava flows—just a few thousand years old and clearly visible on the way to Panguitch Lake. At this point, the road rides along the highest step on the so-called **Grand Staircase** (see sidebar, below), a massive geological feature centered on the Four Corners region of the United States. Look around from this perch and, on clear days, the view extends for hundreds of miles, with Arizona visible to the south beyond the descending Grand Staircase.

Once at **Panguitch Lake**, ahh—take a breath of thick air, for the elevation is but a paltry 8,400 feet on the Markagunt Plateau! With very little tall vegetation surrounding this broad **Dixie National Forest** lake, it has quite an open feel. Named by the Southern Paiutes, Panguitch roughly means "big fish," and indeed sizeable rainbow trout can today be fished from these waters during the summer months. During the cold winters here, fishermen erect ice fishing huts.

The strong presence of rainbow trout actually came about after the entire lake was treated with rotenone, a broad-spectrum pesticide and insecticide, to remove a non-native chub species. As this agent kills all fish, and not just the targeted non-native chub, the lake had to be restocked with 20,000 rainbow trout in 2006. A natural lake by origin, Panguitch used to have a surface area of roughly 780 acres, but that was expanded by about 60 percent with the installation of a dam.

Infrastructurally, the Panguitch Lake environs are pretty much undeveloped. Several campgrounds are open during the summer for those who want to stick around for a while and explore. If you're hungry, snoop around, as convenience stores and a few lodge-style restaurants keep visitors and locals fed and happy. Some of these sit along UT-143 in close proximity to the lake. Those wishing to make a loop around the lake may take Forest Service Road 080 north from UT-143—a paved detour that, together with UT-143, encircles this small lake. Those making this short side trip will come across **Rocky Point Boat Dock** on the northwestern tip of the lake. If you have your tackle and fishing license along, you can try your luck; if you don't have either, a summer float offers a pleasant break from the drive. Because of the open, unpopulated nature of the Markagunt Plateau, this corner of Utah lends itself to snowmobiling, cross-country skiing, and snowshoeing on backroads during the white months.

Less than 20 miles northeast of Panguitch Lake, the highway swoops to the northeast, and then ends in US-89. At this junction sits the actual

Bryce Amphitheater National Park

Technically not a canyon, Bryce is actually an amphitheater. Whereas canyons, by definition, have been carved top-down by streams eating into parent rock, Bryce was eroded from the bottom up, as low waters ate away at the plateau above. Regardless of geological definition, this particular area of Utah might stand alone as one of the most distinctive and visually striking geological features in the state.

1,600-person town of **Panguitch,** elevation 6,660 feet. Joining the National Register of Historic Places in November 2006, this settlement can indeed claim some beautiful and well-preserved brick homes as well as some truly cool old western-style storefronts. Panguitch offers more amenities in the way of lodging and dining than any other town in the Bryce Canyon region.

Main Street is littered with motel-style lodging. Locally owned, these modest accommodations thrive on the business brought to them by their location in "Canyon Country"—but many are open only May through October. A few B&Bs can be found in town as well. One of these, the **Red Brick Inn,** a 1920s-era Dutch Colonial house, offers a more homey stay with a family. Guests enjoy evenings sitting on the porch or making s'mores at the fire pit in the backyard. Located right in the heart of this quiet town, it requires no detour to reach.

The dining, like the lodging in Panguitch, exudes small-mountain-town charm. Most eateries can be found along Main Street, are easily spotted, and serve lots of meat. A couple of café-style restaurants offer coffee and causal meals; a few national-brand chains also serve up quick bites. Look around and take your pick. Before leaving town, be sure to fuel up the car, as townships from here on out are small and far apart.

Next up is **Bryce Canyon National Park**, south of Panguitch on US-89 for 7 miles, and then southeast on UT-12 toward Boulder. UT-12 offers much more than just a means to get to Bryce; it is one of the state's most stunning roadways, touring a major section of the **Grand Staircase-Escalante National Monument**. Here it enters this national monument atop the tall and expansive Paunsaugunt Plateau, blanketed in high-altitude evergreen and sage. This highland flows uninterruptedly until suddenly—as if it were the edge of the earth—it falls steeply away, exposing thousands of vertical feet of strangely eroded, brilliantly colored sandstone layers. Glowing orange, white, red, and yellow, this special area came under protection as a national monument in 1923, and later was made a national park in 1928.

In comparison with many of Utah's other spectacular sandstone formations, Bryce's features are quite different. Its walls are not narrow and tall like those in Zion National Park; it has no buffed Navajo Sandstone windows as in Arches; and it lacks the lofty Wingate towers and fins of Canyonlands National Park. Rather, this broad, scooped-out bowl is filled with thousands and thousands of soft, spiny-looking sandstone spires that resemble red sugar drippings.

In this peculiar forest of rock stand features that are weirder yet—the **hoo-doos.** These buggers are recognizable as thin rock pillars topped precariously with broader capstones and boulders. Resembling humans or even aliens, these form when sturdy layers of rock sit atop more erosive layers. The tougher capstones wear away less quickly than their supporting strata. Despite the unlikely nature of these hoodoos, they can sometimes reach heights of 200 feet. Though spires and hoodoos are the main theme of this park, a few stone arches and fins do exist here, however stylized with Bryce Canyon's knobby flavor.

Amazingly, given the local desert climate, different peoples have lived in the area for roughly 10,000 years. Artifacts from the Basketmaker and Pueblo-period Anasazi have been recovered in the area. The Paiute entered the region roughly 800 years ago, leaving behind artifacts of their own, including petroglyphs tapped into varnished sandstone faces.

The first descendants of Europeans to live in the immediate vicinity were the Mormon family of Ebenezer Bryce, who ran a small cattle ranch at the base of the "canyon" during the 1870s. Persistently inhospitable conditions—including harsh winters, spring

Caitlin Hutter

BRISTLECONE PINE ON
POWELL PT NEAR BRYCE CANYON

flooding, summer drought, and self-caused overgrazing—forced the family to throw in the towel after just a few years, and they relocated to Arizona in 1880. For more information on the geology, history, or ecology of the region, visit the **Bryce Canyon Natural History Association**, which runs a bookstore inside the park's visitor center. Created in 1961, this nonprofit assists with educational and scientific activities within the park.

Leaving Bryce Canyon, continue along UT-12, now trending east-southeast; next up is the turnoff to **Kodachrome Basin State Park**, named by the National Geographic Society for the fact that Kodak films replicate the wonderful red and yellow colors of this area. (Kodak's classic competitor, Fujifilm, typically excels with greens and blues.)

Just when you think Utah couldn't possibly offer any more variety in its strange sandstone earthscapes, along comes Kodachrome. Here, sixteen peculiar cylindrical sandstone spires, or "sedimentary pipes," jut high into the sky from stone platforms atop flat, grassy fields. It should be immediately obvious to the observer why this has been designated a state park—by all appearances, it is nature's own sculpture garden, with bright colors, spires, arches, and other peculiar formations backdropped by a basin of brightly colored earth. In the roughly 5,000 acres of the park, visitors can camp (for a fee), hike, mountain bike, horseback ride, or simply relax. To reach Kodachrome Basin State Park, look for **Cottonwood Canyon Road** departing to the south (right) from UT-12, about 4 miles south of Tropic; follow signs to the park from here.

Grosvenor Arch, 10 miles east-southeast of the Kodachrome Basin (farther along Cottonwood Canyon Road), is a worthy detour if time isn't limited. This distinctive, gothic-looking double arch has been carved naturally by desert winds. From top to bottom, the red rock fades into pale tan as it nears the earth. The pullout for the arch should be easy to spot, as a short sidewalk leads directly to its base from a pit toilet and picnic tables. The National Geographic Society named this arch after the society's onetime president, Gilbert Hovey Grosvenor.

Toodle back north to UT-12, and continue in a northeasterly direction as it crosses into **Grand Staircase-Escalante National Monument** just before arriving in the town of **Escalante**. GSNM and Escalante are both showpieces of the region, with the national monument encompassing 1.9 million acres of land, and Escalante serving as an outpost for desert enthusiasts to decompress and restock.

Though this drive "ends" here, another route (detailed in chapter 11 of this book) also begins right here. From Escalante, it continues through the Grand Staircase-Escalante National Monument, past Boulder and Capitol Reef National Park, and eventually up toward I-70.

IN THE AREA

Accommodations

RED BRICK INN, 161 North 100 West, Panguitch. Open May through October; reservations accepted year-round. Very affordable. Call 435-690-1048. Website: www.redbrickinnutah.com.

Attractions and Recreation

BRIAN HEAD RESORT, 329 South UT-143, Brian Head. Open in winter and summer. Call 435-677-2035. Website: www.brianhead.com.

BRYCE CANYON NATIONAL PARK, P.O. Box 640201, Bryce Canyon. Day-use fee per vehicle (with an exception on certain government-determined days; see website); America the Beautiful pass accepted; additional fees for camping. Call 435-834-5322. Website: www.nps.gov/brca.

CEDAR BREAKS NATIONAL MONUMENT, intersection of UT-148 and UT-143, Brian Head. Entrance fee per individual visitor over the age of 16; America the Beautiful pass accepted. Call mid-June through mid-October 435-586-0787. Website: www.nps.gov/cebr.

KODACHROME BASIN STATE PARK, P.O. Box 180069, Cannonville. $8 day-use fee per vehicle; additional charges for camping. Call 435-679-8562. Website: www.stateparks.utah.gov/parks/kodachrome.

ROCKY POINT BOAT DOCK, Forest Service Road 080, Panguitch Lake. Rates vary per size of boat and length of rental (half- or full-day). Open in summer months only, weather depending. Call: 435-676-2205. Website: www.rockypointboatdock.com.

Other Contacts

BRYCE CANYON NATURAL HISTORY ASSOCIATION, P.O. Box 640051, Bryce. BCNHA is a nonprofit organization established in 1961 to assist with the scientific, educational, and interpretive activities within the park. Call 1-888-362-2646. Website: www.brycecanyon.org.

DIXIE NATIONAL FOREST. Presiding over the bulk of the land along this route. Call 435-826-5400. Website: www.fs.usda.gov/dixie.

GRAND STAIRCASE-ESCALANTE NATIONAL MONUMENT, Kanab Headquarters: 669 South UT-89A, Kanab. Call 435-644-1200. Website: www .blm.gov/programs/national-conservation-lands/utah/grand-staircase -escalante-national-monument.

NAL MORRIS, expert on Parowan Gap petroglyphs. Website: www.paro wangap.org.

PANGUITCH LAKE VISITOR GUIDE. Website: www.panguitchlake.com.

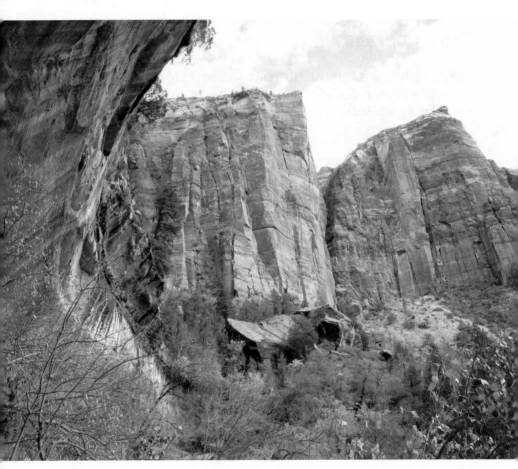

WEEPING ROCK

13

ST. GEORGE TO ZION NATIONAL PARK

ESTIMATED LENGTH: 50 miles each way

ESTIMATED TIME: A few hours with no hiking

HIGHLIGHTS: St. George is Utah's retirement community for a reason. Surrounded by beautiful red rock desert, it enjoys a nearness to Las Vegas, both in terms of distance and climate. Yet it has its own, much more conservative culture and small-town accouterments. In and around St. George are endless opportunities for recreation, from golf and biking, to hiking and climbing in **Snow Canyon State Park**.

Reaching **Zion National Park** takes less than an hour and, though it requires some travel on I-15, most of the drive takes place on relatively scenic, low-traffic highways. **Springdale**, just before Zion's west entrance, serves visitors with lodging, gear rentals, and restaurants. And Zion National Park is yet another of Utah's spectacular and unique geological phenomena. Carved by the **Virgin River**, this deep, narrow canyon has sheer sandstone walls sometimes in excess of 1,000 feet, towering above a pleasant, sandy, cottonwood-tree-lined canyon bottom.

GETTING THERE: St. George, Utah, sits at the far southwestern corner of the state, right on I-15, and just north of Arizona's Virgin River Gorge. St. George is just about 120 miles of interstate northeast of Las Vegas, and a very quick 300 I-15 miles south of Salt Lake City. Given speed limits between 75 and 80 miles per hour, the trip from Salt Lake City should take less than four hours.

Those coming up from the south on I-15 (and through the Virgin River Gorge) should be advised that this is an exceptional piece of freeway. Much windier that most, this very narrow canyon climbs quite steeply and twistily, with reduced speed limits for a reason. There is no cell phone service or gasoline in the gorge, so be sure to tank up on gas in Mesquite, Nevada, before attempting to ascend this stretch of road.

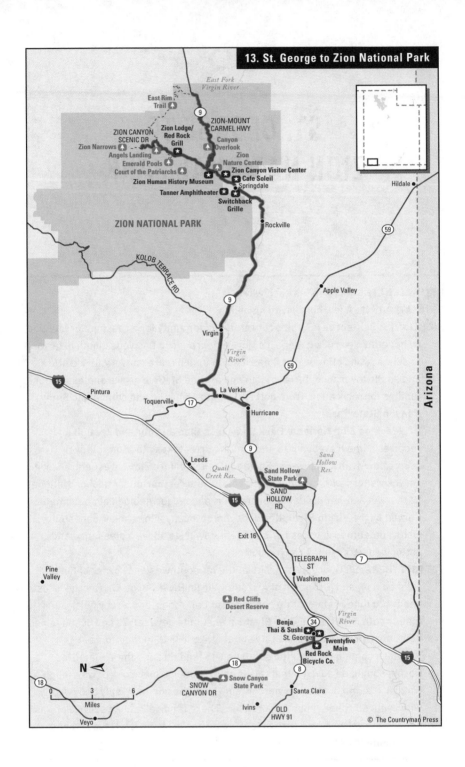

East Fork
Virgin River

East Rim
Trail

9

ZION-MOUNT
CARMEL HWY

ZION CANYON
SCENIC DR

Zion Lodge/
Red Rock
Grill

Canyon
Overlook

Zion Narrows

Zion
Nature Center

Angels Landing

Emerald Pools

Zion Canyon Visitor Center

Court of the Patriarchs

Cafe Soleil

Zion Human History Museum

Springdale

Hildale

Tanner Amphitheater

Switchback
Grille

ZION NATIONAL PARK

Rockville

59

KOLOB TERRACE RD

Apple Valley

9

15

Virgin

Virgin
River

59

Pintura

La Verkin

Toquerville

17

Hurricane

Leeds

Quail
Creek Res.

9

Sand
Hollow
Res.

Sand Hollow
State Park

SAND
HOLLOW
RD

15

Exit 16

TELEGRAPH
ST

7

Pine
Valley

Washington

Red Cliffs
Desert Reserve

Benja
Thai & Sushi

34

Virgin
River

St. George

Twentyfive
Main

Red Rock
Bicycle Co.

15

N

18

Snow Canyon
State Park

8

SNOW
CANYON DR

Santa Clara

0   3   6

Miles

Ivins

OLD
HWY 91

Veyo

Arizona

© The Countryman Press

Snow Canyon State Park

Those who haven't seen the famous Red Rock Canyon Scenic Drive (west of Las Vegas), and don't necessarily have the time to get there, should check out **Snow Canyon**. Though not technically a part of this chapter's drive, Snow Canyon is virtually in St. George and is therefore hardly out of the way.

Unlike many state parks around the nation, this is extremely well maintained and sparkly clean. Cozy in feel, it nevertheless offers some of St. George's best multipitch rock climbing, picnicking, hiking, biking, and camping. Roughly 18 miles of trail exist within the park so, though it's not an endless backpacking destination, it provides well more than a day's worth of exploration. The scenery is dominated by orange Kayenta and Navajo Sandstones topped with black basalt. Just about 7,500 acres, this park is actually a subsection of the more-than-62,000-acre Red Cliffs Desert Reserve.

St. George is the southwesternmost city in the state, barely within Utah's boundaries. Its nearest major attractions are **Zion National Park**, **Cedar Breaks National Monument**, **Brian Head Resort** and, a bit farther afield, **Bryce Canyon National Park**. Despite its nearness to these destinations, St. George is hardly a tourist town; it has a thriving local economy of its own, based largely in retirement, recreation, and construction. Headquartered here are SkyWest Airlines, Dixie State College, and a major hospital. Located precisely on I-15, which runs directly from Salt Lake City to Las Vegas, it is easily accessible. Yet, roughly 120 miles from Las Vegas and about 300 from Salt Lake City, it has an identity and character all its own.

Since the 1848 Mormon inception of Salt Lake City, this southern region of Utah has always had the name **"Utah's Dixie"** or just Dixie. The origins of this name are controversial in Utah's history. Many nostalgically reminisce that this nickname hails back to the region's early settlement as a cotton-farming outpost with warm climes; others believe that this handle alludes to the area's early LDS mission leader and the Mississippi plantation culture from he came. Historians now document that Robert Covington, appointed by the church to bring twenty-eight families south from Salt Lake City to settle this land, was a Confederate sympathizer and former slave driver that bragged of mistreatment and outright cruelty to the slaves he had once owned.

Regardless of Dixie's exact namesake, within a few years of establishing roots in Salt Lake City, the Mormons had already begun colonizing more widely in the region. By 1851, the first Dixie settlement in present-day Parowan, called the Iron Mission, had been established by a group of 168, led by Parley Pratt. By 1857, New Harmony, Santa Clara, and Washington (just north of, and touching, St. George) had all been settled. Dixie's roots were lain. Not a fly-by-the-seat-of-the-pants group, the Mormons calculated each

LEAVES IN VIRGIN RIVER SAND

new development, beginning each city with an organized infrastructure, including an irrigation plan and street layout. Since that time, all of these communities have fleshed out, and more have filled in around them.

In recent decades, the population of St. George and Washington County has been growing remarkably quickly. Between 1990 and 2000, it actually grew almost 1 percent more than Las Vegas, edging it out for fastest-growing metropolis in the United States for that period; and it earned the second-place title in 2005 (behind Greeley, Colorado). From 2000 to 2015, the population grew more than 60 percent to roughly 156,000 residents. Census Bureau experts have projected a population of more than 700,000 by 2050 if nothing changes between now and then.

Sand Hollow State Park

Yet another short detour, this little state park sits just south of UT-9. Historically it's been popular among ATVers, dirt bikers, and dune buggyers who ride its sand dunes. A reservoir attracts fishermen and seals the deal on its designation as a state park. Beaches and picnic areas make this family friendly. Utah's newest state park, this was dedicated in 2009. Open for day use and camping.

Tanner Amphitheater

Fire up the computer and take a look at this venue's online schedule. During the summer, this **Dixie State College** facility hosts many musicians in a fabulous open-air setting underneath the cliffs of **Zion Canyon**. Seating options include bench-style seats as well as chairs with backrests. Each show usually features two or more acts, and the stage lights up almost weekly during the summer. Be sure to check the weather, though; there is no covered seating, so any rain falling from the sky will land on the audience. There is an indoor backup hall, but the experience there is much less special than the open-air treat of the main stage.

For a tasty bite of fresh ingredients in generous portions, with plenty of flavor and salt to quench post-exercise cravings, what could be more fulfilling than a Thai/sushi/Asian-fusion combination restaurant? A bit pricier than peer restaurants in larger cities, **Benja Thai and Sushi** is located right in historic downtown, in Ancestor Square, among boutique shops and brick walkways. This popular eatery has been a St. George go-to for years.

If you are leaving town in the daytime and wishing for a quick lunch, coffee, or breakfast, stop in at **TwentyFive Main**—a fleshed-out, creative, espresso-serving café that dishes up breakfast, paninis, salad, pizza, and famous cupcakes. Each week has a set cupcake schedule, with different varieties being offered every week and multiple choices each day; check online for the schedule.

Mountain bikers should know that the roads between St. George and Zion are virtually crisscrossed by some of the state's best, most scenic bike trails—much more user-friendly than their slickrock counterparts near Moab. Additionally, the side roads themselves can make for a great on-pavement bike trip. Those planning to ride and needing to rent a bike might as well do it in St. George. **Red Rock Bicycle Co.** has a rental fleet with men's and women's options in both road and full-suspension mountain bike varieties. In addition to the rentals, there is a retail side with a full selection of accessories from tubes to pumps, sports foods, maps, and locks—even trunk and hitch racks for hire. Even people with all necessary bikes and accessories should consider a stop here to visit with the staff and get tips on the best, most suitable trail or road ride for the circumstances. The most famous rides are **Gooseberry Mesa**, **Hurricane Rim**, and **JEM**; **Snow Canyon State Park** has good riding, too. The first three (and the most noteworthy) are more or less right on the drive into Zion.

To leave St. George, simply get to I-15 and head north. Not long after entering the interstate, the route departs via Exit 16 to the well-signed UT-9. This route busts dead east to **Hurricane** at first, and then begins squiggling up through **La Verkin** and **Virgin** before coming to **Rockville** and eventually

Springdale. This final town directly abuts the western entrance of the park, just about 30 miles past I-15. Along the way, this fairly serious highway climbs slopes and dips into valleys as it approaches Zion. On this drive eastward, the area's many mountain bike trails can be picked up by way of side roads. Finding and following these trails is fairly intricate, so it's best done with a map and more detailed directions. One of the most popular means to find these trails (and others all across the state) is the free website www .utahmountainbiking.com. This long-standing, amazing resource offers mini-guides and route descriptions by region, supplemented with photos, videos, GPS coordinates, route lengths, and elevation gains. Based on personal experience, the descriptions can sometimes have errors, but keeping alert and following intuition can help you avoid derailment.

After heading through **Hurricane** (pronounced "Hurricun" by locals), UT-9 cuts across the desert, ascending quite distinctly in places as it gains higher benches. Approaching Rockville and Springdale, it winds along the Virgin River bottom, with cottonwood trees growing out of the red sands, and crumbling buttes on either side. **Rockville,** the last town before Springdale, has remained a quiet, residential town with little intention to forge a business in tourism. Its old-fashioned, genuine charm almost causes second-guesses as to whether Zion is actually ahead. Even the streetlights here are antiquated, with single bulbs hanging from wires suspended across the street.

Up next is **Springdale,** the obvious gateway to Zion, with restaurants, hotels, outdoors shops, and cafés galore—all dressed in desert, outdoorsy motifs. A few places stand out as worthy pit stops. For a quick pick-me-up, **Cafe Soleil** specializes in breakfast and lunch, but also serves lighter dinners. Equal parts restaurant and espresso bar, this café offers a generous selection of fresh, speedy eats. Breakfast can be light or hearty, with options in pastries, frittatas, sandwiches, and burritos. Lunchtime comes with wraps, paninis, gyros, pizza, and smoothies. Dine in or outside, or take a boxed lunch to go. If you are lucky, you may even catch live music there one evening.

For a hearty yet gourmet dinner (or breakfast or lunch), try the **Switchback Grille.** Serving American and Continental cuisine, this particular establishment stands out for its fresh seafood, USDA Prime beef, wild game, wood-fired specialty pizzas, and free-range poultry. They even offer a cigar menu. A family-friendly place, it also has a children's menu. Located within the same facility is Jack's Sports Grill, an all-ages establishment with a much more casual menu featuring appetizers, burgers, sandwiches, chili, Mexican food, steaks, and breakfast served all day.

Heading east out of Springdale leads immediately to the west gate of **Zion National Park.** Carved by the **Virgin River, Zion Canyon** has been visited by people as far back as 8,000 years ago. The ancestral Pueblo, the Anasazi, came to be the first human residents in the area roughly around 6000 BC. Small family groups of these seminomadic, basket-making people lived in

Angels Landing

Looking around the canyon, it's clear that these sandstone walls are absolutely sheer. Closer inspection also reveals cracks and other weaknesses running the entire height of many of these faces. Therefore, these cliffs are popular among rock climbers, both aid climbers and free climbers alike. What's the difference? Aid climbers actually pull gear to ascend the rock; free climbers ascend the rock purely by their own power, using gear and ropes only to catch themselves in the event of a hypothetical fall. (*Free climbing* is a term often improperly used for "free soloing"; free soloing is when climbers ascend the rock without any gear whatsoever, meaning that they lack protection in the event of a fall.) Both free climbers and aid climbers use stoppers and cams, but aid climbers also use hooks and any other device that can hold weight but will likely not protect them in case of a fall.

AUTHOR WITH
CLIMBING GEAR

That said, the vast majority of people don't have the interest or technical skills required to climb these walls. Fret not, though. Reasonably fit persons can access virtually the same head-spinning exposure simply by hiking the nontechnical **Angels Landing Trail**. This feature, located right in the "pinch" of the river's biggest bend, is a peninsula of vertical sandstone walls. To ascend Angels Landing, this built-up trail makes many switchbacks, and is augmented by steps, chain handrails, and the like. So, even though it's technically just a walking trail, it provides phenomenal excitement.

(In the event of snowy or icy conditions, be sure to avoid the last, highly exposed portion of this trail. Short sections of trail flanked by sheer drop-offs and unprotected by handrails could prove lethal in slippery or stormy conditions. When in doubt, ask a ranger or fellow hikers, or simply turn around.)

the valley and traveled with the seasons to find food and livable climates. A subsequent group, the Parowan Fremont, lived there as well, but left around AD 1300, to be replaced by a completely separate group, the Southern Paiute. They arrived completely independently of their predecessors, and were the last residents of the canyon before the Mormon arrival to the area. In 1858, Mormon Euro-Americans first saw the area, led by a Southern Paiute guide.

A few years would pass after Zion's "discovery" before Mormons would actually settle here. In 1865, Isaac Behunin began farming corn, cotton, and tobacco in Zion Canyon proper. He and his family spent summers in the canyon (near the modern Zion Lodge), and would winter in a broader section of the canyon, where Springdale is today. Already by 1909, the land was recognized as special and designated as the **Mukuntuweap National Monument** by President William Howard Taft. "Mukuntuweap" was its first European given name, when Major John Wesley Powell dubbed it that during his 1872 visit, thinking it was its Paiute name. In 1916, though, the name was changed to Zion, as its original name was unpopular among local Mormons. On November 19, 1919, it was officially established as **Zion National Park**.

Over time, Zion has become the most popular park in Utah—more visited than Bryce Canyon, Arches, Capitol Reef, and Canyonlands National Parks, and Monument Valley Navajo Tribal Park; it receives almost 3.7 million visitors a year, a figure that keeps climbing. To put this in perspective, Yosemite National Park, one of the nation's most famous and celebrated parks, gets just around 4.1 million visitors a year—almost as many as Zion!

Due to the enclosed nature of Zion and its limited roadways, the Park Service initiated a free shuttle system in 2000. These buses run between April and October every year and are the mandatory means for transport within the park during that time. Arriving frequently and stopping at many places throughout the park, they actually seem to be an asset rather than a hassle, as they eliminate traffic jams and allow visitors to rubberneck without having to focus on the road. In the off-season, buses still run, though less frequently. If visiting during peak season, keep your eyes peeled, starting in Springdale, for shuttle bus stops and associated parking areas. As most visitors are not local, the stops have been deliberately made readily visible and hard to miss.

One of the first points of interest inside the park is hardly past the fee station, reached by following the first right-hand spur. This is the **visitor center**. Interesting in its own way, this architectural gem has been cleverly designed to have the least environmental impact possible. Operating almost purely on just natural light and solar power, its heating and cooling tasks are accomplished with deliberately angled windows, cooling towers, and wall aspect and placement. Anyone interested can read up on it on plaques surrounding and adorning the building. Also at this site is the **Zion Canyon Wilderness Desk**, which doles out permits to backpackers, rock climbers, and generally anyone who wishes to spend the night out and away from the main, pay campsites.

Right on this first turnoff is the **Watchman Campground**, one of only two in-park Zion Canyon camping areas. The other is **South Campground**, accessed just a bit farther along the main drive (also to the east of the road). The South Campground driveway also serves as the access to the **Zion Nature Center**. Largely a curriculum-based organization, this center serves to educate mostly elementary school groups on the goings-on of Zion Canyon and on nature as a whole. A word of warning: Zion's campgrounds fill up virtually every night between the middle of March and November; the first-come, first-served spots at South Campground usually disappear by lunchtime. If you'd like to be guaranteed a site, be sure to make a reservation (weeks or even months) in advance at Watchman Campground.

The next stop back on the main road (and to the left) is the **Zion Human History Museum**, opened in 2002. For those interested, this offers some visual displays and explanations of the various human groups who have lived in and been affected by Zion. A free, short film narrates this story. Permanent and traveling displays of artifacts, photographs, writings, and replicas illustrate the roughly eight thousand years of the park's human habitation—from prehistory to Mormon "discovery" and its modern existence as a popular national park. At no cost, this is a fully worthwhile stop.

The park's road system is quite simple, but soon it forks into two separate branches. One option heads to the north; the other goes east. Both are more fully described below. The first, a continuation of the **Zion Canyon Scenic Drive**, heads up through the Angels Landing area and eventually to the famous Zion Narrows. The second, the **Zion-Mount Carmel Highway**, passes through the famous **Zion Tunnel** that, as part of a massive public works project, allowed this road to connect to the eastern end of the park. Opened in 1930, the tunnel was then the longest of its kind in the United States. Outside of the tunnel, this highway makes many switchbacks along the way past the **Canyon Overlook Trail** and toward the eastern entrance for the park.

ZION-MOUNT CARMEL HIGHWAY

Heading east along the **Zion-Mount Carmel Highway** leads quickly to the famous Zion Tunnel (in which no bike traffic is allowed). In the 1920s, the Park Service felt the increasing need to connect Springdale to the eastern end of the park; at that time, to reach Mount Carmel (the town) or any of the surrounding villages, drivers had to circumvent the park in a big way. Either to the south or to the north, it took hours of circuitous navigation to reach the town of Mount Carmel. Zion Tunnel, 1.1 miles in length, went into construction in the mid-1920s, and was finally completed in 1930. The opening up of this eastern passageway also renders Zion National Park a much

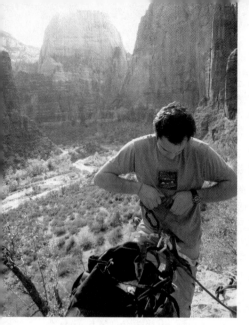

BENEATH MOONLIGHT BUTTRESS, 9 PITCHES

easier stop on the tour of southern Utah's other national parks like Bryce Canyon and Canyonlands.

Along this road is the **Canyon Overlook Trail**. This short trail, just half a mile each way, climbs a good bit to reach generous views of **Zion and Pine Creek Canyons**. Topping out just above the Great Arch, hikers on this trail cannot actually see this feature from the overlook. Beyond that, and just before the **east entrance**, the **East Rim Trail** departs to the north, lacing around the **White Cliffs** and heading toward the northern end of the park, splitting into various trails after **Stave Spring** (for these options, it is best to refer to a detailed topographical map or a Utah gazetteer).

ZION CANYON SCENIC DRIVE

To continue north and head toward Angels Landing and the Narrows, drivers must turn left. About a mile north of the junction is the **Court of the Patriarchs** pullout, to the right. These "patriarchs," visible across the road (to the west), form an alcove of monstrous monoliths. They are also religiously named: Abraham, Isaac, and Jacob.

The next stop, on the right-hand side of the road, is the **Zion Lodge**. This historic structure houses the only in-park indoor lodging. Open all year, this hotel offers a selection of rooms, suites, and cabins. Also at the lodge is a gift shop and restaurant. Reservations are highly recommended for peak-season visits.

Speaking of this restaurant, it goes by the name of the **Red Rock Grill**. This eatery takes advantage of regional flavor and flare to embellish a bit on American cuisine. Fresh trout and sea fish, steaks, poultry, pasta, and the like, done well. The restaurant takes steps to maintain environmental responsibility, such as indicating items made with sustainable ingredients on its menu, not automatically serving water, and selecting local or farm co-op meats and certified sustainable fish when possible. Like the lodge, the restaurant remains open year-round, and serves breakfast, lunch, and dinner. Dinner reservations are required!

Across the river from the Zion Lodge, trails depart to the **Emerald Pools**.

Naturally set up for any level of fitness and agility, these three tiered pools can be reached by hikes of increasing distance and elevation gain—from the lower to the middle and finally to the upper pool. The higher the trail climbs, the more rugged and steep it becomes—though it is still easily passable by able bodies. Though the stream that flows between the pools is not always running, the pools themselves always contain water, and the mossy, jungle-like environment they create in the desert is quite (literally) cool.

Though Angels Landing hasn't been visible from the roadside yet, the famous trail departing to this formation begins at the **Grotto**, just half a mile up the road from the Zion Lodge. To access this hike, cross the Virgin River at the footbridge there and head north on the **West Rim Trail**. Prepare for some remarkable exposure and thrills on the way up! No simple footpath, this is rather a highly developed and reinforced construction with guard chains, cut steps, handrails, and switchbacks. This particular trail is to be avoided in bad weather, particularly in high winds, snowy conditions, or thunderstorms. But any rain also renders the path slippery, which can be dangerous with these kinds of drop-offs.

As the road continues to the north, be on the lookout for rock climbers ascending the canyon walls—particularly where the Virgin River enters an S-curve in the Angels Landing vicinity. This has some of the park's highest concentration of climbs, from single-pitch to dozen-plus-pitch routes. One of the more famous (and easily recognizable) climbs, called **Moonlight Buttress**, ascends a very sheer, smooth pillar on the other side of the river, just northwest of the second bus stop in the S-curves. This was free-soloed (i.e., climbed with no rope or gear for protection) in 2008 by a professional climber.

The final stop is at the very terminus of this road (and the driving route). Those who wish to extend the journey a bit may do so on foot by hiking into the **Zion Narrows**, where Zion Canyon pinches down to a size much too small to be shared by the road and river. Though a popular hike, it is certainly not a trail; this route follows the actual Virgin River. That said, this is best hiked in late summer or fall, when the temperatures are still warm but the water is low. A sturdy strap-on sandal is the best footwear, as usually about half of the journey involves wading or even swimming. (Given the sandy nature of this trail, be cognizant of your foot skin. It wouldn't hurt to bring along some blister care supplies, as well.) About 16 miles of river can be walked before the canyon becomes no longer passable. Just as Angels Landing provides great exposure to nonclimbers, this provides a semi-slot-canyon experience for noncanyoneers; along the way, walls can be as high as 2,000 feet, with the canyon floor as narrow as 30 feet. It is extremely important to avoid this hike if there is any precipitation in the area, even out of sight; storms upstream can cause flash flooding totally inescapable in such a narrow, sheer-walled canyon. Inquire with the park rangers at the visitor center if there is any doubt.

To return to the St. George area, simply head back exactly as you came. But to continue on and check out more drives or national parks, head east out of the park on the **Zion-Mount Carmel Highway**. In **Mount Carmel** (just outside of the park), UT-9 joins with US-89. This road heads north and from here, it is possible to join up with chapter 12's drive (Parowan to Escalante), and then farther on, chapter 11's drive (Escalante to Capitol Reef), and beyond.

IN THE AREA

Accommodations

ZION LODGE, about 2 miles north of the park's Springdale entrance, on Zion Canyon Scenic Drive. Pricey. Guest rooms, suites, and cabins available; reservations highly encouraged. Call 435-772-7700 or 1-888-297-2757. Website: www.zionlodge.com.

Attractions and Recreation

SAND HOLLOW STATE PARK, 4405 West 3600 South, Hurricane. $10 admission and varied camping fees. Day use approximately restricted to sunlight hours. Call 435-680-0715. Website: www.stateparks.utah.gov/parks /sand-hollow/.

SNOW CANYON STATE PARK, 11 miles west of St. George by way of Bluff Street, 3.5 miles farther west on Snow Canyon Parkway, and then a signed right for Snow Canyon Drive. Open daily, year-round; no holiday closures. $6 daily admission fee for cars; $4 for pedestrians/cyclists. Call 435-628-2255. Website: www.stateparks.utah.gov/parks/snow-canyon/.

TANNER AMPHITHEATER, west end of Lion Avenue, Springdale. Outdoor venue with no rain cover; mixed benches and seats with backrests. Call the Dixie State University Box Office at 435-652-7800. Website: www .octannershows.com.

ZION HUMAN HISTORY MUSEUM, 0.5 mile into Zion National Park, on the west side of the Zion Canyon Scenic Drive. Call 435-772-0146.

ZION NATIONAL PARK, Springdale. Call 435-772-3256. Website: www.nps .gov/zion.

Dining

BENJA THAI AND SUSHI, Ancestor Square, 2 West St. George Boulevard, St. George. Cheap to moderately priced. Serving Thai and sushi. Open Monday through Saturday for dinner; closed Sundays. Call 435-628-9538. Website: www.benjathai.com.

CAFE SOLEIL, 205 Zion Park Boulevard, Springdale. Very affordable. Open daily for breakfast, lunch, and dinner. Call 435-772-0505. Website: www.cafesoleilzionpark.com.

RED ROCK GRILL, in the Zion Lodge, about 2 miles north of the park's Springdale entrance, on Zion Canyon Scenic Drive. Moderately priced. American cuisine with regional ingredients and flare. Reservations required for dinner; open year-round, three meals a day. Call 435-772-3700. Website: www.zionlodge.com.

SWITCHBACK GRILLE AND JACK'S SPORTS GRILL, 1149 South Zion Park Boulevard, Springdale. The Grille is appropriately pricey. American and Continental cuisine. Open for dinner only. Kids menu offered. Dinner reservations encouraged. Jack's is much less spendy and much more casual; no reservations required. Open for lunch and dinner. Days of operation for both facilities vary per season. Call 435-772-3700. Website: www.switchbackgrille.com.

TWENTYFIVE MAIN, 25 North Main Street, St. George. Serving breakfast, espresso, paninis, salad, pasta, pizza, and famous cupcakes. Very affordable. No reservations required. Call 435-628-7110. Website: www.25main.com.

Other Contacts

RED ROCK BICYCLE CO., 446 West 100 South, St. George. Open daily, with shortened hours on Sunday. Road and mountain bike rentals and retail. Call 435-674-3185. Website: www.redrockbicycle.com.

UTAHMOUNTAINBIKING.COM. Free mini-guides and route descriptions with photos, GPS coordinates, ride lengths, elevation gains, and more.

14

WEST DESERT

Delta to Great Basin National Park

ESTIMATED LENGTH: 105 miles (each way)

ESTIMATED TIME: A short half day; a full day with return trip

HIGHLIGHTS: An utterly desolate and lonely stretch of highway, US-6 and US-50 stretches from Utah's main north–south corridor, I-15, though the forgotten West Desert and into Nevada. With views utterly uninterrupted by civilization, this landscape of dry lake beds and alternating rugged peaks has an otherworldly feel. Ending at **Great Basin National Park**—just on the other side of the Utah-Nevada border—this route provides a peek at the geologically unique **Great Basin** and a chance to imagine what Utah was like before it was irrigated and paved.

GETTING THERE: Delta sits just 30 miles west of I-15 as the crow flies. If coming from the north, take UT-32 south from Nephi, linking up with US-6. Southern arrivals should depart from I-15 in Holden, heading northwest on US-50.

Unlike most townships in Utah, **Delta** wasn't settled until after 1900—and also unlike most townships, it came about as a result of agriculture being brought to the area, and not by colonizing efforts of the LDS Church. Alfalfa farming was already in full swing nearby to the east, fed by the **Sevier River** running through the valley between the **Wasatch Plateau** and the **Pahvant Range**. A group of thirty-four local entrepreneurs became interested in the potential farming opportunities to the west and organized themselves in the effort of diverting water from the Sevier River westward.

A site was selected for the township in 1906, and settlers began laying roots. Tracts of land 320 acres each were doled out under the provision that

LEFT: VIEW SOUTHEAST FROM THE SHOULDER OF NOTCH PEAK

14. West Desert: Delta to Great Basin National Park

6
125

Ashton
Burger Barn ⭐ Delta
El Jalisciense ⭐ ⭐ Great Basin Museum
Taco Shop
Woodrow ● Oasis
● Deseret
Hinckley ●
257
⭐ Fort
Deseret
Abraham ●
● Clear Lake

⭐ Gunnison Massacre
Monument

6
257
Sevier
River
Cricket Mountains
Black Rock ●

Telescope ⭐
Array Project

Sevier Lake
(dry)

NOTCH PEAK
LOOP RD
6
Sawtooth
Canyon
House Range
Skull Rock
Pass
Topus
Mountain

◆ Notch Peak
Trailhead
Stinson's ⭐ ◆ Marjum
cliff dwelling Canyon
Ibex
Wells
Tule Valley
Hardpan
✛ Notch
Peak

Tule Valley

Confusion Range

6

Eskdale ●
21
Gandy ●
Snake Valley Garrison ●
159
Nevada
487

⭐ Baker Archaeological Site
● Baker
488
Lehman
Caves
GREAT BASIN
NATIONAL PARK
WHEELER PEAK
SCENIC DR
N ◄
Snake Range
0 5 10
6
✛ Wheeler
Peak
Miles

© The Countryman Press

No Services Next 100 Miles

Before leaving town, tank up the car; roughly 100 miles of civilization-barren pavement stretches from Delta to **Baker, Nevada**, just north of Great Basin National Park. It'd be a strange day when someone else didn't drive by, but, having actually had car problems on this road myself, I can say that it might be a while before a ride back into town avails. Also know that most things in rural Utah don't open on Sunday, including mechanic shops.

they become irrigated within a 3-year time period. A diversion dam was built, financed by stockholders, and interested families began moving in.

By the 1920s, Delta was one of the largest alfalfa producers in the nation and had erected a sugar factory as well. Accompanying businesses were founded, and people continued arriving by way of the nearby railroad. The town weathered the Great Depression quite well; its cattle ranching industry even grew during this time. Mining of fluorspar was added to the list of commerce. Also called fluorite, this mineral has a variety of uses and, depending on the grade, can be used in smelting metals, reducing chromatic aberration in lenses, and in the production of hydrofluoric acid.

Despite all this, present-day Delta has few amenities to offer the passerby. For eats, there is a collection of fast food dispensaries, convenience stores, and one supermarket. For something different, **El Jalisciense Taco Shop** is Delta's coolest local restaurant. Starting very early each day (5:30 AM!—except on Sundays, when they open at 7 AM), they dish up classic American and Mexican breakfasts; in the evening, out come the tacos, *mariscos*, enchiladas, and combination platters. If you feel in the mood for a burger or brat, try **Ashton Burger Barn**. They offer a variety of burgers, sausages, hot and cold sandwiches, and other dishes. A kids menu is offered, as well as a salad list. And they have free Wi-Fi all day.

Also in Delta, the **Great Basin Museum** is a small-town affair, but one that details some of the unobvious tidbits of information on the area. Worth a stop, as there is no charge (however, donations are appreciated). On display are fossils, geological specimens, and human history artifacts dating from prehistory to early settlers, all illustrated with local photographs and writing. Also featured in the museum is a darker chapter in the country's history, the **World War II Topaz Relocation Center** (also called the Central Utah Relocation Center). Here 8,500 Japanese Americans, largely hailing from the San Francisco area, were detained from 1942 through 1946. The museum holds various vestiges from this camp.

Heading out of Delta, drive west right on Main Street (also US-6 and US-50). The road goes through the even smaller township of **Hinckley**. Take a quick

John W. Gunnison Massacre

In the fall of 1853, John W. Gunnison was appointed leader of an exploratory mission to the west-central part of Utah. His team's duty was to survey the region, making topographical maps and gathering data on plant and animal life and geology. Gunnison, an army engineer and West Point alumnus, knew Utah well and was quite fit to lead this team. Totaling eleven men, this group included a botanist, a topographer, an artist, a guide, and more.

This research journey, however, found itself in the heat of the **Walker War**, named for the ongoing battles and skirmishes involving Chief Wakara of a band of Utes, the Pahvant Indians. In light of this, the Gunnison group had been warned that the natives might be hostile. Having traveled past **Fillmore**, they reached a point along the Sevier River, just southwest of present-day Delta, and set up camp. At night, a troop of what appeared to be thirty Pahvant warriors descended on this group, killing all but four men.

However, this story is not as simple as it sounds. Martha Gunnison, widow of Captain John Gunnison, believed that the attackers were not Utes of any kind. Rather, she maintained that the attack was carried out by a group of militant Mormons, the **Danites** (see sidebar, page 198). She believed this order was given by Brigham Young, Utah's chief for the Bureau of Indian Affairs, who is alleged to have feared the advent of the **Transcontinental Railroad**, lest it deliver more non-Mormon settlers to the area.

Martha wrote to Utah's Federal Supreme Court appointee, Justice W. W. Drummond, who agreed with her based on witness and informant testimonies and depositions. Accounts by Pahvants and white settlers alike convinced Drummond that Mormons dressed as Indians had attacked this group. Brigham Young arrested the alleged Ute attackers but never punished them. It is said that Brigham Young cut a deal with the Indians, paying them to take the blame for the crime. Of course, intervening time, deceased witnesses, and lack of records render this all hearsay. At this point, nothing can be proven, and there are many conflicting and divergent stories on record.

Today a place marker stands at the site of the massacre, located south of US-6 and US-50 on an unmarked road. To get there, take a left and head south on the first road (less than a mile) west of the intersection of 2500 South and US-6/US-50, just out of Hinckley. The monument is located along the Sevier River at the end of this roughly 2-mile road. Looking at a map will clarify these directions.

detour to the south on UT-257 to **Fort Deseret**, located near mile marker 65 (on the southern end of Hinckley and about 5 miles south of Delta; located right off the highway). In 1865, during the Black Hawk War, this fort was built by almost 100 men, for the purpose of protecting white settlers in the region from Indians. As the US government was quite involved in the Civil War at the time, this was conceived of and erected by Mormons.

Opened after just 18 days of construction, this 550-square-foot structure with 10-foot-high walls successfully protected the area's people and livestock when Chief Black Hawk arrived in the spring of 1866—a time of predicted hostility. After the threat passed, this structure's function shifted to a cattle pen. What remains today is a fairly large adobe structure whose gun ports are still in place in the outer walls.

Back on the main route (US-6 and US-50), resume the westward drive. Check for rations and fuel, as Hinckley truly is the last bit of civilization until

Space!

W hile driving into the desert, keep scanning to the left and the right for what looks like misplaced double beds in the desert. This "furniture" is actually part of a multimillion-dollar international undertaking called the **Telescope Array**, a collaborative project among institutions and universities in Japan, Russia, Korea, Taiwan, China, and the United States. The experiment is designed to study cosmic rays, which are high-energy particles entering the earth's atmosphere from space. Cosmic rays originate from events on our own sun, as well as from other, still-unknown happenings in the far reaches of the universe. Until the advent of nuclear testing in the 1950s, cosmic rays had maintained a constant level of carbon 14 (used in carbon dating) in the earth's atmosphere. The rays have a number of effects on the earth's atmospheric composition, as well as provide data from which physicists can calculate the inner workings and histories of the stars that created them. Because of this, cosmic rays have been the subject of many studies worldwide since their discovery by Victor Hess in 1912 (who later won the Nobel Prize in Physics in 1936 for his discovery of cosmic radiation).

The Telescope Array Project aims to measure these high-energy particles, and its observation field is set up in none other than Millard County, Utah. Some 576 particle counters (the bedlike objects on either side of the road) have been placed in a 1.2-km-square array. Three telescopes look out into space from the grid. Together these are used to gather the most information possible about these particles—electron, positron, muon, and more—entering the atmosphere. The telescopes can "see" the fluorescence created by the particles entering the air; the counters observe the showers' footprints.

A small office in Delta (right on the northern side of US-6) is the local headquarters and research facility for this project, where faculty and graduate students from the participating nations process data and maintain the particle counters. Plans to create a much larger observatory in Delta are in progress—but meanwhile, visitors are encouraged by project supervisors to stop in and check out the work behind the scenes.

APPROACHING THE HOUSE RANGE FROM THE EAST

about 13 miles into Nevada. Not only will there be no gas stations, but there will also be patchier and patchier cell service until there is none at all; if off the main highway, do not expect any type of phone to work, save for a satellite phone. Once you leave the trees and green lawns of town, the landscape quickly becomes more moon-like. The first mountain range you pass is the **Cricket Mountains**, on the southern side of the road. Beyond this gateway sits **Sevier Lake**, completely dry—though a mirage often makes it appear to be full of water. Situated between the Cricket Mountains and the **House Range** (to the west), this massive lake has actually been full recently enough to have been witnessed by early settlers—who claimed it supplied water for their farms, as well as for the indigenous Pahvant Indians.

The **House Range**, which runs north–south on both sides of the road, is impressively large—yet bizarre in appearance because of the very sparse vegetation that speckles it. Scattered throughout the hills are old mines, completely invisible from the road. This range has a fair bit of quirky history owing to its mining, hermit, and shepherd activity over the years. It also includes **Notch Peak**, famous for its northwest limestone face, which has one of the tallest sheer cliffs in the nation at roughly 3,000 feet high. The peak has an elevation of 9,654 feet, so in total it stands roughly 4,400 feet taller than **Tule Valley**, below.

While a dozen or so technical routes ascend the cliff face of Notch Peak, nonclimbers can enjoy the mountain as well. Just past Sevier Lake's westernmost ledge, look for **Notch Peak Loop Road** to the north. This may or may not be signed; anyone planning to visit the backcountry in this area should bring as detailed a map as possible, with a gazetteer being the minimum standard in detail. Indeed a loop, this road heads north, eventually turning west, and then south again to return to US-6 and US-50. However, this is where the map comes in handy: This "loop" is hardly a clean, well-signed route. Many, many roads head in and out of the desert, and few are signed. Firsthand experience confirms this.

Surprisingly, the nontechnical hike to **Notch Peak**'s summit takes just a few hours, and the views from atop the cliff give flight to everyone's stomach butterflies. Nearly a mile of airspace beneath one's feet is quite dizzying. To get there, take this eastern portion of Notch Peak Loop Road, heading west toward **Sawtooth Canyon**. Park where the road becomes impassable, and begin by walking up a dirt road. In about half a mile, follow the fork to the left, and follow gulches and the mountain shoulder until you reach

Crotalus Oreganus Lutosus

Common name: **Great Basin rattlesnake.** When hiking, be aware that this subspecies of western rattlesnake makes its home in western Utah. It lives in grasslands, desert, and forest. Though it typically hangs out on the ground, it will occasionally climb a bush or tree. Fortunately, these snakes prefer to avoid humans, eating mainly smaller dishes like birds, lizards, and mice. They hibernate during the cold months in sheltered areas: small holes and dens. In spring, they begin emerging, seeking sunlight to warm their cold-blooded bodies.

Typically they reach a maximum length of 3 or more feet and have, much like the dry desert dirt, light gray or yellowish tan skin with darker oval spots on their backs, as well as a viper head (the jaw of which is significantly wider than the body). Though these aid with recognition, the tail's rattle is the number-one clue. When threatened, these snakes coil up and shake their tails quite rapidly, sounding like a baby's rattle on overdrive. They prefer not to encounter people, but when forced they will strike, injecting a potent venom especially undesirable to have in the body whilst in the backcountry. Medical experts often disagree with respect to the best means of field care for a bite victim. But if you do plan to explore the Utah desert, it is advised that you do some research ahead of time and develop a plan for what you will do to help yourself or your companions in the unlucky event of a bite.

the top of Notch Peak from a southeasterly direction. Once at the top, those brave enough can peek over the edge and spot rock climbing anchors at the top of the face. Again, a detailed map will be extremely useful in the entire off-pavement undertaking, as no roads off US-6 and US-50 are paved, few are signed, and there are no official trails.

Instead of taking the entire Notch Peak Loop, those on the driving detour should turn west (south of the loop's apex) and enter **Marjum Canyon**. Heading into this gap is entering into superb solitude. Imagine living here alone for twenty years, as a man named Bob Stinson did from the mid-1920s until 1946. Back in those days, US-6 and US-50 did not exist, and Marjum Pass was the only option for east–west travel through the area. After his service in World War I, legend has it that Stinson returned to Delta to find that his wife had married another man. Destroyed, he moved to the canyon, found a natural spring, and built a small cliff dwelling—which is still largely intact today. He used the spring water to keep a garden and even make moonshine. Here he worked maintaining the road, clearing rockslides, and keeping travelers company. Eventually US-6 and US-50 was built and Stinson, now out of work, moved back to Delta. This road's surface is made up almost entirely of coarse, sharp limestone rocks and should be taken slowly.

To the south of Notch Peak, across US-6 and US-50, extends **Tule Valley**. To access this region, keep an eye out for a left-hand turnoff just west of **Skull Rock Pass**. As with most other parts of this "anarchy land," Tule Valley can be accessed via numerous dirt roads, but the main turnoff is the first in this case. A few miles of southern travel on this bring explorers to the eastern edge of a dried-up lake bed. Much smaller than Sevier Lake, this hardpan still stretches more than 5 miles north to south, and more than a mile east to west.

Driving west across the hardpan leads to the central camping area for what is known as **Ibex Wells**. Completely rugged camping, this valley has absolutely no amenities, rangers, fees, or seemingly laws. A fantastically beautiful lunar landscape, this area also features nationally famous bouldering and some multipitch sport and traditional rock climbing routes. Quartzite, the rock type here, is incredibly compact and strangely aesthetic—globular and splotchy. Of course, quartz, found in quartzite, is a valuable mineral with numerous uses. Farther south is **Topus Mountain**, where a massive quartz mining operation is underway. As recently as 15 years ago, this mountain was fully intact; today this is obviously no longer the case. Do *not* drive across this or any hardpan if it is raining, has rained (even remotely) recently, or will rain. This surface may look dry, but it can hide vehicle-eating mud underneath it. If there is any significant moisture, any car will become stuck and require an expensive extraction by military vehicle.

The last major mountains standing before Nevada belong to the **Confusion Range**, running parallel to, and immediately west of, the House Range.

VIEW INTO THE CHASM IN FRONT OF NOTCH PEAK'S CLIFFS

Danites

Formed in **Far West, Missouri**, in June 1838—about ten years before the Mormons would even arrive in Utah—the **Danites** were a vigilante fraternal group of Latter-day Saints. At this time, Far West (in present-day Caldwell County) was the headquarters of the Mormon Church. Joseph Smith preached that nearby Jackson County was actually the Garden of Eden, and when Adam and Eve were banished, they came to Caldwell County.

The peace wouldn't last long here for Smith and his group. Just like at every stop along the way, the Mormons found conflict with their neighbors. In the early summer of 1838, several escalating skirmishes took place between Missourians and Mormons. That June, the Danites formed as a secret society and were the key force in the Mormon-instigated attacks. In reaction, the Missouri governor commissioned a 2,500-man army to end the Mormon rebellion. In October the Mormons surrendered and were forced to leave the state.

However, the end of the **1838 Mormon War** did not end militias in the Latter-day Saints. Other bodyguards of church leaders and protective armies were given different names, such as Avenging Angels. But many historians believe that this secret brotherhood in fact moved westward with the church, carrying out cruel attacks on groups the Mormons disliked.

As in the House Mountains, a large network of wild roads trace the areas of the range that are topographically possible to drive. Numerous small sets of hills, valleys, and deserts lie farther west toward Nevada. **Snake Valley** is the largest of these, straddling the Nevada border.

Cross over this line, into Nevada, drive another 3 miles, and head south toward Baker on NV-487, about 5 miles farther along. About a mile before town, look for signs indicating the **Baker Archaeological Site**. Excavated in the early 1990s, this **Fremont Indian village** is roughly nine hundred years old. A collection of pit houses and adobe buildings—fifteen in total—has stored clues for researchers. Here the story told is that of a people who gathered and stored local vegetables, traded minerals and stones with other groups, and possibly even irrigated for agriculture.

The village has an organized, well-planned layout uncharacteristic of most Fremont settlements. Unfortunately for viewers today, the sites have been refilled with the same dirt that was excavated, in order to preserve the structures' remains for posterity and future studies. Markers have been placed on top of the covered buildings to suggest their subterranean layout. Recovered artifacts are now held at the Brigham Young University Office of Public Archeology Museum in Provo.

From here, drive just over a mile into **Baker**. This town sits in White Pine County and has fewer than seventy residents. This settlement grew up out of ranching, beginning in the 1870s. Today this town serves primarily as the gate to Great Basin National Park; the businesses are small, often kitschy, and have seasonal hours. Baker has a limited selection of basic hotels.

Great Basin National Park definitely stands apart from the other ranges on this drive—looking almost like a misplaced Glacier National Park. Huge mountains rise dominantly from the valley floor out of the dry desert, into evergreen forest, and finally out of vegetation altogether, with exposed, rocky peaks. A vertical transition of several thousand feet accomplishes more than a thousand miles' worth of travel—from Nevada desert to Idaho-looking forests to Canadian Rockies peaks. Massive cirques are adorned with sheer, towering cliffs, steep talus fields (atop which often lie snowfields), forests, and lakes. Marked by immense girth and spectacular vertical relief, these mountains rise from the valleys below, more than 1.5 vertical miles, to a maximum height of 13,063 feet at **Wheeler Peak**.

Though the rock shares similar origins to that which makes up the House and Confusion Ranges, it has here been sculpted into massive turrets and horns—a striking view above the green forests. In addition to spectacular mountain scenery, this park is the location of caves and natural arches. Here also grow bristlecone pines, some still living at more than five thousand years of age.

To get inside the park, take NV-486 west from Baker. This main road leads directly to the **Lehman Caves** less than a mile beyond the park border. These caves may only be entered on a guided tour. Visitors may choose between two different tours (the **Lodge Room** or **Grand Palace** options); each occurs multiple times a day, with eleven total daily tours in summer and four total daily tours in winter. Cave temperature remains constant at 50°F, so dress accordingly. Tickets are priced per person per tour (with varying rates) and can be purchased in person or in advance by calling the park (Monday through Friday only).

After the cave, retrace the drive just a few hundred yards and head northwest on the 12-mile **Wheeler Peak Scenic Drive**. Topping out at more than 10,000 feet above sea level, this road tours up and out of the dry, inhospitable desert into an island of abundant plant and animal life. Rising from about 7,000 feet above sea level at the park boundary, it passes through sagebrush, pinyon pine, and curl-leaf mountain mahogany, and into evergreens like ponderosa pine and Douglas fir—not unlike those in the forests of Montana—and finally up into aspen groves at an elevation of 10,000 feet.

Such a dramatic elevation rise causes rapidly cooling temperatures, with plant populations changing completely in as little as 500 vertical feet ascension. Climes found higher select different species into existence and allow moisture to remain in the soil longer. Additionally, any range so prominent squeezes precipitation from the sky, gathering extra moisture for its inhabitants.

Great Basin National Park, being such a vast wilderness expanse, offers seasons' worth of outdoor activities. Biking is allowed only on pavement within the park; that said, the Wheeler Peak scenic drive should provide a relatively safe, very challenging road bike ride. Abiding by Nevada's conservation laws, visitors can fish any number of creeks in the park. Rock climbing is permitted, too, but climbers must register with the park.

Great Basin National Park marks the end of this route and leaves visitors pretty far out there. To return to the Salt Lake City area, consider driving a bit farther west to Ely, Nevada, and then north to West Wendover. Along the way are two sizeable sections of the **Humboldt-Toiyabe Mountains and National Forest**, a beautiful, craggy range with high rocky peaks and glacial lakes, as well as primitive and developed campgrounds. Though most people overlook rural Nevada, any who have explored it would agree that its mountain ranges rising high above the desert provide amazing backcountry playgrounds similar to those in Montana, Idaho, or Wyoming. Plus, returning to Salt Lake City this way links into the **West Desert Salt Flats and Bonneville Speedway Route** (as described in chapter 15 of this book), from West Wendover to Salt Lake City.

IN THE AREA

Attractions and Recreation

BAKER ARCHAEOLOGICAL SITE, Great Basin National Heritage Area, Baker, NV. Located 1 mile north of Baker on NV-487. Call 775-234-7331. Website: www.greatbasinheritage.org.

GREAT BASIN MUSEUM, 328 West 100 North, Delta. Open limited hours, variable per season. Free entry. Call for tours or to request a special visit time. 435-864-5013. Website: www. greatbasinmuseum.com.

GREAT BASIN NATIONAL PARK, 100 Great Basin National Park, Baker, NV. No entrance fee; fees charged to tour Lehman Caves and camp. Call 775-234-7331.Website: www.nps.gov/grba.

THE SALTAIR, Exit 104 on I-80, Magna. Call 801-250-6205. Website: www .thesaltair.com.

Dining

ASHTON BURGER BARN. 304 North US-6, Delta. Open Monday through Saturday, 10–9. Call 435-864-2288.

EL JALISCIENSE TACO SHOP, 396 West Main Street, Delta. Open daily, breakfast through dinner. Call 435-864-3141.

Other Contacts

GREAT BASIN BUSINESS AND TOURISM COUNCIL. Online tourist information. Website: www.greatbasinpark.com.

HUMBOLDT-TOIYABE NATIONAL FOREST OFFICE, 1200 Franklin Way, Sparks, NV. Call for maps and information; consider ordering maps from home before departure. Call 775-331-6444. Website: www.fs.fed.us/r4usda .gov/htnf.

TELESCOPE ARRAY PROJECT, University of Utah Millard County Cosmic Ray Center, 648 West Main Street, Delta. Visitors encouraged to visit Delta station; call ahead to be sure they're open. Call University of Utah Cosmic Ray Group, 801-581-6628. Website: www.telescopearray.org.

15

WEST DESERT SALT FLATS AND THE BONNEVILLE SPEEDWAY

ESTIMATED LENGTH: 120 miles from West Wendover, Nevada, to Salt Lake City, Utah; 175 miles with the Silver Island Mountain National Backcountry Byway detour

ESTIMATED TIME: Half a day with stops

HIGHLIGHTS: This is a tour of the **Great Basin Desert**—a unique part of the western United States with no outlet to ocean. This wicked dry place is saturated with history, ranging from the Donner Party's crossing to World War II bomber testing, archaeological sites containing eleven thousand years of human history, and the setting of world land-speed records. During various ice ages, the **Salt Lake Valley** and beyond was filled with an enormous body of water, **Lake Bonneville**. Today, the **Great Salt Lake** is just a diminutive memory of that—though plenty of evidence remains. On this drive, keep an eye out for the still-visible ancient shoreline on the mountainsides— several hundred feet higher than the current valley floor. Imagine, too, that the **Bonneville Salt Flats** were once also at the bottom of this massive lake. This lonely drive is almost completely devoid of humanity but tours one of the most distinctive and desolate landscapes of the western United States.

GETTING THERE: Located on the Utah-Nevada border, right on I-80, no city could be simpler to reach than West Wendover, Nevada.

Conspicuously located just west from the Utah-Nevada border, **West Wendover**, Nevada, is a small town with Vegas-like lights. Despite its isolation, West Wendover actually has quite a hold on its neighbors in their socially restrictive state. A shuttle bus runs between Salt Lake City and West Wendover, bringing gambling-deprived and liquor-law-repressed Utahans to natural-resource-deprived border town Nevada. As hokey as this town would

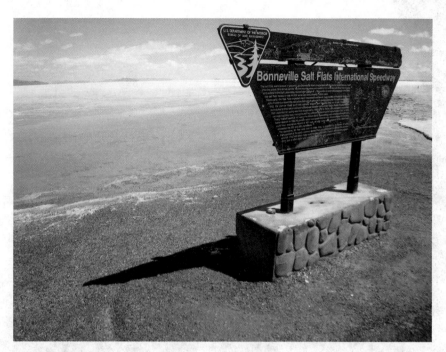

BONNEVILLE SPEEDWAY

seem, many people amuse themselves quite happily in West Wendover, with its ample casinos, hotels, gas stations, and liquor stores. Given its flashiness, it may come as a surprise that this town has fewer than 4,500 residents.

Heading east into Utah and toward Salt Lake City, travelers pass this town's Utah sister, **Wendover**. This community seems to be just the lackluster tailings of its Nevada sibling—for what's a lonely desert town without gambling? Don't scoff just yet; in and around Wendover are natural and man-made points of interest that can be appreciated by informed travelers, including the Silver Island Mountain Byway, Danger Cave archaeological site, Bonneville Speedway, and Historic Wendover Airfield.

The longest detour departing from Wendover is a 54-mile scenic byway loop, the **Silver Island Mountain National Backcountry Byway**. This road tours along the Silver Island Mountains (surprise!), named such as they truly appear to be an island in the expansive, shimmery Great Basin salt flats. Shaped like an 8, this double-loop route provides an excursion into the wilder parts of these flatlands. Though the byway has numerous entrance and exit points, the easiest access is via I-80's Exit 4 (for Bonneville Speedway). When the road makes a 90-degree bend east for the speedway, stay straight, heading slightly left (and away from the speedway) to enter this range. Take a look at a map before heading in; though there is no singular attraction for this route, it allows for a deeper, off-interstate exploration of

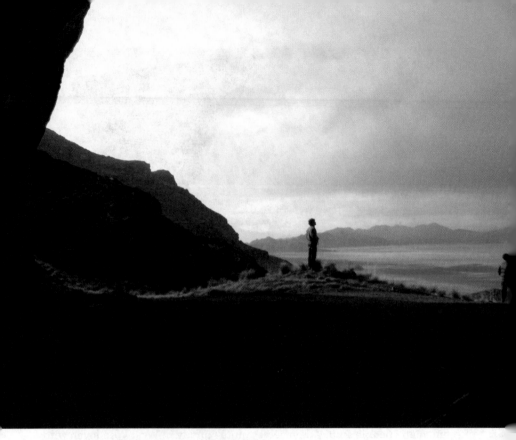

VIEW OVER DESERT FROM CLIMBING CAVE NEAR WENDOVER

the incredible salt flats of western Utah. Overland hikes into **Silver, Donner, Lost,** and **Cave Canyons** are possible; check online or purchase a Utah gazetteer for more help with navigating this backcountry route.

At the apex of this 8-shaped byway is **Donner-Reed Pass**, part of the **California National Historic Trail**. Though not *the* famous Donner Pass of the Sierra Nevada, this was nevertheless a stretch of the Donner Party's westward journey. The ill-fated group attempted to travel from Independence, Missouri, to California. They followed the well-traveled Oregon Trail westward until Fort Bridger, Wyoming. There, they departed to the south and headed across Utah, a difficult route called Hastings Cutoff. Along the way, numerous obstacles resulted in the loss of lives, wagons, and livestock, and created divisions within the group. Making it all the way through the Wasatch and across the Bonneville Salt Flats, the group got as far as the Sierra Nevada in California—quite near modern-day Truckee and Lake Tahoe—where tragedy struck in the winter of 1846–1847. Eighty-seven people had arrived in the Sierra Nevada in December 1846. But stranded by severe winter storms, only forty-eight remained by February 1847, when rescue parties could finally reach the group. During this time, many of the survivors had resorted to cannibalism.

Off the same exit (I-80's Exit 4) is **Danger Cave**, a national historic landmark since 1961. This site is actually a multiple-cave archaeological site containing evidence of human presence dating as far back as 9500 BC—more than 11,500 years ago. Ancient peoples from the Desert Great Basin cultures lived in the area for an estimated 10,000 years, first visiting these caves at the conclusion of the last ice age. Various stone tools and weapons from hunter-gatherer cultures have been found in the cave, including knives, drills, and arrow points. Nearly seventy plant species, various animal bones, and basket remnants have also been recovered from the site.

When he excavated these caves in the late 1940s and early 1950s, Jesse Jennings set a new standard for meticulous digging and record taking. His research surprised peers with some of the oldest samplings found in all of

"Restore Old Lake Bonneville"

This is the slogan on a cultish bumper sticker, rarely to be spotted in the Utah area anymore. What does it mean to "Restore Old Lake Bonneville"? Partly poking fun at other regional bumper stickers, this does not promote an environmentalist cause. Instead, it is a dark-humored joke about covering many of Utah's northern valleys with hundreds of feet of water.

During the last ice ages—a time when the area's climate was much cooler and wetter—huge lakes formed in the Intermountain West. The Great Basin was a perfect tub for these; with no outlet to the ocean, it grew and shrank with changing climates several times until a natural earthen dam burst twelve thousand years ago, draining it once and for all. The last time it was full, Lake Bonneville spanned a huge portion of the Great Basin, with shorelines as much as 980 feet higher than those of today's **Great Salt Lake**. Its waters covered an area roughly half the size of present-day Utah (nearly 20,000 square miles). Today, its various shorelines are still visible along the foothills and mountains of the area, with distinct parallel bands marking the different surface levels of the lake throughout its history. Keep an eye out for these across the entire northern portion of the state, from Logan to Tooele, Provo to Tremonton, and beyond.

It is believed that at one point the lake grew large enough to accept the waters of the **Bear River**. Its volume grew too quickly, and the earth at **Red Rock Pass** (near the Utah-Idaho border I-15), suddenly gave way. When this natural dam burst about 12,000 years ago, it unleashed a catastrophic flood that swept westward across southern Idaho through the **Snake River Plane**—a 410-foot-tall wall of water still traveling about 70 miles per hour as it crossed Idaho. The flow was estimated to be an incomprehensible 15 million cubic feet per second—more than a thousand times the flow of the Colorado River's pumping Cataract Canyon.

North America. Evidence uncovered in the caves suggests that these people were concerned only with survival; gathering food and water apparently was all-consuming, leaving no time for structure building, rituals, and art. Here, too, some of the oldest pinworm larvae have been found in human coprolite, or fossilized poop. Dating back to 7800 BC, this has helped to trace this parasite's path around the world and its coevolution with humans.

Now a Utah state park, this cave can be visited as part of a pay guided tour (reservations required). To get there, take Exit 4 from I-80. Turn left (north) and a quick left again (west) at the first available turn. This paved road turns to dirt and continues roughly another 1.5 miles and ends at the side of Wendover Mountain. Visible from the road, the caves are located on the eastern side of this mountain, with Danger Cave being the northernmost and Jukebox being the southernmost. These trails require agility and fitness of visitors, as grades can get steeper than 40 percent for portions of the hike. Additionally, approaching the caves with a high-clearance vehicle is recommended due to a mandatory trench crossing en route. For protective purposes, the entrances to the caves have been blocked with iron grates.

Also reached by heading north from I-80's Exit 4 are the famous **Bonneville Salt Flats**. World-renowned for the speedway on which land-speed records have been set for more than 100 years, this remarkably flat area has come into existence by a combination of unique factors. As recently as twelve thousand years ago, this sat at the bottom of Lake Bonneville, half the size of present-day Utah (see sidebar on page 63). Part of the Great Basin, a landlocked depression with no connection to the ocean, this area collected water with no outlet but evaporation. As streams ran from surrounding environs into the lake, they carried along soluble materials, including various salts. Without a way to drain the water, the lake collected these salts that could not evaporate. Hence the surface of these flats—salty from the trapped solubles left behind by waters of yore, and almost perfectly flat, as they were once at the bottom of a huge lake.

Over time, an area tends to get windswept and eroded into a less flat expanse—but the varnish-like property of the salt keeps nature from taking away too much soil. Additionally, each winter a film of water collects on the flats, polishing out any surface irregularities. By spring it evaporates, leaving behind a freshly buffed surface. Plants, too, have been unable to disrupt the surface, as the high concentrations of magnesium, lithium, sodium chloride, and potassium make the flats inhospitable to flora.

However, the salt flats are not impervious to the powers of nature, and slowly the surface is changing. When measured in 1976, they were roughly 26,000 acres—down from an estimated original expanse of 96,000 acres. Industry, such as massive salt-mining operations (nearly a hundred years old), was thought to be responsible for decreasing the surface area as well as defacing the remaining flats. A thinning top layer, as well as the appearance of holes and stress lines, suggests an unnatural disturbance. Regardless of

SALT AT SPEEDWAY

actual cause, this environment should be treated with care. Though Bonneville looks as barren as a piece of concrete, it is in fact fragile, and visitors
should remain on prescribed driving paths.

As far back as 1896, this was recognized as a possible surface for high-speed
racing. W. D. Rishel, who was scouting for a racecourse for cyclists, first saw
this potential. Eighteen years later, he returned with daredevil Teddy Tetzlaff.
In 1914, Tetzlaff drove a Blitzen Benz 141.73 miles per hour across Bonneville for
an unofficial record. By the 1930s, land speeds were pushing 280 miles per hour,
but were mostly being tested on beaches like Daytona. Needless to say, a flat-
ter, firmer surface would be required to push the record much further. In 1935,
Bonneville hosted a record at just over 300 miles per hour, sustained for 1 mile.
Perfect for land-speed records, these salt flats provide ample space to accelerate
to a vehicle's full potential without concern for limitation of the course.

By the late 1940s, the area was the standard course for setting land-speed
records. Barriers kept being topped by hundreds of miles per hour, reaching
over 600 miles per hour by the 1960s. Presently, the British Thrust SSC car
holds the record at 763.035 miles per hour—faster than the speed of sound
in some temperature and pressure conditions. This is quite a lot faster than

the 1898 record of 39.24 miles per hour. Today (and since the 1930s), the speediest vehicles have all been jet-propelled. There is no one standard for measuring speed—but most records today (and the ones listed above) are the speed a car sustains for 1 full mile.

The World of Speed, a four-day festival for racers and onlookers alike, takes place every year during the middle of September; check the **Utah Salt Flats Racing Association**'s website (www.saltflats.com) for current listings. Many different categories of vehicles are raced—even the bizarre: racing *barstools*, which go in excess of 70 miles per hour. Spectators should wear plenty of sunscreen, sunglasses, hats, and also bring lots of hydrating liquids. Ear protection enriches the experience, as do binoculars. There are no grandstands, so bring a camp chair and a radio to catch commentary on AM. The time is long between races, and short during the action, so it's a good idea to come with friends or some other kind of entertainment. To get there, take Exit 4 and head north 5 miles, staying on the paved road, to the gate.

To the south of the same exit is the **Historic Wendover Airfield** (sometimes also called the Wendover Field Bomber Training Base or Historic Wendover Air Force Base). In 1940, Wendover, Utah, was a town of just more than 100 people, surrounded by miles of uninhabited salt flats. Needing space for a bombing and gunnery range, the US Army Air Corps began acquiring land and erecting structures that would become the Wendover Airfield. The total size of the field was huge: on average, 27 miles wide and 86 miles long— thought to be the largest of its kind in the world.

The Wendover Air Force Base was officially opened on March 28, 1942, as a training center for B-17 and B-24 heavy bombardment. In all, more than a thousand crews were trained at the base. Here, too, the Manhattan Project was researched, with "Little Boy" and "Fat Man" being tested on the range. After 155 test drops at this site, and one high-altitude simulation drop in New Mexico, Colonel Tibbets flew a B-29, Enola Gay, on August 6, 1945, to Hiroshima, Japan, to deliver Little Boy. On August 9, Fat Man was dropped by Major Charles Sweeney over Nagasaki. A third bomb (another Fat Man) had already departed from Wendover onboard another B-29 when the Japanese surrendered on August 14. With this news, that plane was intercepted and returned to Utah.

Today it is possible to arrange for extended tours of the airfield (by calling ahead), and also to visit its museum, open 7 days a week. On display are models, military memorabilia, and photographs illustrating the history of the airfield and base. Outside stand the original barracks, shack-like dwellings of the enlisted men during this time. A very powerful history for such a quiet, dreary-seeming place.

Finally leaving this Exit 4 and its attractions, head east on I-80. Unmistakably visible 25 miles east of Wendover stands **Metaphor: The Tree of Utah** (commonly called the "Tree of Life"), an 87-foot-tall mixed-media sculpture that was built by Karl Momen between 1982 and 1986. This Iran-born Swedish American artist funded the entire project himself, hoping to add color and the appearance of life to the otherwise pristinely stark background. As the story goes, Momen was driving across the desert toward California and envisioned a tree growing there; years later, he realized that vision. The sculpture is made up of 225 tons of concrete, 10,000 pounds of welding rod, roughly 2,000 ceramic tiles, and various rocks and minerals coming from Utah. Apparently there is quite a lot of speculation among passersby as to what exactly this structure should be. Guesses range from UFO "power pole" to cell tower in disguise or even an expensive memorial for a wealthy person who perished in a car wreck at the location.

The tree used to stand alone, but vandalism has now forced the State of Utah to encircle it with a barbed-wire-topped chain-link fence. Now owned by Utah, the tree is believed to have cost Momen more than $1 million to complete. On the base of the tree is a plaque inscribed, "A hymn to our universe, whose glory and dimension is beyond all myth and imagination."

Exit 41 is for **Knolls**, Utah. A small town until sometime in the 1970s, Knolls no longer exists. The main attraction for the exit is actually the **Knolls Recreation Area**, so named for the rolling hills and sand dunes of the area. This 36,000-acre playground is beloved by dirt bikers and ATVers. With very sparse vegetation and many natural features, the park is perfect for challenging riding as well as doing jumps and tricks. Riders can often be seen from the interstate, as many popular jumps sit almost adjacent to I-80; sometimes the highway itself is even (illegally) used to gain speed for a jump.

Do not exit for **Clive**, Utah (the next along the way), unless you're interested in visiting a privately owned nuclear waste site. Clive's claim to fame is having one of few sites in the nation that will accept commercially generated byproducts—the others being in Barnwell, South Carolina; Richland, Washington; and (one pending) in Fort Hancock, Texas. The owner of the Clive site signed an agreement with then-governor Jon Huntsman in 2008 saying he would accept only Class A nuclear waste (the lowest radioactivity classification), and only a limited amount of it.

Move right along and take Exit 56 for a quick tour of the ghost town **Aragonite**. Head south from the interstate about 2 miles, and turn left, continuing about 3.5 miles on a high-quality dirt road. At this point appear abandoned buildings (some of which are still in fairly good condition), mine shafts, and one old vehicle. This village operated as a mining town for just a handful of years in the early 1900s. It fell quickly out of fashion as its quarried stone, aragonite, had little use but decoration in buildings. With little else to support its economy, this remote town collapsed. Mining resumed decades later, but only under the power of commuting workers; the homes and buildings were never used again. Because it was haphazardly abandoned, this site contains uncovered pits and shafts; pay attention and be careful.

Continuing eastward, glance to the right at Exit 70 at **Delle**. Like Aragonite, this is also a ghost town (or very near to it). Instead of growing up on mining, though, this came to be as a railroad village on the Western Pacific Line. Delle's original name, Dalles Spring, was shortened and slightly altered by railroad workers for the sake of easier telegraphing. Families of rail employees lived here for about 20 years, approximately from 1920 to 1940, piping in water from a spring more than 10 miles away. But changing rail technology and the inhospitable salt-flat environment led these families to all but desert this town. Originating in the San Jose (later Oakland) area of California, the Western Pacific Line scooped north and east through northeastern California, northern Nevada, and across Utah toward Salt Lake City. The shortness of this railroad (only about 1,000 miles on its the main line), and the high-maintenance nature of the mountainous route, only allowed it to be in full-swing operation until the deregulation of railroads in 1980. Unable to compete with major lines in the area, Western Pacific was purchased by Union Pacific at the end of 1982. Today in Delle there still exists a small Sinclair gas station as well as a dusty-looking hotel and café. A de-wheeled, de-everythinged red bus sits eternally parked there as well, covered with various murals.

UT-196 shares Delle's same interstate exit ramp (Exit 77). Taking this road about 37 miles to the south leads to **Dugway**, the gateway to the **Dugway Proving Ground** (see chapter 16). Founded in 1941, this was a US Army test field for chemical and biological weapons. It is believed that more than a thousand different chemicals were tested here. Dirty bombs were said to have been dropped, as well as biological weapons and chemicals released into the air and deployment of weapons of mass destruction. Needless to say, much of the activity here has been secretive.

Continue eastward on I-80 into **Grantsville** for a visit to the **Donner-Reed Museum**. Unlike many of the mining and railroad towns in the West Desert area, Grantsville was founded as a satellite Mormon community in 1850, under the direction of Brigham Young, shortly after the LDS arrival in Salt Lake City in the summer of 1848. The history of this town was therefore always interlaced with Utah's unique Mormon story.

The actual museum is a small affair, dedicated to telling the story of the famous party that became stranded in the Sierra Nevada in late 1846, some of whose survivors resorted to cannibalizing the dead in order to make it through the bitter winter. Prior to their arrival and snowy entrapment in California, they encountered great difficulties on the Hastings Cutoff, a southern spur route that departed from the standard Oregon Trail at Fort Bridger, Wyoming, and cut across Utah. This "shortcut" was much more challenging and vastly less traveled than the standard Oregon Trail, forging through the high Wasatch Range east of Salt Lake City and across the Great Basin salt flats. Hastings Cutoff was roughly parallel to (but much more squiggly than) modern I-80. Lansford Hastings, the route's namesake pioneer guide, was supposed to help the party, but he apparently gave misleading information about the ease of the route and then left them stranded.

During the worst part of the summer, the party had to cut a road in the Wasatch Mountains for miles through willows, only to find they had to turn around and return the way they had come. The Great Salt Lake finally came into sight in late August, and travel across the Great Basin Desert proved much quicker. Still, oxen died of exhaustion and dehydration crossing these blazing-hot salt flats, and these dead animals, as well as "extra" wagons and supplies, were left behind. The extreme difficulties of crossing Utah in 1846 slowed the party greatly, causing them to arrive finally in the Sierra Nevada in December of that year—much too late for passage through such a massive range. Trapped by blizzards, the party sent members away to request rescue, but they remained unaided until February of 1847.

Today the museum holds the remains of five abandoned wagons, horse shoes, yokes, tools, jewelry, and other miscellaneous items, found in the Salt

TOOELE AFTER A RAIN STORM

Lake Desert in the 1920s—preserved remarkably well here, despite utter exposure to the elements, by the arid climate. Though it is possible some of the items were left behind by miners taking the Hastings Cutoff in 1849, these items were most likely abandoned by the Donner-Reed Party 3 years prior. If you are interested in visiting this museum, be sure to call ahead (435-884-3767) to schedule a tour. (At the time of publication of this book, this museum was temporarily closed for renovation. If this is the case during your trip, consider visiting its nearby neighbor, the **Grantsville Daughters of Utah Pioneers Museum**, which holds a modest collection of locally relevant antiques. Just a block west of the Donner-Reed Museum, this facility has limited hours but offers tours by appointment.)

Tooele is the next major stop along the way. This requires yet another detour from the main drive, but for those interested in speed, the **Utah Motorsports Campus** could be a logical destination after visiting the Bonneville Speedway. This race complex has something for nearly every genre of vehicular racing and competition. On the premises is a modern-day, high-speed, paved track used by racecars and knee-dragging motorcyclists. Additionally, short-course, off-road racing events take place off the track once in a while. And there's even an "extreme rock crawling" course in which some vehicles invariably roll in every competition. Contestants span from amateur to professional, but all races are typically quite high-speed and lively—even the amateur events. Plus, race days typically feature a full spectrum of levels—so with one entrance fee, you'll be able to see amateur races to seasoned pros. If you have the time (and you visit between April and October), consider renting their go-karts, which reach speeds up to 50 miles an hour. (Call ahead to arrange for a session.) To get there, take UT-36 south about 3 miles, turning right on UT-138. Follow this west for almost 5 miles and, guided by signs, bear south on Sheep Lane for another 2 miles.

After Tooele, it's pretty much a straight shot to Salt Lake City without a heck of a lot in between. Notice the **Great Salt Lake** to the north; the low-tide-like smell sometimes wafting south should serve as a reminder. On its south shore about 20 miles west of central Salt Lake City is the **Saltair**, a massive, unique structure that has been built, destroyed by fire, and rebuilt three times in its history since first opening in 1893. Not just a victim of fire, it was also flooded when the Great Salt Lake reached epic heights in 1983. Called a "Coney Island of the West," earlier generations of the structure indeed resembled an ocean wharf—absolutely massive and almost spooky in historic photos. In its earliest days, it was a full-blown resort, catering specifically to Mormons who wanted to vacation at a place with a good reputation, high moral standards, and clean activities. Located directly on a train line, it attracted people from around the region. Today this much-simplified building functions as a concert venue and is in a much less grand scale than its original format and made of nonflammable concrete.

Arriving in Salt Lake City completes the day's journey. Luckily, Salt Lake City is the state's major hub, with an international airport and two interstates running directly out of it. From Salt Lake City, the nearest drives are through the **Little Cottonwood Canyon**, **Big Cottonwood Canyon**, and the **Alpine Loop** (detailed in chapters 1, 2, and 3 of this book).

IN THE AREA

Attractions and Recreation

BONNEVILLE SALT FLATS, Bureau of Land Management Salt Lake Field Office, 2370 South Decker Lake Boulevard, Salt Lake City. Call 801-977-4300. Website: www.blm.gov/utah.

BONNEVILLE RACING, Bonneville Salt Flats. Check online for racing schedule. Website: www.bonnevilleracing.com.

DANGER CAVE ARCHAEOLOGICAL SITE, Utah State Parks. Website: www.stateparks.utah.gov.

DONNER-REED MUSEUM, 90 North Cooley, Grantsville. Call ahead to schedule a tour. Visit the website for history of the party, particularly the Utah (or Hastings Cutoff) portion. Call 435-884-0824 or 435-884-3411. Website: www.donner-reed-museum.org.

HISTORIC WENDOVER AIRFIELD, 345 South Airport Apron, Wendover. Museum open daily; arrive at least 1 hour before closing. Call 435-665-2308. Website: www.wendoverairbase.com.

GRANTSVILLE DAUGHTERS OF UTAH PIONEERS MUSEUM, 378 West Clark Street, Grantsville. Open Friday and Saturdays 12–4 PM or by appointment; call 435-840-1585.

UTAH MOTORSPORTS CAMPUS, 2901 Sheep Lane, Tooele. Call 435-277-7223. Website: www.utahmotorsportscampus.com.

SILVER ISLAND MOUNTAIN NATIONAL BACKCOUNTRY BYWAY, Exit 4 on I-80, UT. Website: www.recreation.gov.

UTAH SALT FLATS RACING ASSOCIATION. P.O. Box 27365, Salt Lake City. Organizers for World of Speed; admission charged daily or for entire event. Call 801-485-2662 or 801-583-3765. Website: www.saltflats.com.

RUSH VALLEY

16

GRANTSVILLE, RUSH VALLEY, AND DUGWAY

ESTIMATED LENGTH: Almost 100 miles exactly to complete this loop around the Stansbury Mountains

ESTIMATED TIME: Just over 2 hours with no stops; longer with detours for photographs. Up to a full day or even longer for those hiking in the Stansbury Mountains or camping

HIGHLIGHTS: This route showcases the open and wild expanses of the Great Basin Desert, tracing through the Rush and Skull Valleys, and forming a complete loop around the Stansbury Mountains. To the east of the Stansbury Range are the Oquirrh Mountains, an impressive mountain chain that separates this stark, Wild West landscape from the bustling metropolis of the Salt Lake Valley. With that urban expanse completely hidden from view, this byway gives visitors a chance to imagine Utah's high plains and salt-flat deserts before the influx of Western civilization. Along the way, visitors encounter the small communities of Grantsville, Rush Valley, and Terra before passing by Dugway. History buffs will recognize this town as the home base for the Dugway Proving Grounds, an army facility purposed with the testing of chemical and biological weaponry since 1942. This facility's shadowy military legacy includes the Dugway sheep incident of 1968, in which thousands of Skull Valley sheep suddenly perished.

GETTING THERE: This route begins in Grantsville, Utah. From Salt Lake City, head west on I-80 toward Tooele. The least congested route to Grantsville is via Exit 88, heading due south on Burmester Road; alternately, drivers can take Exit 99 in Tooele, heading southwest on UT-36 for 3 miles, and turning southwest (right) onto UT-138. The difference in travel time between the routes is insignificant. Bear in mind there are no gas stations along the route beyond Grantsville, thus you should tank up there or in Tooele. Furthermore, plan to bring your own food and water because once you leave Grantsville, you'll find no grocery stores along the way.

Great
Salt Lake

Delle

Exit 77

80

80

Exit 88

138

BURMESTER
RD

138

Cedar Mountains

196

Grantsville DUP
Museum

Donner-Reed Museum

Grantsville

36

112

Skull Valley

*Stansbury
Mountains*

Iosepa

FR-171

Stansbury
Loop
Campground

*Tooele
Valley*

Tooele

+ *Deseret Peak*

Deseret Peak
Wilderness

Skull Valley
Indian Reservation

Clover Springs
Campground

Stockton

MORMON TRAIL

Penny's

Terra

*Fisher
Pass*

Rush
Valley

73

199

*Onaqui
Mountains*

Dugway
(English Village)

Dugway
Proving Ground

36

Vernon

*Dugway
Range*

*Simpson
Mountains*

Dugway
Geode Beds

*PONY EXPRESS RTE/
SIMPSON SPRINGS-CALLAO RD*

Fish Springs
National
Wildlife
Refuge

N

0   5   10
Miles

© The Countryman Press

The Stansbury Range soars high above the desert floors of the Great Basin, yet it is set far enough away from the urban conglomerate of the Wasatch Front that it remains largely unvisited and underdeveloped by civilization. Its predominant ridgeline runs from north to south, and it is flanked by Skull Valley to the west and Rush Valley to the east. The Skull Valley Indian Reservation—population 31 and 28 square miles in size—is located on the southwest slopes of this range, just north of Dugway. Of the Stansbury Mountains, Deseret Peak is the tallest at 11,031 feet, and stands almost exactly at the midway point of this range; surrounding this crest is the Deseret Peak Wilderness, a 25,508-acre allotment created in 1984 by Congress. Here you may explore the area on foot, and possibly even spot a herd of wild horses residing in Big Creek Canyon. Due to official wilderness restrictions, motorized vehicles and mountain bikes are prohibited off established roads.

Stretch Your Legs

The most commonly visited portion of the Stansbury Mountains is accessed via South Willow Canyon's Loop Campground and Trailhead. From here, an established trail climbs to Deseret Peak. This mountaintop stands roughly 5,800 feet above the valley floor below, giving it the fourth-greatest valley-to-summit rise of all the impressive mountains in Utah. Of these 5,800 feet, your vehicle will have climbed approximately 2,000, leaving you a "mere" 3,600 feet to ascend over 4 miles.

Those opting to tackle this hike will depart from the campground heading west on the Deseret Trail; approximately 0.7 mile into the hike, there is a stream crossing. Just after this, the trail forks at a signed junction. To continue toward the Deseret Peak summit, stay left. (The right fork leads to South Willow Lake; this relatively mellow hike requires a gain of nearly 1,700 feet over about 3.6 miles, for a total round-trip distance of just over 7 miles. If you're not feeling up to the strain of Deseret Peak, consider this scenic alternative.)

About 2 miles beyond the intersection, the trail ascends to the base of a glacial cirque, after which switchbacks lead up to a saddle and another junction; stay right here to reach Deseret Peak. From this summit, excellent panoramic views can be had of the salt flats and Great Salt Lake, Oquirrh Mountains, and the surrounding Skull and Rush Valleys. Though it is possible to return to the trailhead by a different trail, forming a loop, it is recommended that hikers retrace their steps unless they are familiar with this area. Though the trail to Deseret Peak is usually well marked and easy to follow, hikers are encouraged to arm themselves with a trail map in the event that any trail markings are missing. Also, be sure to come prepared with warm clothing; the high elevations and mountain winds can be surprisingly chilly even during the warm summer months.

It is between the Oquirrh and Stansbury Ranges that this route begins. If you wish to skip the rather minor congestion of Tooele, depart from I-80 at Exit 88, and head south on Burmester Road. After 6.4 miles, you will land squarely in the center of Grantsville, population 9,617. Settled in 1848 by LDS pioneers, this town was originally called Twenty Wells in observance of the area's numerous artesian springs. Predating Mormon settlement, the Goshute tribe occupied the area, drawn there and sustained by the plentiful springs.

In the center of town, the Donner-Reed Museum stands in a repurposed historic schoolhouse, and serves as an eerie commemoration of the famously doomed Donner Party. (For more on the Donner Party, see page 206.)

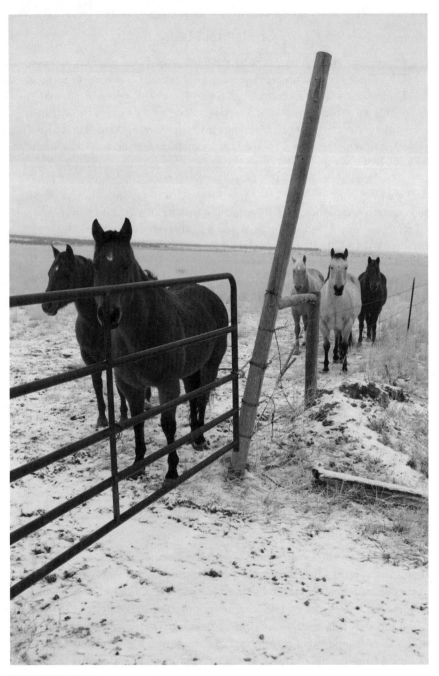

HORSES IN RUSH VALLEY

To continue on this route, head south from Main Street onto South West Street on the western side of town; this road becomes Mormon Trail as it leaves town. To locate this street, keep your eye out for the Grantsville City Cemetery; this occupies the northeast corner of the intersection of South West Street and Main Street.

Hikers, fishers, and campers will want to pay attention 5.1 miles south of this junction: South Willow Road departs to the west and presents the most popular and user-friendly access to Stansbury Mountain's outdoor recreational opportunities along this loop. Quickly after leaving Mormon Trail, this road changes its name to South Willow Canyon Road/FR-171. Deseret Peak, the tallest point in the Stansburys, is most easily approached by this road. After 7.1 miles of westward travel (the last 3.9 of which is dirt), South Willow Canyon Road terminates in the Loop Campground, the most commonly used hiking trailhead and campground in the Stansbury Mountains (see "Stretch Your Legs" on page 219). Camping here is permitted late May through early October (exact dates contingent on the snowpack); in the event that all nine campsites are occupied upon your arrival, consider pitching your tent at the numerous other campsites scattered along this road. For more information regarding hiking and camping opportunities in the Stansbury Mountains, contact the Uinta-Wasatch-Cache National Forest (see Other Contacts, below).

FISHER PASS

With each subsequent mile south of Grantsville, traces of civilization continue to fall off, leaving the road itself and ranch fences among the only evidence of settlement. To either side of the road, sagebrush and grasses speckle the valley floor, growing ever thicker as the slopes rise to gain evergreen trees and meet the foothills and mountain slopes.

Approaching the town of Rush Valley, very large power lines appear on the left side of the road. Quickly thereafter, Mormon Trail turns into Main Street, along which inhabited residences and historic, deserted farmhouses and outbuildings line the shoulder. Founded in 1854, this town currently claims just under 450 residents. A total of 19 miles south of Grantsville, turn right to head east on UT-199. With the Oquirrh Mountains in your rearview mirror, and farmhouses and wooden barns looming alongside the road, you may get the feeling of traveling back in time.

Historic Lincoln Highway

Originally spanning 3,389 miles from New York City's Times Square to San Francisco's Lincoln Park, this highway traversed through Pennsylvania, Chicago, Denver, Salt Lake City, and central Nevada—following roughly the same path as I-80. One of the first transcontinental roads for automobiles in North America, this was the brainchild of Carl Fisher. His vision was not only to create an interconnected network of major cities but also to establish a model of enduring highway systems that would stimulate both agriculture and commerce.

Prior to this highway and Route 66 (which now approximates I-95) being established, roadways were primarily local phenomena, with interstate travel being almost entirely reliant on railways. Furthermore, in that time, automobiles were largely reserved for the wealthy, and it was a widely held belief that were interstate roads to be developed, they, too, would be in service of the elite. Fisher, who had long been an avid automobile enthusiast, innovator of headlight technology and raceway owner, believed that the automobile would fail to progress as a societal tool without proper roads on which it could operate.

Though his idea for the Lincoln Highway was first conceived in 1912, it was only 1 year later that the highway was officially dedicated. Famously quoted as saying, "Let's build it before we are too old to enjoy it," Fisher set about voraciously raising money from private parties, securing $1 million (approximately 10 percent of the estimated requirement) in less than a month. Interestingly, Henry Ford (the largest manufacturer of automobiles at the time) refused to contribute, citing his belief that the funding should come from the government rather than from individuals. When it came time to dub the highway, Fisher rejected the notion of naming the road after himself (and turned down other suggestions as well), but instead sought for it to be named after Abraham Lincoln, a personal hero of his.

At the outset of the project, the endpoints of San Francisco and New York were established; the goal of the project was to connect these two cities via the most direct and best route. The portion on the eastern side of the country proved relatively simple to complete, as the many established roadways there required little extra work to connect. However, the western half of the country, with vast rural expanses and inhospitable stretches, proved much more challenging. From Detroit, Fisher and others traveled as the "Trail-Blazer" crew, riding in two trucks and seventeen cars across the open wilderness. Because the trip was widely publicized, the crew received warm greetings in each town they encountered. Yet hazards such as mudflats, floods, sand dunes, and mechanical breakdowns proved challenging in the intervening spaces. Nevertheless, the trip took the crew only 34 days. As of September 14, 1913, the exact course of the route was announced, and would cover 3,389 miles. Since its October 31, 1913, dedication, this highway's route has been modified and its length shortened to 3,142 miles. Today, this highway still overlaps with many historic routes, including the 1675 Dutch colonist highway of New Jersey, sections of Brigham Young's Mormon Trail, portions of the Pony Express Trail and Overland Stage Line, and the famous Donner Pass of the Sierra Nevada.

After about 6 miles of westward travel, the road ascends sufficiently to reach the tree line. As it does so, it winds back and forth, rolling pleasantly upward and downward as it weaves toward Fisher Pass (see "Historic Lincoln Highway," below). Though this road is newly surfaced, brightly painted, and well maintained (even in winter), be sure to take the speed advisories seriously around its tightest curves (sometimes recommending top speeds of 20 miles per hour). After about 9 total miles of travel on UT-199, you will reach Clover Springs Campground on the left. This campground offers ten single sites ($12/night) and one group site ($45/night). Administered by the BLM, this campground is typically open May through October, depending on snowpack and weather conditions. Marked by natural springs and cottonwood trees, this relative oasis offers something of a reprieve from summer heat. From this small campground, a short trail leads to the namesake springs. Additionally, miscellaneous jeep trails and footpaths depart from the southwestern corner of the campground, as well as to the north side of

CLOVER SPRINGS CAMPGROUND

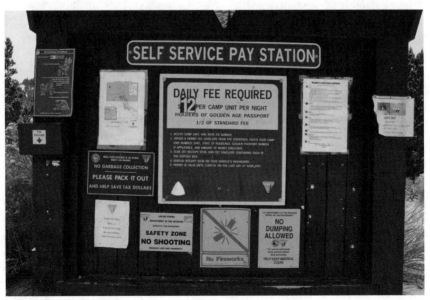

UT-199. Though there is water available at the site, it is not potable; be sure to bring plenty of your own. Contact the BLM (see Other Contacts, below) for more information regarding these recreation opportunities.

Another 6 miles west of Clover Springs Campground, UT-199 winds back down Fisher Pass to the minuscule village of Terra. A small grid of homes located along dirt side roads, scattered behind trees and mostly out of sight, this town offers no public amenities. Beyond Terra, the highway continues linearly southwest to land at the entrance to Dugway after 9 more miles. The secured army gate serves as the far eastern entry to the Dugway Proving

Sheep Kill

The **1968 Skull Valley sheep kill**, also known as the Dugway sheep incident, is an event in which 6,200 sheep belonging to Skull Valley ranchers (just east of the Dugway Proving Ground) suddenly perished. The ranchers lost approximately $300,000 worth of livestock (which, adjusted for inflation, would be just over $1.9 million today). On March 13, 1968, three separate testing operations took place, including burning a nerve agent, firing a chemical artillery shell, and spraying a nerve agent by jet plane. Most believe the jet plane test is responsible for this sheep incident. Based on reports, the jet's spray nozzle malfunctioned, causing the plane to release toxins into the air as it climbed up to an altitude safe for spraying. However, other reports raise a bit of suspicion—at least as to exactly what chemical killed the sheep. Though the sudden mass death of so many thousands of grazing animals was clearly not natural, some of the sheep observed to be alive after the incident appeared to be suffering from something other than nerve gas exposure—according to witnesses, they were bleeding internally and refused to eat, yet their breathing was normal. Additionally, it seems that only sheep were affected, while other wildlife and livestock reportedly survived.

Intervening time and lack of official records regarding these details will leave the incident forever cloaked in mystery. The army did not officially admit guilt for this massacre, but they did bury a few thousand of the dead animals and also replaced much of the lost livestock for the ranchers. Regardless, President Richard Nixon, reacting in the face of international exposure, banned all open-air testing of chemical weapons the following year. And in a 1970 report (finally made public in 1998), the army conceded that nerve agent VX was responsible for the killing of the sheep. In this report, it was said that the agent was indeed found present in grass and snow samplings taken from Skull Valley following the sheep's death. Though the army granted that the agent was indeed sufficient to kill the sheep, it still did not claim negligence or responsibility. An article in *Time* magazine, "Toxicology: Sheep & the Army," published April 5, 1968, details much of the veterinarians' reports and news conferences before time faded them.

As one *Houston Chronicle* reporter, Tony Freemantle, said,

> Dugway Proving Ground is a massive firing range that for 50 years was the U.S. Army testing ground for some of the most lethal chemical, biological and nuclear weapons ever made. A slope of the mountains to the east is pockmarked with hundreds of fortified bunkers storing enough toxin to eradicate mankind. . . . This was where the Cold War was waged, not on battlefields in foreign lands, but in factories, laboratories and testing ranges.

Though many of the details of Dugway's past will never be resolved, and rumors will always compete with disclosed facts and secrets, this place nevertheless contains fascinating history punctuated with tinges of excitement.

Grounds. Established by the US Army under President Franklin D. Roosevelt in March of 1942, this site came to be as a consequence of the December 7, 1941, Japanese attack on Pearl Harbor. Some 126,720 acres in size at the complex's inception, these isolated grounds fulfilled the military's need for a secure and secretive testing facility for biological and chemical weapons and defenses against them. Over the decades, the site has undergone many

A RAFTER OF WILD TURKEYS CLIMB THE HILLSIDE ABOVE FISHER PASS stages of activity and deactivation, and has grown almost 700,000 acres, to approximately the size of Rhode Island. The town of Dugway itself remains out-of-bounds behind the security gate, so is inaccessible to the general public. Yet just beyond this checkpoint live approximately 1,800 people. This village for military personnel and their families has been called the English Village.

A shroud of mystery has long surrounded this site, arising from factual and fictitious incidents alike. One of the most famous happenings was the sheep kill of 1968; in the days leading up to this eerie event, three different nerve agent operations were conducted at Dugway. Just 27 miles from the site, 6,200 Skull Valley sheep died over the course of just a few days following those operations. (See "Sheep Kill," below.) More recently, scandal struck again in 2015 when twelve Dugway personnel underwent investigation after it was discovered that 194 labs across the United States and the world received small quantities of live anthrax bacilli in shipments from Dugway that were supposed to have exclusively contained dead anthrax. As of the publication of this book, the results of this investigation were still pending.

Wild Bird Enthusiasts and Rock Hounds

Though public access ends at the gates of the Dugway Proving Grounds, those with enough time and supplies can take a very long—60 miles (120 miles round-trip)—gravel road detour by turning south from the western terminus of UT-199 at the obvious BLM sign onto the Pony Express Route/Simpson Springs-Callao Road. This road continues across the barren landscape in a southwesterly direction to the Fish Springs National Wildlife Refuge. Established in 1959, this sanctuary spans roughly 18,000 acres—10,000 of which are wetlands. This striking area of moisture in the Great Basin Desert is supplied with water by an alluvial aquifer and associated fractures in the earth's crust. Though wildlife of all varieties is present, the diversity of birds in the area is the most remarkable, and provides observation and photography opportunities year-round. For more information regarding which types of birds are best viewed during each season, contact the refuge.

If rockhounding is more up your alley, you can cut the drive a little shorter and head approximately 45 miles down this road, stopping 15 miles shy of the refuge. To the north of the main road, multiple short spur roads branch north to reach the Dugway Geode Beds. As the name suggests, geodes are what you can expect to hunt here. Reaching the beds is very casual and requires little navigational skill once you leave the car, due to the utter scarcity of vegetation on this landscape. If you plan to extract some treasures from this site, be sure to bring appropriate tools, such as picks, chisels, gloves, and a bucket.

The most direct route to these beds is to turn north off the main gravel road 44.1 miles after departing from UT-199. During pleasant weather, you may be surprised to find several other people out for the weekend to pick rocks and camp. Be aware that BLM land abuts private property here; signs on the site should help you navigate property lines.

Regardless of your destination along this detour, it would be savvy to view a detailed map before leaving pavement, and to bring a Utah gazetteer along with you. There are multiple junctions along the way; though the intersections are somewhat well-signed, some road signs become worn or go missing from season to season. It would also be a very good idea to come well prepared to this extremely remote area (with a fully inflated spare tire and all the fluids topped off), as you will not have any cell service for major stretches of this detour.

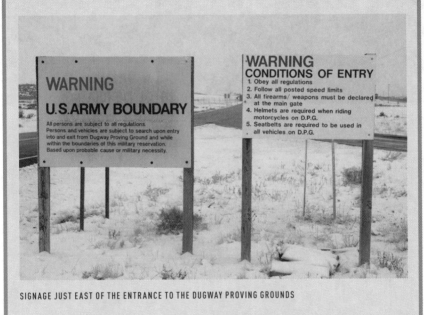

SIGNAGE JUST EAST OF THE ENTRANCE TO THE DUGWAY PROVING GROUNDS

Further stoking the imaginations of many are fantastical rumors of UFOs being associated with the site—however, these accounts have never been confirmed. Nevertheless, they include reported sightings and even claims that multiple UFOs have been stored underground in the area. Some people even go so far as to call Dugway "the new Area 51" or "Area 52." ("Proof" of these claims can be viewed on YouTube.) Currently, the US Army insists that the only research being done at the facilities is defensive in nature: protective equipment and detection systems. Regardless of where the truth lies on the spectrum of rumors and official reports, it is nevertheless fun

TOP: SKULL VALLEY SIGN
BOTTOM: RANCH LANDS OF SKULL VALLEY

to imagine that some of the far-fetched stories may be true. Those wary of driving too close to this facility may take comfort in the claim that outdoor experimentation with live agents ended in the '60s, followed by the cessation of biological weapons testing in the '70s and of outdoor chemical weapons in the '90s. When you drive north from Dugway today, you will observe hundreds or even thousands of cattle being raised on the extensive grounds of Skull Valley's Ensign Ranch with no apparent health problems whatsoever. Additionally, antelope, deer, falcons, hawks, and even wild turkeys are common sightings in the area.

Turning north on UT-196 from UT-199, you will enter the Skull Valley Indian Reservation after just 8.3 miles. A small plot just 28 square miles in size, this requires just 5 miles of highway driving to traverse. This is Goshute land, and it has recently become a proposed temporary repository for nuclear waste. Much controversy surrounds this motion, and activism has succeeded in stopping the project for the time being. However, the situation seems tenuous, owing to the fact that a lease has already been signed for a storage site.

About 21.5 miles along UT-196 north of its junction with UT-199 (and 8.1 miles from the northern border of the Skull Valley Reservation), take a right

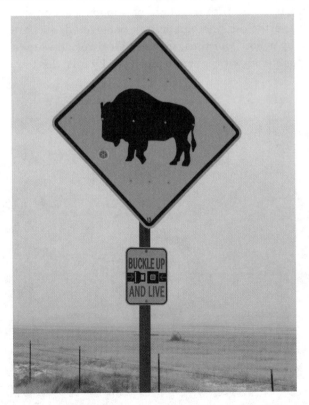

BUFFALO-CROSSING SIGN ON THE SKULL VALLEY INDIAN RESERVATION

onto a dirt road (immediately after Skull Valley Road departs to the left) for a short detour to a ghost town with a unique history. After just 0.4 mile, the road splits; take the left fork. In another 0.4 mile, take another left. At this junction stands the abandoned village of Iosepa. Settled in 1889 by LDS Polynesians, this town was inhabited for 28 years. At its maximum size, it was home to more than 200 Native Hawaiians. Emigrating from their homeland to Salt Lake City following conversion to Mormonism, they found themselves out of place, segregated and mistreated by white members of the Mormon Church in the Salt Lake Valley. As a result, they sought a location elsewhere at which they could establish their own community. However, many of the desirable locales in the region had already been claimed by preceding LDS pioneers. After surveying the remaining options, the Pacific Islander pioneers selected this site, and forty-six settlers moved there on August 28, 1889. They named the town Iosepa (Hawaiian for "Joseph") after Joseph F. Smith, among the first LDS missionaries to contact the Hawaiian Islands, and with whom they maintained correspondence in their native language even after arriving in Utah.

The new settlers found life on this land to be quite challenging. In addition to the extreme dryness of the region, winter came as a brutal shock to the new settlers, bringing with it a blight of whooping cough that killed many children. Nevertheless, the community persevered, encouraged by faith and driven by need. Over time, they corralled spring water and were able to irrigate their town with concrete pipelines. By 1911, this town was dubbed

METALWORK OF IOSEPA

SIGN OF UT-196 MARKING THE NORTHERN ENTRANCE TO IOSEPA

the most progressive in Utah. Yet mysteriously, the town was completely vacated just 6 years later, at which point all the buildings, farms, and animals were abandoned and subsequently sold off by the LDS Church. Although it is believed that Joseph Smith told the settlers they must return to Hawaii to build a temple in Laie, the details of this correspondence and the impetus behind his command remain sealed in church files.

Today the town of Iosepa is all but gone excepting a graveyard, the network of irrigation canals, a cave high in the hillside with whale and sea turtle petroglyphs, and a modern pavilion at which a luau is held annually on Memorial Day by Hawaiians who live in Utah in honor of their Pacific Island ancestors. Though much of this land here is currently managed by BLM, some is owned by Ensign Ranches. If you decide to leave your vehicle and explore, be sure to observe signs marking private property.

From this abandoned community, continue in a northerly direction, and the dirt road will return you to UT-196 after 1.1 miles; this junction with the state highway will be marked with a colorful ALOHA IOSEPA sign adorned with small sculptures. Further north 4.2 miles on UT-196, you will see an obvious network of OHV (off-highway vehicle) roads crisscrossing the hillsides. If it is not a weekend or otherwise busy time, you may enjoy a quiet night of wild camping here. Though it is not particularly scenic and it lacks any amenities, this area is essentially unregulated and there is no charge to spend the night here. From

FARM IN SKULL VALLEY

here, just 9.2 miles of northward travel on UT-196 will return you to I-80. Once at the interstate, Salt Lake City is only about 30 minutes to the east, and Wendover is just over an hour to the west. If you decide to head west, you will meet up with chapter 15's scenic drive; if you head east to Salt Lake City, you will arrive in the vicinity of the routes described in chapters 1, 2, and 3. Be warned that no services exist between Grantsville and Wendover; if going that way (west), make sure you have more than 80 miles' worth of gasoline in your car.

IN THE AREA

Accommodations

COMFORT INN & SUITES, 8580 North UT-36, Tooele. Affordable. Clean, modern hotel with indoor pool, free Wi-Fi, and breakfast. Call 801-250-3600. Website: www.comfortinntooele.com.

HOLIDAY INN EXPRESS & SUITES, 1531 North Main Street, Tooele. Moderately expensive. A pleasant, standard hotel with fitness gym, free Wi-Fi, and hot breakfast. Call 435-833-0500. Website: www.ihg.com/holidayinn express.

Attractions and Recreation

DONNER-REED MUSEUM, 390 West Clark Street, Grantsville. Call ahead to verify the reopening of this museum, and to schedule a tour: 435-884-3411. Website: www.donner-reed-museum.org.

FISH SPRINGS NATIONAL WILDLIFE REFUGE, 60 miles southwest of Dugway. Call 7:30 AM–4 PM. Monday through Friday: 435-693-3122. Website: www.fws.gov/refuge/Fish_Springs.

GRANTSVILLE DAUGHTERS OF UTAH PIONEERS MUSEUM, 378 West Clark Street, Grantsville. Open Friday and Saturday 12–4 PM or by appointment; call 435-840-1585. Website: www.grantsvilledupmuseum.com.

Dining

PENNY'S, 7760 South UT-36, Stockton. $. Open Monday through Thursday 8 AM–7 PM, Friday through Saturday 8 AM–8 PM, and Sunday 8 AM–3 PM. Classic American cuisine with hearty breakfast, and a lunchtime and dinner emphasis on burgers.

Other Contacts

BUREAU OF LAND MANAGEMENT, Salt Lake Field Office. Responsible for much of the lands outside of the Deseret Peak Wilderness, including the land surrounding Clover Springs Campground. Call 801-977-4300. Website: www.blm.gov/utah.

UINTA-WASATCH-CACHE NATIONAL FOREST. Oversees the Deseret Peak Wilderness, including its trails and campgrounds. Call 801-733-2676. Website: www.fs.usda.gov/uwcnf.

Index

Note: Italics indicate photographs

B

Baker, NV, 191, 200
Baker Archaeological Site, 198, 200
Balanced Rock, 85–86
Bald Mountain Pass, 67, 70, 74
Bannock Indians, 12
bear attacks, 49
Bear Lake, 53–55, 63
Bear Lake Raspberry Days, 64–65
Bear Lake State Park, 64
Bear Lake Valley, 53–55, 64
Bear River, 63
Bear River Range, 53–54
Bear River Range Canyon, 55
Beaver Creek, 71
Beaver Creek Lodge, 55, 61, 64
Beaver Mountain, 60–61, 64
Beef Basin, *112*
Beef Basin Road, 110–11
Benja Thai and Sushi, 179, 187
Big Bend, 95–96
Big Cottonwood Canyon, 19–21, 26, 29–35
Big Spring Canyon Overlook, 114–15
bison, 139
Blacksmith Fork Canyon, 55
Blanding, UT, 117, 126–27
Blondie's Eatery & Gift, 136–37, 143
Blue Coffee Pot, 119–120, 129
Blue Lake, 74
Bonneville desert, 12
Bonneville Racing, 215
Bonneville Salt Flats, 203–15
Bonneville Speedway, 203–15, *205*, *209*
Boulder, UT, 131, 140–42, 145, 149, 151–161
Boulder Mountain, 155–58
Boulder Mountain Lodge, 156, 159
Brian Head Peak, 166
Brian Head Resort, 163, 166, 172, 177

Bridal Veil Falls, *42*, 43–45
Bridal Veil Falls Tram, 44
Bridger, Jim, 61–63
Bridger Campground, 57
Bridger Jack Mesa, 110–11
Brigham Young University, 38, 41, 51, 58, 198
Brighton ski resort, 35, 43
Broken Arch, 88–89, 91
Bryce Amphitheater National Park, 169
Bryce Canyon, 167
Bryce Canyon Arch, *162*
Bryce Canyon National Park, 43, 149, 153, 163, 167, 170, 172, 177
Bryce Canyon Natural History Association, 171, 173
Buckeye Lake, 74
Bullfrog Ferry, 141, 143
Bullfrog Marina, 140
Bullfrog Visitor Center, 141, 143
Bull Mountain Market Pizza and Deli, 137, 143
Bureau of Land Management Salt Lake, 77
Bureau of Land Management Salt Lake Field Office, 233
Bureau of Land Management Vernal, 77
Burr, John Atlantic, 140
Burr Trail, 131, 140–42, 149, 154
Burr Trail Grill, 156, 160
Burr Trail Outpost, 156, 160
Burr Trail Road, 154
Butterfly Lake, 75

C

Cache Valley, 53–55
Cache Valley Visitors Bureau, 55, 65
Cafe Diablo, 157, 161
Cafe Soleil, 180, 187
Calf Creek, 150–53, *150*

G

Gap Road, 165
Garden City, UT, 64–65
Garden of Eden area, 85
Garden of Eden, 85
GearHeads, 82, 91
geology, 20, 82–83. *See also* Moab, UT
Gifford Homestead, 157
Glen Canyon, 147
Glen Canyon Dam, 136, 147
Glen Canyon National Recreation Area, 125, 141, 143
Goblin Valley State Park, 134, 143
Golden Eagle Pass. *See* America the Beautiful– The National Parks and Federal Recreational Lands Pass
gold rush, 73–74
Gooseberry Mesa, 179
Goosenecks State Park, 117, 123, 127
Gosiute Indians, 12
Grand Gulch Primitive Area, 125, 128
Grand Palace, 199
Grand Staircase-Escalante National Monument, 131–33, 135, 142, 145, 150, 153–56, 160–61, 163, 170–73
Grand Staircase (geological feature), 167–69
Grand View Mountain, 101
Grand View Point Overlook, 114
Grand Wash Road, 159
Granite Mountain Records Vault, 21
Granstaff, William, 95
Grantsville, UT, 212–15, 217–221, 232–33
Grantsville Daughters of Utah Pioneers Museum, 214–15, 233
Great Basin, 12–13, 55, 207–8
Great Basin Business and Tourism Council, 201

Great Basin Desert, 203, 213, 217–18, 226
Great Basin Museum, 191, 200
Great Basin National Park, 189–191, 199–200
Great Basin rattlesnake, 195
Great Basin salt flats, 205, 212
Great Salt Lake, 13, 38, 203, 207, 213–14
Great Western Trail, 43, 51, 154
Green River, 13, 69, 111, 115, 131–33, 143
Grizzly Gulch, 26
Grosvenor Arch, 172
Grotto, 185
Guardsman Pass, 29, 33–34
Guinavah Campground, 58

H

Ham Rock, 85
Hanksville, UT, 135–39, 143, 145, 159
Hanksville-Burpee Quarry, 137–38, 143
Hardware Ranch, 55
Harris Wash, *168*
Hayden Fork, 75
Hayden Peak, 75
Haystack Mountain, 101
hazards, natural, 14
Heber City, UT, 35, 42, 50
Hellgate (rock formation), 19, 25
Hell's Backbone Bridge, 154
Hell's Backbone Grill, 155–56, 161
Hell's Backbone Road, 145, 152, 154
Henry Mountains, 85, *130*, 131, 135–142
Hidden Haven Falls, 165–66
Hidden Peak, 20
Highline, 75
High Uintas Classic, 70, 77
Hinckley, UT, 191–94
history, of Utah, 12–13

Hole in the Wall? (handwritten annotation at top)